A Voice in the Wilderness

Terry Tempest Williams

A Voice in the Wilderness

Conversations
with
Terry Tempest Williams

Edited by
Michael Austin

Willet Drawing by Lee Carlman Riddell

Utah State University Press
Logan, Utah

Utah State University Press
Logan, Utah 84322-7800

Manufactured in the United States of America

Printed on recycled, acid-free paper

ISBN-13: 978-0-87421-634-9
ISBN-10: 0-87421-634-6

Library of Congress Cataloging-in-Publication Data

Austin, Michael, 1966-
A voice in the wilderness : conversations with Terry Tempest Williams / edited by
Michael Austin ; Willet drawing by Lee Carlman Riddell.
p. cm.
Includes bibliographical references and index.
ISBN-13: 978-0-87421-634-9 (pbk. : alk. paper)
ISBN-10: 0-87421-634-6 (pbk. : alk. paper)
1. Williams, Terry Tempest--Interviews. 2. Naturalists--United States--Interviews. 3.
Environmentalists--United States--Interviews. 4. Authors--United States--
Interviews. 5. Human ecology. I. Title.

QH31.W626A5 2006
508--dc22
2006009473

For Karen, Porter, and Clarissa

Contents

Acknowledgments

In editing this collection, which relies almost entirely on the talents of others, I have incurred more debts than I could ever discharge. My greatest debt, of course, is to Terry Tempest Williams herself. Her extraordinary talent made this book possible, and her graciousness at every step of the process made the book a pleasure to compile. I am also indebted to my collaborators on this project, the authors, journalists, and radio hosts who conducted the original interviews that I have gathered for reprinting. I am deeply gratified by the unselfishness that these interviewers displayed in allowing me to reprint their work. The project would also have been impossible without the support of three amazing women at Shepherd University: Linda Tate, my colleague in the English Department, who suggested this collection to me in the first place; Theresa Smith, the interlibrary loan librarian at the university library, who tracked down and obtained the texts of more than forty interviews; and Ashley Hutson, my editorial intern, who transcribed radio interviews, corrected scans, and edited the entire document several times with amazing competence and professionalism. Ben Spiker, also a Shepherd University student, provided critical assistance in the final stages of the project. Special thanks are also due to John Alley at Utah State University Press, who displayed incredible wisdom and patience, without which this book would never have existed; to Monette Clark, who proofread the entire manuscript and suggested key improvements; and to Cecilia Konchar Farr and Laura Bush, who read the manuscript cover to cover with a scholarly perspective that I found invaluable. And, to my wife Karen, the most important figure in my life, I give my thanks accompanied by my undying love.

A Life Engaged

A Critical Introduction

Michael Austin

Paradox is life. It's the same thing as balance. You can't have one with-
out the other . . . Tell me what you fear most and then we can talk about
what we desire most. Then this "third thing," which in this case is con-
versation or understanding, becomes the creative expression of an idea.
— Terry Tempest Williams to Derrick Jensen (p. 44)

Critics describe Terry Tempest Williams as a paradox. In the introduction to a
recent book of essays devoted to her work, Katherine R. Chandler and Melissa
Goldthwaite note that "tensions and oppositions abound in her work . . . As critics, we have set our sights on ferreting out how those contradictions contribute to
a coherent vision."[1] This is a daunting task: Williams is a feminist, a Mormon, a
scientist, an environmentalist, an activist, and a writer of great beauty and passion.
In the final interview for this volume, I asked Williams specifically about some of
these contradictions. "There are so many Terry Tempest Williamses," I queried,
"the writer, the activist, the naturalist, the wife, the speaker, the educator—how

---

1.   Katherine R. Chandler and Melissa A. Goldthwaite, eds., *Surveying the Literary*
     Landscapes of Terry Tempest Williams (Salt Lake City: University of Utah Press,
     2003), ix.

1

does writing integrate with other facets of your life?" Her response was as simple as it was sublime: "I only know one me. I don't know those other people that you're talking about. It's one life and it's a life engaged" (p. 180).

Many readers—and most literary critics—have become accustomed to working with prepackaged critical and cultural narratives with well-established boundaries. By refusing to be trapped in these narratives, Williams demands the full attention of her readers. Invariably, this means abandoning many of the standard tools of literary criticism—analysis, categorization, comparison, and detached observation—and entering into an honest dialogue with the words on the page and with the woman who wrote them. To read Terry Tempest Williams well, one must enter into intimate conversations with the texts, dialogue in the margins, interact with the words. The literary interview is a logical extension of this reading process.

The purpose of this volume is to showcase some of the most extensive and valuable conversations that Terry Tempest Williams has had with scholars, critics, journalists, readers, and friends during her literary career. The 17 interviews in this collection were drawn from some 40 print or radio interviews that Williams has given since 1989. Williams's interviews, like her books, are suffused with the passions of her life—her family, the land, the power of words, and unwavering courage and personal integrity—and can be read profitably as primary works of literature in their own right. Those familiar with Williams's books will find that the interviews offer insights unavailable in any other source. What follows below is a brief introduction to some of the recurring themes, arguments, and ideas of Williams's work, with an emphasis on how they interact with the interviews in this volume.

Desire, Intimacy, and the Erotics of Place

How does our intimacy with each other, or lack of intimacy, affect our intimacy with the land? Like death, I think our sensuality is something we're afraid of and so we have avoided confronting it. I am interested in taboos, because I believe that's where the power of our culture lies. I love taking off their masks so we can begin to face the world openly. I believe that will be our healing.

—Terry Tempest Williams to David Petersen (p. 20)

In both her books and her interviews, Terry Tempest Williams weaves together the strands of her life—fully embracing the contradictions that they create. Consider the following passage from *Refuge* (1991), Williams's most well-known book, about the impact of Utah's desert landscape on her sense of spiritual connectedness:

It's strange how deserts turn us into believers. I believe in walking in a land-scape of mirages, because you learn humility. I believe in living in a land of little water because life is drawn together. And I believe in the gathering of bones as a testament to spirits that have moved on.

If the desert is holy, it is because it is a forgotten place that allows us to remember the sacred. Perhaps that is why every pilgrimage to the desert is a pilgrimage to the self. There is no place to hide, and so we are found.

In the severity of a salt desert, I am brought down to my knees by its beauty. My imagination is fired. My heart opens and my skin burns in the pas-sion of these moments. I will have no other gods before me.

Wilderness courts our souls. When I sat in church throughout my grow-ing years, I listened to teachings about Christ in the wilderness for forty days and forty nights reclaiming his strength, where he was able to say to Satan, "Get thee hence." When I imagined Joseph Smith kneeling in a grove of trees as he received his vision to create a new religion, I believed their sojourns into nature were sacred. Are ours any less?[2]

This single passage merges most of the recurring images in Williams's early work: the desert landscape, Mormonism, community, spirituality, the power of narra-tive, and the integrity of bodily experience. A specific landscape—the desert—is the starting point for a large constellation of ideas and values. By its lack of water, the desert produces community; by its solitude, reflection; by its fire, passion; by its remoteness, a refuge. It is tempting to see the desert as a metaphor for many other things in Williams's work, but to do so would commit the fatal error of not taking the land seriously as itself. For Williams, the land is not simply a metaphor for ideas; it *is* an idea and, as such, forms an integral part of the mosaic of ideas, truths, stories, and desires that she weaves into her work.

In her interviews, Williams employs three overlapping concepts to define her approach to place. The first of these is a *poetics of place*, an aesthetic that begins with a landscape—and with the cultures that grow out of it—and, as she works it onto the page, honors that land, its culture, and its stories. Williams's early literary efforts—children's books entitled *The Secret Language of Snow* (1984) and *Between Cattails* (1985)—are deeply rooted in her poetics of place. Her first work for adult readers, *Pieces of White Shell: A Journey to Navajoland* (1985), frames traditional stories through the landscape of the Navajo Nation, and her second, *Coyote's Can-yon* (1989), continues the project in the desert of her native Utah. "I think each of

---

2.   *Refuge: An Unnatural History of Family and Place* (New York: Pantheon, 1991), 148–49.

my books has turned on a question," Williams tells Ona Siporin. "With *Pieces of White Shell* it was 'What stories do we tell that evoke a sense of place?' In many ways, the Navajo sent me back home. And with *Coyote's Canyon* it was 'Okay, do I have those stories within my own culture?'" (p. 70).

In *Refuge*, Williams's notion of landscape broadens to include that of her family, religion, and culture. In the process of this shift, her *poetics of place* grew into a *politics of place*, as her writing combined its initial emphasis on the narrative gifts of the land with a sense of urgency in speaking on the land's behalf. Unlike the gradual, often undetectable changes in a writer's ideological orientation over time, this one occurred during the course of a single conversation—a conversation with her father that forms the basis of the essay that concludes *Refuge*: "The Clan of the One-Breasted Women." In her interview with David Petersen, she describes the momentous impact of that conversation: "For years, every time I went south into the desert, I would have these horrifying dreams of nuclear explosions. But it wasn't until a year after Mother's death that my father told me I had in fact witnessed such an explosion. Suddenly, all the pieces of the puzzle came together for me. I realized we, too, were downwinders. Suddenly, my poetics of place evolved into a politics of place. It was then that I made the decision to write *Refuge*" (p. 19).

Soon after the publication of *Refuge*, Williams's attention shifted to her third conceptual framework, which she calls the *erotics of place*. Perhaps no phrase in Williams entire oeuvre has evoked as much critical commentary—or misunderstanding—as this one. With strong echoes of the notion of Eros as defined by Plato in the *Symposium*, Williams posits erotic longing as the foundation of connection. Eros develops from the realization that we are incomplete and fragmented—that the mask of wholeness that we present to the world is an illusion. Even if our minds do not acknowledge this incompleteness, our bodies understand it, sensing that, as isolated organisms, we are not whole. We long for connection, for completion, and this is the starting point of desire. When we focus on relationships, "we are engaged, we are vulnerable, we are both giving and receiving, we are fully present in that moment, and we are able to heighten our capacity for passion which I think is the full range of emotion, both the joy and sorrow that one feels when in wild country" (p. 75). For Williams, the erotic algebra of longing and desire is rooted in the land. Meaningful intimacy between people and meaningful intimacy with the natural world proceed from the same sense of longing. As she tells Justine Toms, "our lack of intimacy with the land has initiated a lack of intimacy with each other" (p. 32).

There is a key distinction for Williams, as for other feminists and social theorists, between the erotic and the pornographic. The erotic is based on genuine connection to, sharing with, and acceptance of another's whole being, on intimacy.

Pornography involves domination, control, and the perception of another as a mechanism for satisfying desires. In her essay "The Erotic Landscape," Williams quotes Audry Lorde to define "pornography" as "sensation without feeling."[3] In her interviews, she expands on the notion. "When love is only one-way," she tells Derrick Jensen, "eventually it becomes pornographic, a body that is used, rather than a body that is shared" (p. 36). When the pornographic impulse—the desire to subjugate, use, and control—is transferred to the land, the result is strip mining, pollution, mountaintop removal, sprawling development, extinctions, and, ultimately, the destruction of wildness, whose value can never be understood within the confines of a pornographic relationship.

Writing the Body

The body does not lie. Therefore, if we write out of the body, we are writing out of the truth of our lives. This creates a language that is organic and whole . . . The body is the realm of the story. And it is in story that we bypass rhetoric and pierce the heart. We feel it first and understand it later. Memory resides in the body. Memorization resides in the mind.
—Terry Tempest Williams to Jana Bouck Remy (p. 151)

In both her writing and her interviews, Terry Tempest Williams takes seriously the work of French feminist scholars—foremost among them Hélène Cixous—who exclaim that women should write from the body. "Write yourself," Cixous writes in *The Newly Born Women*, "your body must make itself heard. Then the huge resources of the unconscious will burst out. Finally the inexhaustible feminine Imaginary is going to be deployed."[4] In many ways, *Leap*, Williams's follow-up to *Refuge*, is about the discovery of the body. After she sees the *Garden of Earthly Delights* for the first time in the Prado, Williams remembers that she had seen two of the three panels before:

We turned, and there we were, confronted with El jardín de las delicias, The Garden of Earthly Delights, by Hieronymus Bosch. At that moment, I realized I knew the painting, or at least part of it: the panels of Paradise and Hell. My grandmother had thumbtacked these prints above the bed where we slept as children. What I didn't know . . . was the whole center panel, the panel of

---

3.   *Red: Passion and Patience in the Desert* (New York: Pantheon, 2001), 108.
4.   Hélène Cixous and Catherine Clément, *The Newly Born Woman*, trans. Betty Wing (Minneapolis: University of Minnesota Press, 1986), 97.

earthly delights; I never knew that existed. The body, the body of the triptych, my body—and a seven-year search ensued. (p. 116)

In the pages of *Leap*, the center panel thus becomes a figural representation of the body, in the process challenging religious orthodoxies that try to suppress the physical self and undermine both sexuality and femininity.

Williams goes beyond the normal understanding of *ecriture feminine* by joining it with her passion for wild spaces. For her, wildness represents a force that is at once restorative, transgressive, erotic, playful, and deeply intuitive—all terms that French feminist theory applies to the feminine body and to the art that flows from it. *Leap* explores the complicated relationship between art, nature, physicality, and spirituality. All are governed by an ideal of wildness rooted in both body and landscape— connections that she explores further in her interview with Jana Bouck Remy:

> The body carries the physical reality of our spirits like a river. Institutional thinking is fearful of rivers because rivers inevitably follow their own path, and that channel may change from day to day, even though the muscle of the river, the property of water remains consistent, life sustaining, fierce, and compassionate, at once. To write out of the body is to write ourselves into a freedom. It is here we can let go of fear and trust the joy that is held in each movement of the hand, word by word by word. (p. 151)

Perhaps no work better displays Williams's fusion of French feminist theory and the landscape of the American West than her small book *Desert Quartet*, a series of four brief vignettes that she describes in her interview with Ona Siporin as her effort to "write out of the body and to create a narrative where it was of the flesh, and even ask the question, 'What might it mean to make love to the land?' Not in an expletive manner, but in a manner of reciprocity" (p. 70). In this book she showcases what her other works and interviews only describe: a landscape that serves as a touchstone for both bodily desire and the longing for spiritual connection—the very elements that make up an erotics of place. Her thinking here merits careful consideration, as it refuses to simplify either wilderness or Eros. In "The Erotic Landscape," she writes that the erotic "calls the inner life into play. No longer numb, we feel the magnetic pull in our bodies toward something stronger, more vital than simply ourselves. Arousal becomes a dance with longing. We form a secret partnership with possibility."[5]

---

5.   *Red*, 106.

Writing from the body, for Williams, means not only ignoring the censorship of logic and reason, but also overriding the protective mechanisms built into us by evolution and adaptation. She is fond of quoting Cixous's maxim that "the only book worth writing is the book that threatens to kill us" (p. 125). Our defense mechanisms, she believes, become our greatest censors, and our biggest obstacle to writing the truth. In my interview with her, I asked her about the paradox of trying to write from the body while at the same time trying to ignore our natural protective instincts. Characteristically, her answer both embraced and dispelled the paradox:

> We are mammals. We want to survive. It's part of our evolution. But it is also in our evolutionary interest to take risks. Whether we are Mormon, Catholic, Buddhist, or whatever our spiritual tradition is, there are conditionings that create an "ought" and a "should." As writers, we have to bypass the oughts and shoulds to the "what is." I think this really goes to the heart of the matter of exposing our true selves. Inherently, we don't think people are interested in what we have to say, and we don't have any confidence that our voice matters. So writing against our instincts is also believing that maybe we do have something to say. (p. 184)

The Religious Dance

I am a Mormon woman. I am not orthodox. It is the lens through which I see the world. I hear the Tabernacle Choir and it still makes me weep. There are other things within the culture that absolutely enrage me, and for me it is a sacred rage.
—Terry Tempest Williams to Scott London (p. 55)

To acknowledge that which we cannot see, to give definition to that which we do not know, to create divine order out of chaos, is the religious dance.
—*Refuge*, p. 196

For many of Williams's readers, her complex relationship with the Church of Jesus Christ of Latter-day Saints stands as a formidable obstacle to her work. Mormon readers often express frustration with her unorthodoxy and her criticisms of the faith's emphasis on conformity, authority, and patriarchy.[6] Non-Mormon readers, on the other hand, are equally confused by her refusal to reject Mormonism entirely

6.   For an overview of Mormon reactions to *Refuge*, see Michael Austin, "Finding God in the Desert: Landscape and Belief in Three Modern Mormon Classics"

and by her repeated insistences that she is a Mormon woman, an inhabitant of a culture, and an heir to a rich spiritual tradition. This culture and tradition serve as the fountainhead of the values that pervade her work: family, history, spirituality, and connections to the land. As she writes in *Leap*: "I cannot escape my history, nor can I ignore the lineage that is mine. Most importantly, I don't want to."[7]

Williams has carried out her religious dance in full view of her readers, in an extended narrative that develops gradually through her work. In her first two books—*Pieces of White Shell* and *Coyote's Canyon*—her religion remains safely on the sidelines. In *Refuge*, however, it becomes a major focus. As she tells Jana Bouck Remy, her early drafts of *Refuge* attempted to avoid Mormon issues, but her editor pushed her to deal with them explicitly (p. 155). For most of *Refuge*, Williams presents Mormonism in a positive light. It is the source of the family traditions that she honors, and it is also the source of the land ethic that she has always professed. "Genealogy is in our blood," she writes. "As a people and as a family, we have a sense of history. And our history is tied to land."[8] The 19th-century Mormon experience in the Salt Lake Valley provides an extremely rich storehouse for Williams. Early Mormons, as she explains, emphasized such concepts as communitarian economics, the existence of a divine feminine being, and, perhaps most important, the function of wilderness as a place of refuge.[9]

Mormonism does not become a paradox in Williams's work until "The Clan of the One-Breasted Women," where she describes the impact that her knowledge of nuclear testing had on her faith. Though the testing was not, of course, carried on by Mormons, it did cause her to reject the unquestioning devotion to authority that she sees in her faith. Once she discovered that her mother's death may have been caused by this testing, she recognized "that the price of obedience is too high" and concluded, "I could never go back . . . back to the same place in the family, the same place within Mormon culture" (p. 19).

The rupture between faith and authority that comes to the surface in "The Clan of the One-Breasted Women" becomes the main focus of *Leap*, which, she tells Remy, she views as "a sequel to *Refuge* in many ways" (p. 150). *Leap*'s extended meditation on Hieronymus Bosch's medieval triptych painting allows her "to see various patterns and connections within [her] own religion and homeland" (p. 150). Specifically, the three panels of the *Garden of Earthly Delights*, which

---

in *Literature and Belief* 23:1 (2003), 51–52. Williams also brings up some of these critiques in her interview with Jana Bouck Remy on pp. 146–59.
7. *Leap* (New York: Pantheon, 2000), 177.
8. *Refuge*, 14.
9. Ibid., 99–103; 241; 13, 69.

represent *Paradise*, *Earthly Delights*, and *Hell*, correspond to the three "Kingdoms of Glory" in traditional Mormon eschatology: the Celestial, Terrestial, and Telestial kingdoms. Williams told me that "I always imagine that my audience is a Mormon one. *Leap* is a book that certainly has a Mormon reader in mind" (p. 182).

Yet Williams's relationship to Mormonism in *Leap* is very different than it is in *Refuge*. The question that she identifies, to Michael Toms, as the prime mover of *Leap* is "What happens when our institutions no longer feed us" (p. 120)? Whereas *Refuge* focused on the communal and nurturing aspects of Mormon families, *Leap* shines its light on the corporate, conservative aspects of the Church of Jesus Christ of Latter-day Saints. In one of the book's most memorable passages, Williams acknowledges the painful distance between herself and her religious culture. "I weep in the midst of my people," she writes, after describing a jingoistic stadium rally celebrating Mormon pioneer heritage. "I weep because I recognize I no longer believe as I once did. I weep because I do not believe there is only one true church. I weep because within my own homeland I suddenly feel foreign, so very, very foreign."[10]

It is crucial to note, though, as Williams does in both *Leap* and *Refuge*, that there is room in the 150-year-old Mormon tradition for environmental activism, community organization, and even challenges to authority. In the 19th century, Mormons were driven into the Utah desert and adopted it as their own place of refuge. Their persecution stemmed largely from their unorthodox marriage practices. The theology that they espoused held that God was a corporeal being—a deity of "body, parts, and passions." Williams presents her crisis of faith in *Leap* not as a fundamental quarrel between Mormonism and progressive ideology but as a historical conflict between two different versions of Mormonism: 19th-century Mormonism, which was transgressive, erotic, charismatic, and connected to the land; and 20th-century Mormonism, which has become bureaucratic, conservative, conformist, and hostile to the environment. Yet Williams has always held out hope that Mormonism can be reconciled with its roots. To this end, she coedited the volume *New Genesis: A Mormon Reader on Land and Community* (1998), which presents essays by 39 well-known Mormons on environmentalism. Williams tells David Thomas Sumner, "I am convinced there is a broader vision within Mormonism. There is something beautiful and meaningful here on the edges of this 'American religion,' as Harold Bloom has called it. I do not believe that a fundamentalist viewpoint is all that is available to members of the Church of Jesus Christ of Latter-day Saints" (p. 102).

---

10.   *Leap*, 180–81.

Taking Back the Language: The Writer Since 9/11

I believe our country is being run as a business not as a democracy and they don't understand that this is a public process. Whether it's Bush/Cheney's energy policy behind closed doors or the desire to exploit everything they possibly can on every possible level—the environment, social issues or the economy—I think it's devastating. Now there's this atmosphere of war where we aren't allowed to criticize our president. To be called a traitor or a patriot—this is one of the darkest times we've faced in this country.
—Terry Tempest Williams to David Kupfer (p. 161)

Before September 11, 2001 was seared into minds worldwide as the date that terrorists brought down the World Trade Center towers and attacked the Pentagon, it had been scheduled as the publication date for Terry Tempest Williams's book *Red: Passion and Patience in the Desert*. In her own mind, Williams told me, that book is "inextricably tied to that moment" (p. 186). Less than two weeks later—before the American government's response to the attacks had been fully formulated—Williams spoke prophetically in an interview with the New Dimensions Radio Network's "A Time for Choices" series: "I do think that the coming days are going to require strength, courage, and a gathering together for those of us who define patriotism in another way—not just as waving flags, but also as standing our ground in the places we love and continuing to honor the Earth and its wild places" (p. 140).

In the months and years following the attacks, both Williams's writing and her public persona have undergone a perceptible shift—a change that she, in her interviews, relates to her view of the role of a writer in a participatory democracy. As she told me, "there is a strong tradition among writers in this country and abroad to raise essential questions during times of war. And we are a nation at war" (p. 186). Williams believes that writers need to intervene when the politics of war corrupt their medium—language. This concern became central to Williams after the attacks: "I felt that our language after September 11 had been hijacked. And talk about being constricted. We were being restricted at the level of our language: the definition of what a patriot was, what a terrorist was, what a dissident was, the language of war that seeped into our culture" (p. 185).

For Williams, the degradation of language firmly links the destructiveness of warfare and the destruction of the environment. She tells Aria Seligmann, "There are many forms of terrorism and environmental degradation is one of them." Invasions of Afghanistan and Iraq exist on a spectrum that includes assaults on the Arctic wilderness, Middle East oilfields, and the redrock desert of Southern Utah.

All are caused by the arrogance of a powerful few, and all of them require the same response: "Speak. Shatter the silence. Question everything. Redefine. Reimagine patriotism. Reimagine hatred and take back the language" (p. 161).

Unlike some in the peace and environmental movements, however, Williams sees the solution to such problems as something deeply embedded in the American mind, with its devotion to grass-roots democracy. This is the major argument of her first full-length book since 9/11—*The Open Space of Democracy* (2004)—and it was a theme in many of the interviews that she gave long before the attacks on the World Trade Center forced it to the forefront of her writing. In these interviews and her recent writing, Williams adopts a hopeful—and in many ways a utopian— view of the earth's future. It is in such moments that the major strands of her writing—her sense of an erotic longing based on place, her belief in a form of reason based on the body, her concept of community derived from a Mormon heritage, and her understanding of the social function of art—come together in a compelling vision of a possible future based on compassion and cooperation. "I believe capitalism will eventually be replaced by a communitarian ethic where the rights and care of all beings will be taken into consideration," she tells David Kupfer in this volume's penultimate interview. "I do trust that the open space of democracy is ultimately the open space of our hearts and that we can follow our own leadership that carries a long-term view way beyond 'four more years'" (p. 174).

Conclusion

For some time, I have believed that the conversational style of the literary interview is better suited to Terry Tempest Williams than to almost any other writer alive. Throughout her career, she has been engaged in conversations with herself, with her family, with her culture—and, perhaps most importantly, with the land. I began collecting copies of Williams's published and recorded interviews in 1999, soon after Dr. Richard Cracroft and Dr. Eugene England of Brigham Young University asked me to participate in the "Spiritual Frontiers 2000" conference in Provo, Utah—an event for which Terry Tempest Williams was the keynote speaker. At the time, I simply wanted to read the interviews to fill out my own understanding before completing the paper on Williams's work that I intended to present. After I delivered the paper, however, I still found myself compelled to seek out and collect interviews. I viewed each new one with the excitement that I normally reserve for new books by major authors. By the time I had collected 40 interviews, I had hundreds of pages of text and many hours of radio recordings, which had taken several years to track down, secure, and digest. The more I looked at this material, the more it began to resemble a book.

A Voice in the Wilderness

The most daunting task I faced in preparing the manuscript was whittling the list down to its present size (see pages 187–89 for a more complete list of interviews that were considered). In making the selection, I followed several guiding principles that were not always compatible. The time frame of the interviews was an obvious factor, and I tried to select interviews that fairly represented Terry's work at different points in her career. I also tried to include interviews from a wide variety of venues. The 17 interviews in this volume (including two interviews about the 9/11 attacks which have been combined into one) come from scholarly books and journals, popular magazines, specialty publications on environmental and women's issues, progressive radio programs, alternative newspapers, bestselling books, creative writing journals, a journal of Mormon literature, and a food magazine. Where choices between equally representative interviews have been necessary, I have preferred hard-to-find interviews over easily accessible ones, out-of-print interviews over those still circulating, and radio interviews—appearing here in print for the first time—over print ones. The final interview was conducted specifically for this collection and attempts to clarify and expand on some of the issues about writing and the writing process that came up in many of the others.

Memory is the Only Way Home

A Conversational Interview with Terry Tempest Williams

David Petersen, *The Bloomsbury Review*, 1991

A cloudless June day, and already hot out on the bone-white slick-rock north of Moab, Utah. Writer-naturalist Terry Tempest Williams and I, escorted by an entourage of pesky gnats, are hiking out across a rolling sea of sand and sandstone, into a brilliant sun back-lighting the hobgoblin landscape of Arches National Park—Abbey Country—towards a special place I wish to share with Terry.

With no name on the maps, and having been revealed to me by Mr. Abbey himself, I've come to call the place Ed's Canyon. It seems an entirely appropriate backdrop for a long conversation with Terry Williams. After all, it was Cactus Ed who, by his conspicuous absence, introduced us when we, and a few hundred others, attended his memorial service, held near here back in May of 1989.

Arrived at the canyon's abrupt edge, we take gritty seats on a warm lip of sandstone over-looking a 500-foot plunge into . . . what? Abbey knows, of course. And I suspect after having read her latest book, Refuge, *that the woman here with me today may have some clues as well.*

Terry Tempest Williams is an archetypal southwesterner—born, reared, and educated (to the master's level) within sight of the Great Salt Lake; a former teacher on the Navajo

David Petersen, "Memory Is the Only Way Home: A Conversational Interview with Terry Tempest Williams," *Bloomsbury Review* 11, no. 8 (December 1991): 8-9. Reprinted by permission.

Reservation at Montezuma Creek, Utah; and recently ranked by Newsweek *among the score of people most likely to have "a considerable impact on the political, economic, and environmental issues facing the western states in this decade."*

Considering her experientially broad, geographically concentrated background, it's natural that Williams's first two major literary works—the Southwest Book Award-winning Pieces of White Shell: A Journey to Navajoland *(Scribners, 1984) and* Coyote's Canyon *(Peregrine Smith, 1989)—both deal intimately with southwestern land- and mindscapes.*

The skillfully braided subjects of Williams's newest work, Refuge *(Pantheon) are summarized in the big (305 pages) book's subtitle—*An Unnatural History of Family and Place.

The place is the Bear River Migratory Bird Refuge on Salt Lake—which, during the disastrous flooding of the great lake (and a portion of the town of the same name) in 1983, was inundated and threatened with total destruction. Williams grew up with the refuge and its symphony of bird song, and feels its health, or lack thereof, as her own.

The family is the author's maiden Tempest clan. Central to the story is Terry's mother, Diane Dixon Tempest, who learns that she has cancer even as the refuge begins to flood. Williams weaves these two elements—nature and family, both bedrock to her life, both out of balance—into the rich fabric of Refuge.

Williams's mother, however, was not the first Tempest woman to face premature death by cancer, and may not be the last. As it is, at age 34 Terry became the matriarch of the Mormon Tempest clan and lives herself in the shadow of this foreboding legacy of suffering and unnatural death.

In "Clan of the One-Breasted Women," the poignant epilogue to Refuge, *the author explains:*

> *I belong to a Clan of One-Breasted Women. My mother, my grandmothers, and six aunts have all had mastectomies. Seven are dead. The two who survive have just completed rounds of chemotherapy and radiation.*
>
> *I've had my own problems: two biopsies for breast cancer and a small tumor between my ribs diagnosed as "borderline malignancy."*
>
> *This is my family history.[1]*

Why so many early deaths in one family?

Almost certainly because the Tempests were among the "downwinders"—that unfortunate number of people, many now gone, whose collective tragedy was to have been in the

---

1.   *Refuge: An Unnatural History of Family and Place* (New York: Pantheon, 1991), 281.

wrong place at the wrong time, during the 1950s and '60s surface nuclear weapons testing in the desert Southwest. Terry herself was an accidental eyewitness to one such detonation, and the nightmarish image haunted her dreams for decades and clouds her future even today.

But Refuge *is no mere keen of familial suffering, no maudlin plea for sympathy, no angry cry of outrage. It is a brave, engaging, and hopeful story of love and strength, of change in nature and the nature of change. And, most significantly,* Refuge *is about adapting.*

We sit for awhile in silence atop our spectacular cliff-edge aerie, our eyes tracing the wind-and water-sculpted sandstone walls down into the shapely, shadowy void, enjoying a pair of white-throated swifts who circle and dart close by, calling in sweet, wrenlike voices. When the swifts have finished their conversation, we begin ours.

THE BLOOMSBURY REVIEW: When did you first realize you wanted to become a writer?

TERRY TEMPEST WILLIAMS: My life has always been engaged with the natural world, and writing has been an outgrowth of that passion. I don't perceive myself so much as a writer as I do a member of a community of people in the American West who are envisioning what it means to be living here at this time. I believe we are witnessing the opening of a renaissance among a community of western writers who work from the tradition of landscape as literature. I think it's an extraordinary time to be living and writing in the West because we are asking tough questions—and perhaps finding some answers along the way.

TBR: What was the first thing you wrote that was meaningful to you?

TTW: I think it was keeping notes in a bird book, a gift from my grandmother, at about age five. And I've always kept a journal, which is really the bedrock of my voice in terms of perceptions and sense of place. My first published place work was a children's book, *The Secret Language of Snow*, which I did in collaboration with Ted Major, my earliest mentor, whom I met at the Teton Science School in Jackson Hole, Wyoming. That was 1974; I was only a year out of high school. Ted showed me the power of questioning, and that for every question there's an answer waiting in the natural world.

TBR: You are an extraordinary writer. Have you had any formal training?

TTW: I have a bachelor's degree in English, with a minor in biology, and a master's in environmental education. I guess I've always had a love affair with language and landscape. I remember being a student at the University of Utah, in the English department; I was torn because there wasn't enough time to take all the literary requirements *and* all the biological requirements, so I asked my advisor if I could major in "environmental English" [laughter]. "Absolutely not!" he said. So I went over to the biology department and asked them if I could major in "literary biology," and they looked at me and said, "You're completely mad" [laughter]. So I wound up with a straight English major and biology as a minor. Finally, in graduate school, I was able to integrate my passion for the two through story. By exploring narrative, within the Navajo culture, I saw a correspondence between language and landscape.

TBR: You have a unique style—I'm speaking here primarily of *Pieces of White Shell* and *Coyote's Canyon*—in that it's sometimes difficult to tell where the line is drawn between reality and imagination.

TTW: You know, I think it's how you see the world. For me, the line between what is real and what is imagined is thinly drawn. I don't live with such boundaries. Maybe that's the definition of style—how one perceives and writes about place in the world from the vantage point of one's experience.

TBR: Why do you write?

TTW: In great part, to discover that which I don't know. The writers who touch me, who move me, are the writers who are generous not just with what they know, but also with what they *don't* know. For example, as I sit here overlooking this beautifully sculpted canyon, I realize that what I love most about Ed's writing, about Abbey himself, is that he was constantly confronting his own humanness, and that the nonhuman world informed his existence so completely that ultimately his existence didn't matter at all. He was a man whose priorities were intact. This translated to a humility, even a humor, in his writing so powerful that it changed my way of thinking about life. And I love Ed's rage; sharp-edged and cutting. He was not a polite writer.

It's that kind of honesty, that generosity of spirit, that I ask of writers. And it's *difficult*, because you have to be thoughtful, taking nothing for granted, and you have to be willing to risk everything, to write against your instincts. I think Edward Abbey did that. I hope I can.

TBR: What other writers have influenced you?

TTW: Rachel Carson, first and foremost. She was an incredible role model who spoke her truth at great personal cost. In *Silent Spring* (Houghton Mifflin,

16

1962), she wrote with intention and integrity to the biology that was the bedrock of her work. What she had to say about pesticides, people did not want to hear, and so they attacked her personally to undermine her credibility. Virginia Woolf influenced me in terms of taking narrative to the extreme of consciousness.

Passionate women are always feared because they threaten to undermine the status quo—and Rachel Carson and Virginia Woolf are two examples of that phenomenon.

Another writer who has made a difference in my life is Gregory Bateson. In *Steps to an Ecology of Mind* (Aronson, 1988), he explored "the pattern that connects."

Susan Griffen, in her watershed book *Women and Nature* (Harper & Row, 1979), brought forth the idea that the exploitation of land and the exploitation of women both are rooted in the philosophy of the dominant culture. To her I am indebted.

Barry Lopez has been an important mentor and friend. I met Barry when I was twenty-three years old. He set a standard and continues to show me what is possible.

Ursula LeGuin is one of the most passionate voices I know. She refuses to honor any borders of literary genre.

Simon Ortiz, Linda Hogan, Louise Erdrich have had a huge influence on me as native voices of this land.

Jim Harrison—raucous with abandon, a brilliant storyteller, one of the most exquisite men I've ever met.

Doug Peacock in terms of what it means to live an authentic life.

Wallace Stegner is perhaps my greatest teacher, because he has defined the American West as "living space."

But the single most significant influence on my work and my life has not been other writers, but my marriage of nearly twenty years [to Brooke Williams]. That relationship has its own landscape, which informs everything else. It's that solidarity within our home that has enabled me to be really free in my relationships outside the home, both with the land and with other people.

TBR: Those are the primary themes in *Refuge*—your relationships with the land and with your family?

TTW: Yes, in *Refuge*, I looked at the landscape of my family, the landscape of my childhood and the landscape of the Bear River Migratory Bird Refuge adjacent to Great Salt Lake. The story turns on the juxtaposition of events within my family and the refuge. Great Salt Lake was rising and there was nothing to blame it on, nothing to be angry about, nothing to fight—just a complete acceptance that the refuge, those vast priceless wetlands, would be flooded and lost through a natural phenomenon. Similarly, I had to learn and acknowledge and accept the loss of my mother and grandmother. That's the premise of *Refuge*—that an intimacy with the natural world initiates an intimacy with death, because life and death are engaged in an endless, inseparable dance.

In America today, we're terrified of death, have little relationship with it, abrogate our responsibilities to someone else; we enter a hospital, it's antiseptic, it's inhuman, and it leaves us with little choice as to what our relationship to death will be. We turn our deaths over to someone else. In the process, our deaths have little privacy. We lose the spiritual instruction a good death can offer. No death is easy. We are rarely prepared. What I have learned through the deaths of women in my family is that it's not only possible to live well, it is possible to die well. They wanted to face death as part of life. There were no rules when my mother was dying, there was no precedent for us. So we, my family, just walked into that unknown territory with as much trust as possible, our mother our guide.

TBR: Would you, then, describe *Refuge* as a joyful book?

TTW: I think it's an honest book, and there was tremendous pain involved in its writing. But yes, I believe there is an unspeakable joy in being fully present and responding totally to the moment. For me, that's where joy dwells and feeling lies; in fact, I think that's the well of all strength and wisdom—knowing that all we have, all we will ever have, is right now; that's the gift. And I must tell you the Bear River Migratory Bird Refuge is coming back; the birds are returning. It's the nature of life—the land, the animals, humanity—to regenerate itself. So yes, *Refuge* is a joyous book.

TBR: You come from a traditional Mormon family, and yet you say things in Refuge that strongly challenge that tradition, particularly as it relates to women and the land.

TTW: I take my cue from Octavio Paz, who says that both love and criticism are necessary in order to create revolution. I hope *Refuge* exhibits both those emotions. I am interested in a revolution of the spirit. I value the sense of family and community that is the cornerstone of Mormon religion. But I despise the lack of thinking inherent to all orthodoxies, where humanity's responsibility to the here-and-now is abdicated to a blind faith in "the life hereafter."

And yes, I'm openly critical of the traditional historic place of
in Mormon culture. It's a strongly patriarchal society. I think that needs
to be questioned, because it ultimately has to do with how we treat the
land; the repression of women parallels the repression of the earth. But
I do believe the place of women is slowly changing within the Mormon
church—because the women are changing.

TBR: How long was *Refuge* in the writing?

TTW: It began in 1983, so it was seven years. And during all that time, if you
had asked me if I was writing, I would have answered no. But during those
seven years, I filled 22 journals. I guess it was my way of articulating on
an intensely personal level what was happening, and I didn't talk about it.
When you are engaged in the process of dying—helping someone you love
to die—there's work to be done; you just do it. My journals allowed me to
dialogue with death. And *Refuge* came directly out of those journals.

TBR: The way the book is structured, it's as if you weren't aware during the
time your mother and grandmother were dying what the cause of their
cancers might have been—that it all just sort of came together for you, an
epiphany, sometime later.

TTW: Yes. For years, every time I went south into the desert, I would have
these horrifying dreams of nuclear explosions. But it wasn't until a year
after Mother's death that my father told me I had in fact witnessed such
an explosion. Suddenly, all the pieces of the puzzle came together for
me. I realized we, too, were downwinders. Suddenly, my poetics of place
evolved into a politics of place. It was then that I made the decision to
write *Refuge*. And once I crossed that line—physically, at the Nevada test
site, as well as psychologically in the recognizing that the price of obedience is too high—I could never go back . . . back to the same place in the
family, the same place within Mormon culture.

TBR: Do you have another book in mind yet, and will it be as revolutionary as
Refuge?

TTW: My writing comes out of my life. Every one of my books has come to me
as a question. In the case of *Pieces of White Shell*, I asked, "What stories
do we tell that evoke a sense of place?" That book, of course, focused
on traditional Navajo stories and beliefs. In a very real way, the Navajo
people inspired me to return home, to look within my own culture, my
own stories. *Coyote's Canyon* was an experiment in weaving such stories
together. And in *Refuge*, the question was simply, "How does one find
refuge in change?"

A Voice in the Wilderness

The next question I would like to ask will have to do with an "erotics of place," as it relates to our love, or lack of love, towards the natural world. In other words, how does our intimacy with each other, or lack of intimacy, affect our intimacy with the land? Like death, I think our sensuality is something we're afraid of and so we have avoided confronting it. I am interested in taboos, because I believe that's where the power of our culture lies. I love taking off their masks so we can begin to face the world openly. I believe *that* will be our healing.

Wild Heart

The Politics of Place

Justine Toms, *New Dimensions Radio Show*, 1994

Our guest today is Terry Tempest Williams, naturalist-in-residence in the Utah Museum of Natural History and author of Refuge: An Unnatural History of Family and Place, *which chronicles the rise of the Great Salt Lake and the death of her mother from ovarian cancer. Her book,* An Unspoken Hunger: Stories from the Field *is a testament to the continuing power of nature to enrich our minds and our lives. She is the recipient of the 1993 Lannan Literary Fellowship for Nonfiction. Join us for the next hour as we speak of the power of nature to heal and bring us together in healthy community, with our guest Terry Tempest Williams. My name is Justine Toms; I'll be your host. Welcome to* New Dimensions.

Justine Toms, "Wild Heart: The Politics of Place," New Dimensions radio interview, December 30, 1994, program 2460. Produced by New Dimensions World Broadcasting Network. Used by permission.

A Voice in the Wilderness

JUSTINE TOMS: Terry, welcome.

TERRY TEMPEST WILLIAMS: Thank you, Justine, it's wonderful to be with you.

JT: You have said that we are all rooted in a place, something that holds us, that we can comprehend. How did you discover that for yourself?

TTW: I think that a notion of rootedness, of homeland, is in each of us, and each of us defines it differently. For me it's in Utah. Four, five, six generations of my family are deeply rooted in the Great Basin and the American West. My family is Mormon. We literally came over in a Handcart Company in the 1800s and sought spiritual refuge in the Salt Lake Valley. So I've never really been able to separate family, spirituality, landscape, and home. But I think that we all have our own stories. Some of these stories are about rootedness, and some of them may be about rootlessness. But I think that we need to pay attention.

JT: I want to go back to your grandmother, Mimi. You begin your book, *An Unspoken Hunger*, by mentioning Mimi and seashells. And you also share Mimi in your other book, *Refuge*. So I want to talk about her. Tell me the story of Mimi.

TTW: Well, I carry her with me. And, as you know, she is a powerful mentor of mine. I say 'is' because, even though she died in 1989, her spirit is still present, as I think all of our grandmothers' spirits are with us, living or dead. The story that I tell in *An Unspoken Hunger* is something that happened when I was seven or eight. Mimi said, "Terry, I have a wonderful winter project for us." And she brought out this huge, huge bowl of shells that she had collected on her various journeys to the Pacific Ocean in California. And so we got out field guides, picture books, encyclopedias, a blue ballpoint pen, and some adhesive tape, and we would pick one shell and then pore through the field guides until she said, "Ah, here it is—what does this word say? What does this picture evoke?" And we would talk about this white shell with a pink lip, and she would say, "Yes, pink murex." And then we would write the name "pink murex" on the adhesive tape, break it off, put on the mouth of the shell, and put it in the bowl. And we would repeat that process for other shells: olivella shells, angel wings, cowries, melongena. This was a wonderful introduction into taxonomy—not only to naming things, but also to the sensuality of nature in objects. And then, when we were through and it was time for bed, I would take a bath and take the shells with me into the tub—somehow recreating this ocean environment even in the most small, intimate way.

JT: What does the naming do? Can you take us back to you as a seven year old learning the name of something? What does that feel like?

TTW: I think it's about familiarizing ourselves, don't you? We say that the names matter, and then we say that the names don't matter. You know: I see the mountain, I don't see the mountain, I see the mountain. But for me, as a child and now as a woman, as a naturalist, the names still matter to me because it's about recognizing who we live among. So whether it's California gull, black-necked stilt, American avocet, grizzly bear, coyote, or the names of shells—melongena, cowry, pink murex, whelk—one word evokes an entire narrative, an entire story connected to place.

JT: That reminds me of when you met a woman in New York City as you were naming these different animals and rocks and shells. Could you tell us that story?

TTW: Certainly. I was an intern at the American Museum of Natural History in New York, and I worked with a wonderful woman, Lee Miller, who had a very strong sense of place that was rooted in Pelham Bay Park, near the Bronx. It was an extraordinary experience to go out with her. When we went on a collecting trip for the museum gathering invertebrates—killifish, clams, so forth—I got to see the world through her eyes. When I first went out with her I had my Western bias and was horrified at what the people in New York considered "wetlands." But as I began to see the world through her eyes, I realized that it takes so little to sustain life that, even in these wetlands that had been drained, dredged, and dumped in, there was life in all its vitality—even a Black Crowned Night heron standing in the reeds staring at us.

JT: So we can find that sense of place and that sense of the natural wherever we are.

TTW: I think so, don't you?

JT: I do. I keep getting this image of these delicate little plants, delicate little flowers, that will come up through the cracks of the cement. If left alone, they just take over the cement in no time.

TTW: Yes, there are these remnants of wildness all around us. And then I think about the large open spaces of wildness that we still have in this country, particularly in the American West. We still have a chance to do something right by embracing these wild places, by offering legislative protection. If we don't, if we allow everything to become urbanized, if we allow everything to be an object of our exploitations, what will be the cost? What will the loneliness be that we suffer as a result of our lack of attention to wildness?

JT: And I know you speak from a deep-feeling place. Recently, my partner Michael and I traveled up to Oregon by car. I hadn't been up through the Northern part of California in a long time, and it felt so wonderful to be amongst the big trees again, just to be in the presence of these enormous consciousnesses and to see wild elk right off the highway. And this is your life. You go out into nature, into the wilderness, all the time—is that right?

TTW: I can't separate my life from that. And as you speak, as you evoke these images of the Pacific Northwest, of driving into Oregon and feeling the presence of ancestors—the ancient forests—my heart is just pierced because the other side of what you are feeling can be summed up in one word: clearcut. And what is the result? I think about how, for all practical purposes, the Tahoe salmon are gone as we know them, that less than a hundred years ago, stories are told of the native peoples who lived there that you could literally walk across the backs of salmon to reach the other side of the river. Now we're lucky if we see one or two. What does that mean? What does that mean in terms of our idea of community? What does that mean, again, in terms of the sustainability of our relations, deep relations? So more than ever before, I feel both the joy of wildness and the absolute pain in terms of what we are losing. And I think we're afraid of inhabiting, of staying in this landscape of grief, yet if we don't acknowledge the grief, if we don't acknowledge the losses, then I feel we won't be able to step forward with compassionate intelligence to make the changes necessary to maintain wildness on the planet.

JT: You talk about the paradox of feeling the joy in what is still available and the pain of what we are losing. Let's stay with the paradox for a moment. How does it help us to stay there and feel both of those places?

TTW: I don't know, except that I believe it's a dance. And I believe that it makes us more human. I love Clarice Lispector when she writes in her book, *An Apprenticeship*, "and what human beings want more than anything else is to become human beings." If we don't allow ourselves to feel the full range of emotion—deep joy and deep pain—then I think we are less than who we can be.

JT: Right now we are working on how to get along with each other, and, in reading your words, and knowing you, I suspect that you see a connection between really being present to the natural world and really being able to relate to each other as human beings.

TTW: I think that's very true. I think of my uncle, Alan, the subject of the essay in *An Unspoken Hunger* called "The Village Watchman." Though there is no mention of environment or landscape in that essay, and yet I think that he has been one of my most powerful teachers of what an ecological life might mean. He was 10 years my senior, and I remember a conversation that I had with him at my Grandma's house when I was eight or nine. I remember saying to him, "How are you doing?" And he said, "Ask me how I'm feeling." And I said, "Okay, how are you feeling?" And he said, "Right now, today?" "Yes." "I am very happy, and I am very sad." And I remember thinking, how can that be, how can we hold two opposing views in our mind at once? And then he said, "They live in the same house, didn't you know?"

This is paradoxical ability that we have to hold opposing views in our mind at once, in our heart at once. Alan—and he was someone who, in our culture would be called "mentally retarded," or "mentally disabled," and all of the labels we put on people—had such an insight into a life of greater intention. And more than anything else, Alan taught me what it means to live and love with a broken heart. And when you say, "So what good does this do us?" I think that, if we feel these kinds of emotions, it enables us to live in the landscape of compassion and to live in the world with a sense of empathy.

JT: So you're really talking about asking new questions, or asking questions in a different way.

TTW: I think so. And I think that if we could begin to look at the world in the context of "other"—other creatures, other forms of life—that our world would be defined differently.

JT: We live in a society where people are being laid off from jobs, jobs are switching, jobs are changing, companies are downsizing, people are looking for new work and trying to figure out what they are going to do with their lives. And at the same time our communities are having a hard time keeping the systems going—the fire support systems, the school systems, and the libraries, and so forth. We have all of these people-to-people problems to focus on in our communities, and what you are talking is expanding the question to also include something else. How can we afford to do that?

TTW: How can we afford not to do that? I think of two stories, if you don't mind me sharing. First, the Second Morelia Symposium was held this year in Morelia, Mexico. The first Morelia Symposium was held in 1991 in anticipation of the Earth Summit in Rio in 1992. This second symposium was held in January, in anticipation of the conference in Cairo in September, 1994, talking about population and development. At the symposium, writers, poets, environmentalists, scientists, population biologists, and humanists gathered together to think about these things. The symposium produced a declaration. This time, our emphasis was on questions. What questions might we ask? What questions might we set before our world leaders to consider? And we came up with eight. May I share them with you?

JT: Oh please do.

TTW: I think this is a response to your question, "can we afford to do this?" We and our leaders might ask ourselves: 1) How can we consider environmental protection to be a luxury? 2) What will happen if we continue to insist on dominance, instead of balance, at the expense of every other species? 3) Will the child of the next century see a monarch butterfly, a tiger, or a grizzly bear, or walk in the forest in Malaysian Borneo, Mexico's Lacandon Wilderness, or anywhere in West Africa? 4) Why is the production of a machine gun treated as economically desirable, while cleaning a river from which people must drink is considered a costly extravagance? 5) How realistic are official environmental policies that ignore the overconsumption and population crises? 6) Why are we afraid to offer adequate information on reproductive health services to our youth? 7) What will our money be worth when we have turned the Earth into a wasteland? And 8) Do you think these questions have anything to do with you? If so, what can we do about that?

JT: I'm speaking with Terry Tempest Williams, the author of *An Unspoken Hunger*. My name is Justine Toms. You're listening to New Dimensions. [music break]

JT: Those wonderful sounds of our kin were produced—or were taken, they weren't produced—but they were recorded by Paul Winter on an album called *A Prayer for the Wild Things*.

TTW: I love that album. It's so wonderful, speaking of "other." Justine, I was going to say, when you asked about jobs—and so often we bring that idea up when we're talking about the environment. "Well if we preserve the environment, then what about jobs?" There is a wonderful metaphor of this, and an actual example, in one of the rainforests in Central Mexico where there is a sanctuary for monarch butterflies, where they all migrate—23 million, if you can imagine. We were in the middle of this, and, as Bill McKibben was saying, it was as though we were inside the "Mind of God." If you can imagine 23 million individuals . . .

26

JT: You know, I really can't imagine that.

TTW: I couldn't either. Imagine one monarch butterfly flapping its wings, mul-
        tiplied by 23 million. It was a sound unlike anything I have ever heard in
        my life. The only way I can describe it to you is that, when you are outside
        of that sound, you are absolutely gripped with an almost inconsolable
        loneliness. But the villagers there—there are individuals in the village
        whose sole job is to pick up monarchs off of the trail and place them back
        into the arms of the trees. Or, if there is an element of shade on the trail,
        these gentlemen, these children, will pick up the butterflies and put them
        into pockets of sunshine so that their wings become full again.

        I think that is honest work.

JT: Oh, that really takes my heart and opens it.

TTW: Isn't that wonderful?

JT: That reminds me of a woman in Kenya, and you tell a story in your book,
        An Unspoken Hunger, about the planting of trees, about women and plant-
        ing trees. Can you talk about that?

TTW: Yes, Wangari Maathai,[1] I think, is one of the most potent human beings on
        the Earth right now, and it's her vision that one person does make a differ-
        ence and that the gesture looms large in the scheme of things. She started
        the Greenbelt movement in the 1970s with the idea that rural women in
        Africa, in Kenya, were carrying the environmental crisis on their backs—
        literally, in terms of carrying firewood—and that the degradation of the
        earth was literally being carried in their bodies. So she asked, "Why not
        gather indigenous seeds in the folds of our skirts?" Women would gather
        the seeds and plant them in nurseries, and then, as the plants grew, they
        would give these plants back to the women in the villages who would
        plant them on their land. It was an erosional measure, it was about fruit
        trees, and it was about restoring a forest that was in the process of degra-
        dation. And then she placed this in the hands of the children. And now,
        15 years later, millions of trees have been planted in Kenya. One woman's
        vision inspired other women's visions, which inspired the children. I think
        this is a marvelous story, and it gives me great hope and faith for what is
        possible in terms of restoration and healing on the earth.

JT: That reminds me of women in general and the image of the bear. I think
        of the bear as a very female presence, and I think of the ferocity of a

---

1.   Wangari Maathai (b. 1940) was awarded the 2004 Nobel Peace Prize for the ac-
        tivities that Williams describes in this interview.

27

mother bear. People think of the feminine spirit as very gentle, but there's also part that, when stirred, will do anything to protect its young, or to protect something that is important. It can be very fierce. And you have a whole chapter of different facets of the bear in your book, *An Unspoken Hunger*. Can you tell us what the bear represents for you?

TTW: Again, we're talking about mentors, whether it's Wangari Maathai or whether it's a grizzly. For me, the bear embodies these opposing views, that we can be both fierce and compassionate at once. The bear is above ground in spring and summer and below ground, hibernating, in fall and winter—and she emerges with young by her side. I think that's a wonderful model for us, particularly as women. And it's one I've tried to adopt. From the Day of the Dead[2] until April Fool's Day I'm home, and "home" consists of being with my husband Brooke, of writing, of whatever that creative time may be. So I think the bear offers us a model of how one lives with that paradox, of a public and private life, of a creative life as well as a life of obligation.

I also think that the bear encompasses the mysteries—that the fear of women and the fear of bears may be in our refusal to be tamed, the instincts we arouse. So I think the bear encompasses so much of our own mythology, not mention its own natural history, which largely remains a mystery to us. And I think about the places that the bear has inhabited in North America, and of the places now that are quiet because it is no longer there.

JT: I was just thinking of John McPhee writing about observing a bear in Alaska finding something to sit on and actually sliding down a slope. There is a sense of playfulness in bears, of fun, of joy. Other animals seem this way as well—the coyote, maybe, has humor.

TTW: Right! We're so cautious not to place anthropomorphic views on animals, but it's hard not to. Doug Peacock, who is as intimate with bears with anyone I know, has wonderful footage, a film of watching bears in Glacier National Park. One bear that he calls "Happy Bear" is literally trying to walk on ice and keeps falling through, but the delight of that summer morning is conveyed—early, early summer, with the snows melting in the high country. It's hard not to stand back and smile at the absolute sheer delight that we see in landscape.

JT: We have a lot of buzzards around here, and they are up so high, you know, that they can't be looking for food; they're just flying for the sheer

---

2.   The Day of the Dead (*Día de los Muertos*) is celebrated in Mexico on November 1 of each year.

fun of flying. I'm convinced that they are just enjoying the updrafts, the bliss of that.

TTW: That's right. In fact, I've heard stories told by friends who live in Jackson Hole, Wyoming, that they have seen white pelicans . . .

JT: Maybe we can talk about the white pelicans in just a moment. I'm speaking with Terry Tempest Williams, the author of *An Unspoken Hunger*. You're listening to New Dimensions.

[music break]

JT: I'm here with Terry Tempest Williams, and we're talking about the landscape that we live in, that we're connected to, that we're part of. And you were speaking about a climbing guide, a guide who . . .

TTW: I know, I get so excited because we're telling stories. There's a wonderful climbing guide, Jack Turner, who lives in Moose, Wyoming. He told us this story that they were up on top of the Grand Teton, 13,000+ feet, and he heard this clapping sound, and he couldn't imagine what that would be in this landscape of rock and sky. He looked up above him, and there were these circling, spiraling white pelicans. Can you imagine? He was so stunned and in awe of this, and he just held the moment. And when he got back down home, he started reading everything he could about pelicans What could this clicking sound, this clapping sound, be? No mention. And then there was this one citation that said, "Perhaps it is ecstasy; perhaps it is just the sheer bliss of circling at that elevation." And why not?

JT: Why not? You have a reading for us that I'd like you to share.

TTW: This is from "Undressing the Bear," and again, Justine, it talks about the opposing views, the paradoxical response we have to the world that we embrace as human beings and that we see in the animal world:

> Last spring, our family was in Yellowstone. We were hiking along Pelican Creek, which separated us from an island of lodgepole pines. All at once, a dark form stood in front of the forest on a patch of snow. It was a grizzly, and behind her, two cubs. Suddenly, the sow turned and bolted through the trees. A female elk crashed through the timber to the other side of the clearing, stopped, and swung back toward the bear. Within seconds, the grizzly emerged with an elk calf, secure in the grip of her jaws. The sow shook the yearling violently by the nape of its neck, threw it down, clamped her claws on its shoulders, and began tearing the flesh back from the bones with her teeth. The cow elk, only a few feet away, watched the sow devour her calf. She pawed the earth desperately with her front hooves, but the bear was oblivious. Blood dripped from the sow's

muzzle. The cubs stood by their mother, who eventually turned the carcass over to them. Two hours passed. The sow buried the calf for a later meal. She slept on top of the mound with a paw on each cub. It was not until then that the elk crossed the river in retreat.[3]

JT: Such a powerful image. That reminds me, you mention in your book that you spent some time with Edward Abbey, just talking about storytelling—and he was a storyteller, and one that roamed about the rich landscape. Tell us about him. What was your memory and feeling for him? He died in 1989.

TTW: He did. I think that, for so many of us in this country connected with the conservation movement, Edward Abbey spoke to all of us, whether it was *Desert Solitaire*, whether it was the *Monkey Wrench Gang*, or his essays about going down rivers. He embodied a sacred rage, and an outrage. He was completely politically incorrect, which I must say I find very refreshing these days. And he wasn't afraid of humor, and wicked humor. But there was always this core that asked, "How do we live with wildness, what do we do to maintain that, and what is acceptable and what is not." Ed was a man who knew it in his body, from the soles of his feet, literally. I think we're taught not to trust our own experience, and experience is all we have. And if we fail to simplify, to spend time, to slow down, then where does that leave us? We have no memory, and memory fuels great actions. Memories of loss, memories of love, and memories of action can jar us out of complacency. I remember the last time I was with Ed. We were hiking through Mill Creek Canyon, near Arches National Park in Utah, and I said, "So Ed, what's next?" And he said, "I'm thinking of running for governor of Arizona." And I said, "Oh really." And he said, "Yeah, I think the voter turnout has been a little bit too low in my state." I think it's important for us to find ways to jar each other out of complacency and to think about how we can engage in this revolution, this evolution of the spirit. Octavio Paz says that it requires both love and criticism. I think that is powerfully rendered in Edward Abbey's work.

JT: Let's talk about storytelling. You had a wonderful natural occurrence in your life where rocks spoke to you. In fact, you call her "Stone Woman." Can you tell us a little bit about that experience?

TTW: I think I was on an extreme hallucinogenic. Not really; in Mormon culture you're allowed to have visions. This happened on a trip that Brooke and I took in to the Grand Canyon, and there is an extraordinary waterfall

---

3.   *An Unspoken Hunger: Stories from the Field* (New York, Pantheon, 1994), 58-59.

at Stone Creek. I remember walking up to this place, and it wasn't a waterfall, Justine—I saw this *Stone Creek Woman*. And she was so clear to me, and so present to me, that I just sat at her feet. And I think about her at the bottom of the Grand Canyon, relegating the Colorado River. And sometimes she is full, and sometimes she is dry.

JT: When you mention her, I think of the Great Mother—an image of something we can hold that is there and here. She appears in the rocks, and the rocks become alive. Then, with the rocks and the moss and the breathing through the seasons, there is a peace there that is made alive.

TTW: And again, it's letting our boundaries dissolve so that anything is possible.

JT: Would you mind doing another reading?

TTW: *An Unspoken Hunger* [reading]:

> It is an unspoken hunger we deflect between knives—one avocado between us, cut neatly in half, twisted then separated from the large wooden pit. With the green fleshy boats in hand, we slice vertical strips from one end to the other. Vegetable planks. We smother the avocado with salsa, hot chilies at noon in the desert. We look at each other and smile, eating avocados with sharp silver blades, risking the blood of our tongues repeatedly.[4]

JT: That really is connecting us with everything. When do we slow down to have that kind of experience? That's available, just eating. It's so sensual, such an erotic act. And it's just totally being human. It even reminds me of what you read earlier, about the bear, bringing out the calf and feeding her young.

TTW: We are capable of both of these responses: to love, in terms of the bear, and the elk calf, the elk mother watching the sow devour her calf; eating avocados in the desert, risking the blood of our tongues repeatedly. It's life, and it is deeply sensual and deeply erotic. And again, how do we separate? Why would we separate ourselves from the land, from the food, from the body, from blood, from our voice? It's how the poetics of place translates to a politics of place, to an erotics of place.

JT: Go back. The poetics of place to the politics of place—help us make that bridge.

TTW: I think it's where we began our conversation, Justine, with the naming of things: pink murex, melongena, cowry—the shells that suddenly we see in context of a beach, in context of a place, in context of a people holding those shells, digging for clams, eating them, the nourishment of our body. And

---

4.   *Unspoken Hunger*, 79.

31

what happens when that becomes out of balance? What happens when the beaches no longer support those shells, those creatures? What happens when the oil slicks from the Exxon Valdez make impossible that connection between place, creature, and community? I think that the naming of things, the poetics of place, the passion that we feel, is naturally translated to a politics of place—standing our ground in the places we love. And that, too, is sensual because it is about passion, and we are so fearful and frightened of that. Audrey Lord says that we have been raised to fear the "yes" within ourselves. And then we go back full circle to the fact that our lack of intimacy with the land has initiated a lack of intimacy with each other. It's this whole spiral, circle, connectedness of how we live our lives. It's what Abbey was saying.

JT: What about the seasons? You also talk about the connection with the larger picture, too, of the seasons, of the year as it moves around. Maybe that's something that you could tell us about. I know that you said that you take time out in the darker months of the year, but how can we be better with the seasons?

TTW: I only need a quote from DH Lawrence's poem, "The Old Church Knew," talking about "blood knowledge":

> Oh, what a catastrophe for man
> when he cut himself off from the rhythm of the year,
> from his union with the sun and the earth.
> Oh, what a catastrophe, what a maiming of love when it was a
> personal, merely personal feeling, taken away from the rising
> and setting of the sun, and cut off from the magic connection
> of the solstice and the equinox!
> This is what is the matter with us.
> We are bleeding at the roots.[5]

The land is love. Love is what we fear. To disengage from the earth is our own oppression. I really believe that, Justine.

JT: Those are really powerful words: "to disengage from the earth is our own oppression." Tell us your own experience of that.

TTW: If we lose our connection to landscape—if we forget where the source of our power lies—a real power, not power in Washington, not power based

---

5. Lawrence's "poem" here is actually a prose excerpt from his essay *A Propos of Lady Chatterly's Lovers*, (London: Mandrake Press, 1930).

on oppression, but power derived from an authentic life, from a life in balance, from a life of beauty, awe, integrity, compassion, empathy, then how can we know liberty? How can we know the truth of our souls? How can we know other?

JT: And that is something that you don't have to have an education to do, you don't have to have money to do—it's a quality that you're talking about, a quality that's available to all of us.

TTW: Yes. And I think this is the *unspoken hunger*. This is our desire, our yearning, our longing to connect with some place, some one, some thing other, outside, beyond ourselves.

JT: And how do we reach out and do that?

TTW: I don't know, but I fantasize. I think about what would happen if we took an act like the Homestead Act, where everyone had a 160 acre parcel that they fostered—what would happen if we turned that inside out and created the Homestand Act, where as a people in this country, we literally stood our ground, and we really thought about the whole idea of home rule. That we did, in fact, extend our notion of community to include all life forms. And that we began to engage in this politics of place born out of compassion, a deep love, and a deep sense of rootedness.

JT: Oh, you have to tell us about the wild cards.

TTW: Well, this was something that we were thinking about as a group of women: what would happen if, as women, as human beings, as members of this nation, if we were to create a deck of wild cards. And if we saw a landscape that was degraded, we would lay down our card to say, "This is inappropriate." If we saw an act in Congress that we disagreed with, we would absolutely flood the desks of our representatives and senators with the wild cards. If we were at a board meeting, and we saw oppression, if we saw inappropriate policy, we would lay all of our cards on the table, wild cards, saying that the games of women are not the games of men. I would love to see this kind of action that is based both in humor and playfulness as well as a fierceness—a force to be reckoned with.

JT: May it be so. I am speaking with Terry Tempest Williams, the author of *An Unspoken Hunger: Stories from the Field*. Terry, thank you for being with us today.

TTW: Thank you, Justine.

Terry Tempest Williams

Derrick Jensen, *Listening to the Land: Conversations about Nature, Culture, and Eros*, 1995

Terry Tempest Williams has written that "it's strange to feel change coming. It's easy to ignore. An underlying restlessness seems to accompany it like birds flocking before a storm. We go about our business with the usual alacrity, while in the pit of our stomach there is a sense of something tenuous."

Where, Terry Tempest Williams asked, can we find refuge in change? She has answered that question as well, "I am slowly, painfully discovering that my refuge is not found in my mother, my grandmother, or even the birds of Bear River. My refuge exists in my capacity to love. If I can learn to love death then I can begin to find refuge in change."

Terry Tempest Williams is naturalist-in-residence at the Utah Museum of Natural History in Salt Lake City. Her first book, Pieces of White Shell: A Journey to Navajoland, *received the 1984 Southwest Book Award. She is also the author of* Coyote's Canyon, Refuge: An Unnatural History of Family and Place, *two children's books, and most recently,* An Unspoken Hunger: Stories from the Field. *She is the recipient of the 1993 Lannan Literary Fellowship in creative nonfiction.*

Derrick Jensen, *Listening to the Land: Conversations About Nature, Culture, and Eros* (San Francisco: Sierra Club Books, 1995), 310–26. Reprinted by permission.

DERRICK JENSEN: What does the erotic mean to you?

TERRY TEMPEST WILLIAMS: It means "in relation." Erotic is what those deep relations are and can be that engage the whole body—our heart, our mind, our spirit, our flesh. It is that moment of being exquisitely present.

It does not speak well for us as a people that we even have to make the distinction between what is erotic and what is not, because an erotic connection is a life-engaged, making love to the world that I think comes very naturally.

Eroticism, being in relation, calls the inner life into play. No longer numb, we feel the magnetic pull of our bodies toward something stronger, more vital than simply ourselves. Arousal becomes a dance with longing. We form a secret partnership with possibility.

The moment I realized that life is sexual, that death is sexual, *in relation*, was when Mother was dying, in those last hours. We were breathing together. It was a dialogue between mother and daughter, between two women, between human beings.

The permeability of the body was present. I felt her spirit disengage from the soles of her feet and move upward to leave out the top of her head. It was as though she was climbing through her body on a ladder of light. The only analogue I had for that feeling was in making love when you're moving toward orgasm. Again, you are walking up that ladder of light. It's almost like being inside a piece of music, moving up the scale, the pitch gets higher and higher and more intense, more intense. My mother's death was one of the most sensual, sexual, erotic encounters I have ever had.

I don't know why that should have surprised me. It is that immediacy of life, even in death.

That experience changed everything for me.

DJ: What did you do . . .

TTW: After Mother died, our family stayed with her body. Her spirit was very much present in that room. We all felt the peace of that moment, as well as the loss. But again, she was so present that grief was not yet a part of it. I remember when my husband, Brooke, and I finally left, my first impulse once outside was to look up. "Where are you?" How could something so full, so tangible, so alive, be gone and vanish into air? My only solace was to look at the full face of the moon and see my mother's face illumined.

I didn't articulate for a long time what that encounter had been for me. Then one morning, Brooke was waxing his skis and I went downstairs and started to explain to him what Mother and I had shared, what that landscape of death really meant to me.

He said, "I know exactly what you're talking about. I have the same experience whenever I go powder skiing."

I was incensed. At first I thought, what a sacrilege, here I am trying to talk about this profound moment and he's reduced it to powder skiing. And then, suddenly, I realized powder snow is his passion. That is where he lifts off from the face of the earth and moves through an ocean of snow—weight and release, weight and release. He becomes a bird, an angel, mediating between two worlds. Each person has their own intimate connection to the erotic, to the sacred, to that movement. Once again, it's that notion of surrendering to something greater than ourselves.

And of course, the erotic is about love, our deep hunger for communion, where issues of restraint and yearning, engagement and desire enter us.

When I think about the moments in my life when I have felt engaged, it's always about love. With my mother, I was loving a woman who gave me life, realizing this was a dialogue, that here was the woman who not only gave me my body, but helped to nurture and create my soul. I had always felt my indebtedness to her, and suddenly in her moment of death I felt her trust. I think that was the first time I really saw how much she loved me, enough to trust me even with her life, enough that we could breathe her, birth her, into the next world. She allowed me to be a midwife to her soul.

A gift.

Erotic moments. Love. And I believe it is a two-way love, acts of reciprocity, where both parties involved are giving and receiving. When love is only one-way, eventually it becomes pornographic, a body that is used, rather than a body that is shared.

Without feeling. Perhaps these two words are the key, the only way we can begin to understand how our abuse of each other contributes to our abuse of the land. Could it be that what we fear most is our capacity to feel, and so we annihilate symbolically and physically that which is beautiful and tender, anything that dares us to consider our creative selves? The erotic world is silenced, reduced to a collection of objects we can curate and control, be it a vase, a woman, or wilderness. Our lives become a piece in the puzzle of pornography as we "go through the motions" of daily intercourse without any engagement of the soul.

If I am honest, one reason the erotic is so intriguing to me is because in the culture I was raised in eroticism is the ultimate taboo. It isn't your body that is valued; it is your soul. Our souls could always be saved in spite of our bodies. It's not this world that counts; it's the hereafter.

Why is that? What are we afraid of? That's the question I keep asking myself. What is our culture afraid of? Why are we so afraid of the body?

I believe our most poignant lessons come through the body, the skin, the cells, our DNA. It's where our ancestral memory is. It's where the future will be changed. And what we take in we ultimately give away. If we stop the world from penetrating us, what does that mean? The body allows us to be human. It is through the body we feel the world, both its pain and its beauty.

DJ: If we stop the world from penetrating us, we're living in solitary confinement. The only love that can exist is one way.

TTW: I've been thinking about marriage, and what that is in terms of an institution. The oppression of marriage as well as the liberation of marriage, and how it's not something that people really share. Many people have facades of marriages. But are they engagements? Are they marriages in their bodies? Why don't we talk about what it means to be married? What it means to be married to our self? What it means to be married to a lover, a partner? What it means to be married to the earth, to our dreams, to community? What it means to be married to a politics of place that can both inform and inspire us?

When I think about Brooke and I making love, I often think of that deep peace that follows. That's the peace I would love to hold, because of those deep relations and that sense of connectedness, that sense that we are not alone in the world. Every time we make love to a human being, fully, we are making love to everything that lives and breathes. In that sense it becomes communion. It is a sacrament.

This has nothing to do with orthodoxy. Maybe religions have every reason to fear the erotic, because it would take the walls down. The erotic defies convention. Anything becomes possible.

DJ: What's the connection between eros and the land?

TTW: Brooke and I were recently in Spain. As is the case with all travel, one is refreshed by having no responsibilities or obligations. It is a new landscape. We are not residents, we are simply visitors.

We were gone almost a month.. Everything was sensual. Everything was erotic. It's the gift of travel, where everything is infused with meaning, compressed, so you begin to see the golden strand that weaves life together. You are in a constant state of awe.

We drove into Portugal, to a place called Sagres. If Portugal is the face of a woman, and Spain is her hair, Sagres is the tip of her chin. It's a very powerful place, with sea so relentless there is no ocean-beach transition. It's just ocean-cliff. Portuguese fishermen stand on the edge of the cliffs like herons, casting lines of light two hundred feet below with tremendous faith, both that they're not going to be blown off and also that their lines will lure fish that will provide food for their families. I sat next to the fishermen on the cliffs for hours. My body trembled at the beauty of it, at the peace of the fishermen, at their fierce attention, the precarious nature of their stance, the ritual, the dailiness of their lives.

The longer I sat, the more frightened I became. The seduction of the sea was alluring. The pounding waves, the sheer face of the continent, the immensity, the beauty, the fact that the depth of the ocean was unfathomable to me—the whole situation was so arousing it was all I could do not to step off. I had an insatiable, unexplainable desire to leap, to merge. I don't know why I didn't.

Had I walked off the cliff, it would not have been out of despair. It would have been out of beauty, out of my desire to be *one with*. I think about Rilke, when he speaks of beauty as the beginning of terror. That's the edge, that fine line between life and death, the erotic impulse that moves us beyond fear.

DJ: Matthew Fox also quotes Rilke, that beauty "serenely disdains to destroy us."

TTW: How do you make peace with those kinds of contradictions ? At a pivotal moment in the wonderful novel *The Apprenticeship*, by Clarice Lispector, her main character, Lori, says, "I now know what I want: I want to remain standing still in the sea."

That's it. To be able to have that core of serenity in the middle of huge oscillations; to be present in those waves and emotional tides, but to possess a solidarity of soul. That's what I would like to hold for myself.

DJ: I have on my wall at home: "What do we do with contradictory impulses? We play with them. We accept them. Love them. Rejoice in them, and in the fact that we are alive, that we have choices, that the wind mingles with the branches and the snow kisses the soil."

TTW: That is lovely. It is what I so cherish about Great Salt Lake. It is Trickster. It is water in the desert that no one can drink. It is self-proclaimed wilderness with islands too stark, too remote to inhabit. It really is the liquid lie of the West. I love that. No one knows what to do with it.

I wonder why we have to do anything with it at all? Why can't it just be? Why are we always asking so much of ourselves or of these places of power? Is it not enough that they simply exist for their own right, whether it's Great Salt Lake, the ancient forests of the Northwest, or this ocean of sage that covers the Great Basin? Why must we always try to manipulate and control life?

It may be that our task now, as it has always been, is to listen. Simply that. If we really listen, the land will tell us what it wants, and tell us how we can live more responsively.

Just for fun, I made a spontaneous list of the lessons I have learned from the Great Basin. The Great Basin is about exposure. It's about austerity. It's about how nothing is as it appears and it's about aridity and the conservation of water. Again, in the Basin one finds deep relations with all their subtleties. I believe it is also about "deep time." John McPhee has created a beautiful canvas of these ideas in his book *Basin and Range.*

How can we take these qualities of the land and bring them to the table in terms of our politics and negotiations of how we as a people want to live in this desert landscape?

Exposure. Putting our cards on the table. Not being tactical. Not being hidden.

Aridity. Conservation. Conserving water. Conserving our energy. Perhaps living more lightly on this land that is not so forgiving. There is a history of human habitation in the Great Basin that spans ten thousand years. Perhaps we need to study our past to see what was known then that we may have forgotten.

The subtleties. Again, really listening. And time. It will take an enormous amount of time to really find out what habitation means in this country. We're just beginning to get a taste of it. And patience. We don't need to have all the answers right now. We may never have the answers, but as long as we keep driving the questions, or keep finding pockets of humility, maybe it won't seem so overwhelming or so difficult. Then maybe a rancher and an environmentalist can burn their labels and see each other as neighbors.

The environmental movement right now is not listening. We are engaged in a rhetoric as strong and as aggressive as the so-called opposition.

A Voice in the Wilderness

I would love to see the whole notion of opposition dissolved, so there's no longer this shadow dance between "us" and "them." I would love for us to listen to one another and try to say, "What do we want as members of this community? What do we love? What do we fear? What are our concerns? How do we dream our future? How do we begin to define home?" Then we would have something to build from, rather than constantly turning one another into abstractions and stereotypes engaged in military combativeness.

I believe we all desire similar things. The real poison of our society right now is that everything is reduced to such a simplistic level. There is no tolerance or hunger for complexity or ambiguity. Do you want this or that? Black or white? Yes or no? It strips us to our lowest denominator, creating a physics that is irreconcilable just by the nature of polarity. As a result, we miss the richness we can bring to one another in our diverse points of view. It is not about agreement. It is about respect.

Again, when Brooke and I were in Spain, we found ourselves in the Doñana National Park, one of the last remaining wetlands in Europe. We were there during spring migration, so we were able to witness waves of birds from both the European and African continents.

The wetlands happen to be on the edge of a beautiful town called El Rocío. We went on a Sunday morning to see the flamingos and the spoonbills. On the edge of the marsh is a beautiful whitewashed adobe *santuario*. An old woman handed each person a large candle. She said, "Light this candle with your desire in mind, let your desire pierce your heart, and take it home with you."

The people lighted their candles with their desires in mind, then moved into an alcove to put their candle onto a huge iron rack. In this white-tiled room with a statue of the Mother of Dew, each person stood next to their candle and tended to their desire, watching while the wax melted. When the wax had melted sufficiently to make a ball of it, each person took the wax home as a talisman.

The room was searing—there had to be hundreds, even thousands of candles, all burning at the same time, with people attending to their individual desires. It was wonderful. Brooke said to me, "My desire is melting into everyone else's." And that was precisely the point. When you're in that collective space in a ritualistic way, there is no way your desire won't merge with everyone else's desire. They are the desires of our highest selves.

That gives me comfort. Our needs as human beings are really very simple — to love and be loved, a sense of connection and compassion, a desire to be heard. Health. Family. Home. Once again the dance, that sharing of breath, that merging with something larger than ourselves.

DJ: That's a gift, and a contradiction. How does that relate to the houses that are being built in this canyon, to the trees in the Northwest that are going down now, and to women who are being raped right now? It's easy to tell myself to play with contradictions, but this is no spiritual game. Real canyons are ruined, real forests are destroyed, and real women are raped.

TTW: These are ultimately aggressions against ourselves. This is the blockage of time and the blockage of space. And it's building walls, it's building structure. It's whatever we can do to not be in that sacred space with our desires, to not be in that place of pilgrimage.

This is our addiction to speed and time. How can we have any sense of stillness when we have an insatiable appetite, when we have a big void inside because we've forgotten what we're connected to, we've forgotten where the source of our power lies? Everything becomes a substitution, with that hunger never being filled. So we build more houses, cut more trees, rape more women, thinking that will satisfy the yearning. But it only creates a deeper depression of the soul. Nothing is coming in — it's the one-way affection that becomes pornographic— because it's not a dance, it is an assault, an attack, the oppressor.

When we're in that space of oppression, we ultimately destroy that which we love. We fear that which we desire most.

The man who is building these houses in our canyon has more money than he knows what to do with. He is a man who has a deep desire for connection without knowing how to connect. I know this sounds judgmental. But I know him. I grew up with him. We played with his nine children, growing up in our neighborhood.

What if we were to hand this man a candle at El Rocío, on the edge of the migration of flamingos, and if he were to carry that candle into that room to sit with his desire? I'll bet his desire wouldn't have anything to do with money, greed, or power. I'll bet it would have to do with peace. It would have to do with being loved. It would have to do with trying to find his place in the world. One house. One self.

But we don't have time to even consider these things. So what we do is just engage in a speed of "development" that ultimately destroys both the land and ourselves.

To engage in the erotics of place means to engage in time.

DJ: And to engage in the erotics of personhood also means to engage in time.

TTW: We're not willing to give that time, because we might be affected. We might be altered, and that would force us to question the speed factor, the matrix of our very lives. Then what would happen? Would that be so terrible? Again, what are we afraid of?

I love how Edward Weston, the photographer, said he refused to drive faster than 35 miles an hour because he couldn't see. What does it mean that we zoom everywhere at 70 miles an hour? We are losing our ability to see.

DJ: If the ability to see and the ability to listen are not valued, what does this culture value?

TTW: My culture, if I were to define my culture as Mormon, values obedience, and adherence to the teachings of Jesus Christ. It values a work ethic. It values family, which means having children. And it values numbers.

Ultimately, my culture values control, a control which suppresses creative expression. That is necessary because creative expression threatens to undermine the status quo.

What does American culture value? In Washington, D.C., information is valued, because information is power.

DJ: And power within a patriarchy becomes eroticized. Marilyn French has written that women view sexuality primarily as a communication of pleasure, while men within a patriarchy view it primarily as an expression of power.

TTW: That's interesting. I understand what she is saying. Because it is about love, it's about exposure, it's about revealing who you are, and that is about having to change, having to be acted upon. Again, perhaps it is our different ways of defining power—the power with another human being versus power over another human being. One reveals love, the other reveals fear. We are frightened of engagement, of being fully present, because then we risk feeling pain and we feel grief, the grief inherent in life.

It comes back to the notion of time. If we are always busy, if we create an atmosphere of busyness around us, we don't have to penetrate anything in depth. We live on surfaces. We don't have time for connections.

But if we spend time with people, listen, see them for who they are, relationships develop, accountability arrives and stereotypes shatter. Power in the dark sense disappears in favor of cooperation. We face each other as human beings. Suddenly, the world is much more unpredictable, and that is very frightening.

That's why it's so much easier if everything remains an abstraction. "I hate ranchers." "Goddamn those environmentalists." "Don't tempt my heart."

Let's keep things simple.

DJ: I once had a friend who was a rancher. We've only spoken twice in the last couple of years, because each time we talk now he yells at me for being a nature writer. I'm not sure how to respond. We'd been friends for seven years.

TTW: We all feel schizophrenic. Here is a friendship that is being split apart because of an assumed ideology. How do we begin to break down these barriers? What candles can we light for one another to begin the healing? I believe all we can ask of ourselves is that we are as honest as we can be in our relations. I know I have personally been broken open a thousand times because of differing opinions or beliefs within my culture, with the people I love. And it is a very private pain. I don't think we are ever immune from being hurt by those we care about. For me, I must stay in my truth, my center, and that has everything to do with my relationship to the land.

That is also where my grief lies, because of what we are doing to the Earth and its inhabitants. It's almost as though our own personal pain is so intolerable that if we destroy everything that is beautiful around us, we will no longer have a mirror to look at, to remind us of our impoverishment. If the world is only a strip mine, if the world is only a clear-cut, our own impoverishment is easier to bear—there's nothing to remind us of the richness of life, even our own. And again there is nothing to remind us where the true source of our power comes from. What we are doing as a species is an incredible mass abuse of our own spirit: and of the spirit of life around us.

I don't think about hope much anymore. But I do think about imagination. That's where we have the capacity to shift. And that's another aspect of eroticism.

DJ: When you feel love—for an individual person, for a place, for your self, for anything—everything becomes bearable.

TTW: It's in the context of love—love of the universe, in terms of a creation as divine as this, love between two people, the love we have toward our work, our families—that we can really allow ourselves to experience the full range of human emotion. We can experience the beauty and the terror, and we can be both fierce and compassionate at once. It is this honesty of spirit that is completely paradoxical. Once again, I think of Great Salt Lake as my mentor.

DJ: Are beauty and terror, fierceness and compassion, paradoxical?

TTW: Paradox is life. It's the same thing as balance. You can't have one without the other. There's always that creative third, which is where possibility lies. It's Jeannette Armstrong's En'owkin concept—give me your contraire, and we'll have something to talk about. Tell me what you fear most and then we can talk about what we desire most. Then this "third thing," which in this case is conversation or understanding, becomes the creative expression of an idea. Art. Story.

DJ: I'm thinking about grief and about hope. The mass abuse will undoubtedly get worse as we try to hold on to an industrial civilization that can't last. This transition will be very painful for humans and nonhumans alike. I've come to know that one of the most important things we can do through this transition is hold each other, including the land, while many beautiful things die.

TTW: I agree with you. And I've been thinking about what it means to bear witness. The past ten years I've been bearing witness to death, bearing witness to women I love, and bearing witness to the testing going on in the Nevada desert. I've been bearing witness to bombing runs on the edge of the Cabeza Prieta National Wildlife Refuge, bearing witness to the burning of yew trees and their healing secrets in slash piles in the Pacific Northwest and thinking this is not so unlike the burning of witches, who also held knowledge of healing within their bones. I've been bearing witness to traplines of coyotes being poisoned by the Animal Damage Control. And I've been bearing witness to beauty, beauty that strikes a chord so deep you can't stop the tears from flowing. At places as astonishing as Mono Lake, where I've stood knee-deep in saltwater to watch the fresh water of Lee Vining Creek flow over the top like oil on vinegar . . . It's the space of angels. I've been bearing witness to dancing grouse on their leks up at Malheur in Oregon. Bearing witness to both the beauty and the pain of our world is a task I want to be part of. As a writer, this is my work. By bearing witness, the story that is told can provide a healing ground. Through the art of language, the art of story, alchemy can occur. And if we choose to turn our backs, we've walked away from what it means to be human.

DJ: Once you know what it means to be human, you never *can* finally turn your back. Your body won't let you.

TTW: If we don't get it, we keep having the same nightmare over and over. And then you can say, "It was just a dream. Even though I woke up in the night with an incredible sweat, I have no idea what that's about." But if we don't respond to those dreams, to those nightmares, to those numinous moments of our nightlife, the message will move into the body. It's a lot harder to ignore two ruptured discs or bleeding intestines. The body has its own voice and when it chooses to speak, it is very difficult to ignore.

DJ: I had a dream last night. I came upon a fiery car wreck, and as I tried to save whatever was inside, my hands kept catching on fire. Then I heard a voice say, "Beyond hope and despair is play." Waking up from the dream, I knew that each of us is reaching into the fire, trying to pull out whatever we can.

TTW: Yes. Exactly. The last three words of my grandmother's life were, "Dance, dance, dance." That's it. It's those grouse dancing on the sage flats, even in the rain, crazy with desire, their pumping breasts creating the sound of water. It's eros, it's love, that nurtures and feeds our soul.

We're so serious. We're so earnest. We forget, fear, and mistrust our own trickster energy because people don't have time to listen, to notice when we are playing, when we are provoking. Where are our clowns? Where are the Koshare of our tribes?

DJ: The exact moment I understood relationships was when I read a letter that said, "All there is to do is play."

TTW: Through play we develop relations and see each other whole. Through play tension is released, and joy is found. Humor emerges and that can be very intimate. This takes time. The culture at large views play as something frivolous, something that belongs to children. But that's how community is created. If we don't have time to play together, to eat meals together, to make love together, what holds us together? We drive fast in our cars, we have workloads that are unrealistic and horrendous and self-imposed for one reason or another, and we're not creating community. We're creating desperate, isolated, fast-paced lives that give us enormous excuse not to be engaged. We are lonely.

DJ: How can we live, and live in community, if we move every three years?

TTW: I was very fond of Wally Stegner. I always felt he was the one person who really understood what it meant to be Mormon, what it meant to be raised in this valley—both the gift and burden one carries with that.

A few years ago, I was driving Wally and Mary, his wife, to the airport. As we drove down South Temple he gave us a wonderful annotated narration: "This is where your grandfather and I played tennis. This is where I used to go for milkshakes at Snelgrove's. This is where I wrote *Recapitulation*." We parked at the airport, and as I helped them with their bags, I turned to Wally and said, "Thank you so much for coming." He looked at me dead-eye center and responded, "Thank you for staying."

I've never forgotten that. It's given me great courage to live in a place I both love and at times find great difficulty in.

This is my place. It just may be that the most radical act we can commit is to stay home. What does that mean to finally commit to a place, to a people, to a community?

It doesn't mean it's easy, but it does mean you can live with patience, because you're not going to go away. It also means making a commitment to bear witness, and engaging in "casserole diplomacy" by sharing food among neighbors, by playing with the children and mending feuds and caring for the sick. These kinds of commitments are real. They are tangible. They are not esoteric or idealistic, but are rooted in a bedrock existence of where we choose to maintain our lives.

That way we begin to know the predictability of a place. We anticipate a species long before we see them. We can chart the changes, because we have a memory of cycles and seasons; we gain a capacity for both pleasure and pain, and we find the strength within ourselves and each other to hold these lines.

That's my definition of family. And that's my definition of love.

DJ: Bees have blessed me by bringing their relatives into my family. Through them I have become related to willows, dandelions, and wild roses in a very real way.

TTW: Isn't that a way to extend our notion of community to include all plants, animals, rocks, soils, rivers, and human beings? On Brooke's birthday a wonderful wave of Audubon's warblers flew in. "Hello. Happy Birthday." "Welcome home."

It's all so beautiful, so intensely beautiful.

DJ: How do the warblers, the stars, the trees speak to you?

TTW: For me, it has nothing to do with language.

Some people have a hard time picking flowers. I don't at all. There's so much underground, and they live in the land, and then one day it's all right to bring them inside. It's that permeability, the inner and the outer. I love bouquets of flowers in our home picked from our garden.

The doors of this house are always open. I can't tell you the animals that have inhabited our bedroom. Everything from porcupines to lizards to raccoons. We've had bats in this house, and hummingbirds. If we open our doors we receive a constant flow of visitations, or messengers. It's all about the pleasure and acknowledgment of sharing this place. It goes into our bodies, our hearts, our cells.

And I think there are times we rescue each other. When the hummingbird came in, I held her little body with cupped hands and felt her heart beating, beating, beating, beating. She became incredibly still. When I opened my hand outside she stayed for a few minutes to get her bearings, and then she flew.

Each time, it is a privilege to have that momentary encounter, that acknowledgment of other, those seconds of engagement.

It's those times, once again, when borders dissolve, when boundaries dissolve. It's that breath, that erotic moment, that third thing, that merging into something higher.

DJ: Merging, permeability, eros . . .

TTW: And mutability. If we're going to survive we have to learn how to be shape-shifters. This has nothing to do with inconsistency. It has to do with seizing the moment, perceiving what is necessary *in that moment.*

I remember the last time I was at the Nevada Test Site, before the moratorium.[1] Chief Raymond Yowell, a Shoshone elder, was officiating. He stood before the three thousand or more people gathered together, chanting and drumming, chanting and drumming. We had brought huge baskets and bowls of flowers, with the idea that we can throw flowers against evil.

Throwing flowers against evil comes from the Yaqui Easter ceremony. For several weeks during Easter season, Yaqui people reenact the passion play, a ritual they adopted from the Jesuits in the 15th century. Imagine this: a slow, inexorable build-up of evil against the forces of good. The *fariseos*, or pharisees, are dressed in black cloaks. They are masked and

---

1. The Nevada Test Site, a massive outdoor facility of some 1,375 square miles, is located 65 miles north of Las Vegas. The site was commonly used for testing nuclear weapons until October 2, 1992, when the United States declared a moratorium on nuclear tests.

they march to a slow, steady dirge, to the haunting flute music that is accompanying them. They are carrying the weight of evil that is leaning against the village. In their long black capes they forcefully make their way through the crowd of onlookers. Their goal is to literally penetrate the church. They have stolen the body of Christ, they have violated every sense of decency within the community, they have marred and destroyed the sacred.

The *fariseos* charge the church in full run. As they do this, they are showered with flower petals thrown against evil by the children, by the women on both sides of the human gauntlet. The young girls—five, six, seven years old—are adorned in crisp white dresses. They are the final barrier to the community's holy altar that the *fariseos* must penetrate. The *fariseos* charge again. The girls raise boughs of cottonwood and mesquite and wave them over the *fariseos*. The *fariseos* are repelled.

They retreat, take off their black capes and return to the *santuario* in confession.

A deer—the Deer Dancer—the most peaceful of animals, covered with flower petals, dances in the middle of the *fariseos*. The *fariseos* have been "changed to good" and are "forgiven." The universe is restored, health and peace have been returned to the village.

This story was told to me by Richard Nelson, an anthropologist who has attended the Yaqui ceremonies. I asked him if it would be all right to carry this story with me to the Test Site. He felt it would be appropriate, saying, "I think these stories exist for all of us as a means of understanding how to behave in the world."

A few days before the demonstration, my nieces, Callie, Sara, and I decided we would visit all the florists in town and ask if they had flowers they would like to donate to heal the Test Site. The florists opened their arms to us and within a few hours, the car was completely filled with flowers: roses, dahlias, daisies, tulips, irises, lilies, chrysanthemums, every type of bloom imaginable.

We brought the flowers home, laid them out on a white sheet in the middle of our living room, and started plucking the petals. We placed the greenery outside and organized the flowers in big black bowls and baskets.

While we worked, we told stories. We talked about their grandmother, my mother, and their great-grandmothers, and what might have caused their deaths. We spoke about the Test Site, about the whole notion of war, the possibilities of peace, and that we could in fact throw flowers against evil, that something this delicate and beautiful could make an extraordinary difference. We discussed the power of gesture.

I never thought about how we would get the flowers to the Test Site given that we were flying to Nevada. But once we arrived at the airport and people saw the flowers, rules disappeared.

"Of course you can carry more than two pieces of luggage onto the plane," the flight attendants said. They happily (and a bit subversively) strapped baskets of flowers into empty seats.

When we arrived in Las Vegas, various passengers volunteered to carry the flowers outside. The beauty was intoxicating.

Finally, at the Test Site we placed the baskets of flowers around the barbed wire fences and on the platform where Chief Yowell was drumming. The story was retold of the Yaqui passion play and how the community threw flowers at evil. Chief Yowell never wavered, but continued drumming and chanting, drumming and chanting. The children from the audience spontaneously rose and walked toward the bowls and baskets of flowers. They took them into their arms and distributed the petals throughout the crowd. Chief Yowell stopped drumming and spoke, "We will now enter the land like water . . ."

En masse, people moved across the Test Site, ducked under the barbed wire fence, crossed the cattle guard, and infiltrated the desert, sprinkling flowers upon the contaminated landscape.

"There is something older than war," writes the poet Lyn Dalebout.

It's all about being shape-shifters, it's about permeability, it's about malleability, it's knowing what each occasion demands, standing our ground in the places we love. I have tremendous faith in these things.

Through an erotics of place, I believe anything is possible.

The Politics of Place

An Interview with Terry Tempest Williams

Scott London, *Insight & Outlook* Radio Show, 1995

The connection between language and landscape is a perennial theme of American letters. Nature has been a well-spring for many of our finest writers—from Whitman and Thoreau to Peter Mathiessen and Edward Abbey. Terry Tempest Williams belongs in this tradition. A native of Utah, her naturalist writing has been richly influenced by the sprawling landscape of the West. It also draws on the values and beliefs of her Mormon background.

Terry Tempest Williams is the naturalist-in-residence at the Utah Museum of Natural History in Salt Lake City. She was thrown into the literary spotlight in 1991, with the release of her sixth book, Refuge: An Unnatural History of Family and Place. *It tells of how the Great Salt Lake rose to record levels and eventually flooded the wetlands that serve as a refuge for migratory birds in Northern Utah. Williams tells the story against the backdrop of her family's struggle with cancer as a result of living downwind from a nuclear test site.*

For Williams, there is a very close connection between ourselves, our people, and our native place. In the words of the Utne Reader—*who recently included her*

Scott London, "The Politics of Place: An Interview with Terry Tempest Williams," *Insight & Outlook*, National Public Radio, May 1995. Used by permission.

among their 100 leading "visionaries"—her writing "follows wilderness trails into the realm of memory and family, exploring gender and community through the prism of landscape."

In addition to her work as a naturalist and writer, she has been active in the struggle to conserve public lands. She has recently been embroiled in one of the most heated public-lands debates in the West. Together with the Southern Utah Wilderness Alliance, she is pursuing federal legislation that will designate as wilderness 5.7 million acres of land in Utah, to protect it from oil and gas exploration, dams, and other uses.

The following conversation took place in May 1995 in Santa Barbara, California.

SCOTT LONDON: You've said that your writing is a response to questions.

TERRY TEMPEST WILLIAMS: I think about Rilke, who said that it's the questions that move us, not the answers. As a writer, I believe that it is our task, our responsibility, to hold the mirror up to social injustices that we see and to create a prayer of beauty. The questions serve us in that capacity. Pico Iyer describes his writing as "intimate letters to a stranger," and I think that is what the writing process is. It begins with a question, and then you follow this path of exploration.

LONDON: At a recent talk you surprised a lot of people in the audience by saying that you don't consider yourself a writer. That was a very puzzling thing to hear from someone who has written eight books.

WILLIAMS: Yes. Well, it feels so presumptuous somehow. I know the struggle from the inside out and I would never be so bold as to call myself a writer. I think that is what other people call you. But I consider myself a member of a community in Salt Lake City, in Utah, in the American West, in this country. And writing is what I do. That is the tool out of which I can express my love. My activism is a result of my love. So whether it's trying to preserve the wilderness in Southern Utah or writing about an erotics of place, it is that same impulse—to try to make sense of the world, to try to preserve something that is beautiful, to ask the tough questions, to push the boundaries of what is acceptable.

LONDON: One of the underlying themes of your work is the power of place and the importance of a land we can call our own. Tell me about your own homeland.

WILLIAMS: I think the whole idea of home is central to who we are as human beings. What I can tell you about my home is that I live just outside of Salt Lake City in a place called Emigration Canyon. It's on the Mormon trail.

A Voice in the Wilderness

When Brigham Young came through with the early Mormon pioneers in 1847 and said "This is the place," that's the view we see every morning when we leave the Canyon and enter the Salt Lake Valley. So I feel deeply connected, not only because of my Mormon roots, which are five or six generations, but because of where we live. There isn't a day that goes by that I'm not mindful of the spiritual sovereignty that was sought by my people in coming to Utah.

LONDON: You once said that one needs a sense of humor to live in Salt Lake City.

WILLIAMS: That's very true, and increasingly so given the political climate that we see in this country, and especially in Utah. I also think that's true in the American West in general. You can't take yourself seriously very long because you are immediately confronted with big weather, big country, and there is a sense of humility that rises out of the landscape.

LONDON: I've been to Utah several times. The last time I was there I drove through on dusty back roads. I've been to the Sahara and even that seems more hospitable than some parts of Utah! It's so windy, desolate, and barren. I wonder how a landscape can inspire such reverence and poetry in one person and seem so God-forsaken to another.

WILLIAMS: I think it's what we're used to. Home is where we have a history. So when I'm standing in the middle of the salt flats, where you swear that the pupils of your eyes have turned white because of the searing heat that is rising from the desert, I think of my childhood, I think of my mother, my father, my grandparents; I think of the history that we hold there and it is beautiful to me. But it is both a blessing and a burden to be rooted in place. It's recognizing the pattern of things, almost feeling a place before you even see it. In Southern Utah, on the Colorado plateau where canyon walls rise upward like praying hands, that is a holy place to me.

LONDON: In *An Unspoken Hunger* you say, "Perhaps the most radical act we can commit is to stay home." What do you mean by that?

WILLIAMS: I really believe that to stay home, to learn the names of things, to realize who we live among . . . The notion that we can extend our sense of community, our idea of community, to include all life forms—plants, animals, rocks, rivers *and* human beings—then I believe a politics of place emerges where we are deeply accountable to our communities, to our neighborhoods, to our home. Otherwise, who is there to chart the changes? If we are not home, if we are not rooted deeply in place, making that commitment to dig in and stay put . . . if we don't know the names of things, if we don't know pronghorn antelope, if we don't know blacktail jackrabbit, if we don't know sage, pinyon, juniper, then I think we are living a life without specificity, and then our lives become abstractions. Then we enter a place of true desolation.

I remember a phone call from a friend of mine who lives along the MacKenzie River. She said, "This is the first year in 20 that the chinook salmon have not returned." This woman knows the names of things. This woman is committed to a place. And she sounded the alarm.

LONDON: You were talking about the concept of "community." What does that mean to you?

WILLIAMS: Community is extremely intimate. When we talk about humor, I love that you know when you're home because there is laughter in the room, there is humor, there is shorthand. That is about community. I think community is a shared history, it's a shared experience. It's not always agreement. In fact, I think that often it isn't. It's the commitment, again, to stay with something—to go the duration. You can't walk away. It's like a marriage, only I think it's more difficult to divorce yourself from community than it is from a human being because the strands are interconnected and so various.

LONDON: You mentioned Pico Iyer. He has described home as the sense of a bleak landscape—something that inspires the sort of melancholy that only a truly familiar place can evoke. That seems so very different from what you are saying.

WILLIAMS: Having lived in Utah all of my life, I can tell you that in many ways I know of no place more lonely, no place more unfamiliar. When I talk about how it is both a blessing and a burden to have those kinds of roots, it can be terribly isolating, because when you are so familiar, you know the shadow. My family lives all around me. We see each other daily. It's very, very complicated. I think that families hold us together and they split us apart. I think my heart breaks daily living in Salt Lake City, Utah. But I still love it. And that is the richness, the texture. So when Pico talks about home being a place of isolation, I think he's right. But it's the paradox. I think that's why I so love Great Salt Lake. Every day when I look out at that lake, I think, "Ah, paradox"—a body of water that no one can drink. But I think we have those paradoxes within us and certainly the whole idea of home is windswept with paradox.

LONDON: If we go back to your book *Refuge* for a moment, your "refuge" was tied both to a place and to a people, and you were losing them both. You called it an "unnatural history of family and place." In what way was it unnatural?

WILLIAMS: "Natural" in the sense that death is part of our lives—the Bear River Migratory Bird Refuge was being flooded by the rise of the Great Salt Lake; my mother was diagnosed with ovarian cancer; both are natural phenomena. "Unnatural" in the sense of what is imposed on those cycles. In the case of Great Salt Lake, the state of Utah decides to put in a $60 million pumping project to pump the water into the West Desert—hardly natural. In terms of my mother's diagnosis with cancer, what are the options: chemotherapy, radiation. Natural? It's debatable. Then this overlying cloud, if you will, of nuclear testing in the 1950s and 60s which moved all the way up the Wasatch front in Utah. The whole issue of downwind, even being downwinders—natural? Hardly.

LONDON: "Downwinders," what does that mean?

WILLIAMS: Downwinders, meaning those people, individuals, communities that were downwind of the nuclear test site. During those years when we were testing atomic bombs above ground, when we watched them for entertainment from the roofs of our high schools, little did we know what was raining down on us, little did we know what would appear years later. I write about that in *Refuge*—"The Clan of One-Breasted Women." With so many of the women in my family being diagnosed with breast cancer, mastectomies led to one-breasted women. I believe it is the result of nuclear fallout.

This is not peculiar to my family. There are thousands of stories and narratives in the nuclear west that also bear this out. Natural? I don't think so. That's what I was referring to.

LONDON: In *Refuge*, you also talk about the connection between your church and the whole downwinder phenomenon. Perhaps you can expand on that a bit.

WILLIAMS: I think that what I was talking about was that as a woman growing up in a Mormon tradition in Salt Lake City, Utah, we were taught—and we are still led to believe—that the most important value is obedience. But that obedience in the name of religion or patriotism ultimately takes our souls. So I think it's this larger issue of what is acceptable and what is not; where do we maintain obedience and law and where do we engage in civil disobedience—where we can cross the line physically and metaphorically and say, "No, this is no longer appropriate behavior." For me, that was a decision that I had to make and did make personally, to commit civil disobedience together with many other individuals from Utah and around the country and the world, in saying no to nuclear testing. Many people don't realize that we have been testing nuclear bombs underground right up until 1992. President Bush at that time placed a moratorium on all testing in this country and President Clinton has maintained that.

LONDON: How central is your Mormon faith to your identity as a writer—has it had a big influence on your work and ideas?

WILLIAMS: It's hard to answer because, again, I don't think we can separate our upbringing from what we are. I am a Mormon woman. I am not orthodox. It is the lens through which I see the world. I hear the Tabernacle Choir and it still makes me weep. There are other things within the culture that absolutely enrage me, and for me it is sacred rage. But it's not just peculiar to Mormonism—it's any patriarchy that I think stops, thwarts, or denies our creativity.

So the question that I'm constantly asking myself is, What are we afraid of? I think it's important for us to follow that line of fear, because that is ultimately our line of growth. I feel that within the Mormon culture there is a tremendous amount of fear—of women's voices, of questioning of authority, and ultimately of our own creativity.

LONDON: In this culture we tend to draw very distinct lines between the spiritual world and the political world. And yet you don't seem to see any separation between them. You've said that for you it's all one—the spiritual and the political, your home life and your landscape.

WILLIAMS: I think we learn that lesson well by observing the natural world. There is no separation. That is the wonderful ecological mind that Gregory Bateson talks about—the patterns that connect, the stories that inform and inspire us and teach us what is possible. Somewhere along the line we have become segregated in the way we think about things and become compartmentalized. Again, I think that contributes to our sense of isolation and our lack of a whole vision of the world. I can't imagine a secular life, a spiritual life, an intellectual life, a physical life. I mean, we would be completely wrought with schizophrenia, wouldn't we?

So I love the interrelatedness of things. We were just observing out at Point Reyes a whole colony of elephant seals and it was so deeply beautiful, and it was so deeply spiritual. It was fascinating listening to this wonderful biologist, Sarah Allen Miller, speak of her relationship to these beings for 20 years. How the males, the bulls, have this capacity to dive a mile deep, can you imagine? And along the way they sleep while they dive. And I kept thinking, "And what are their dreams?" And the fact that they can stay under water for up to two hours. Think of the kind of ecological mind that an elephant seal holds. Then looking at the females, these unbelievably luxurious creatures that were just sunbathing on this crescent beach with the waves breaking out beyond them. Then they would just ripple out into the water in these blue-black bodies, just merging with the water. It was the most erotic experience I've ever seen. We were there for hours. No separation between the spiritual and the physical. It was all one. I had the sense that we had the privilege of witnessing *other*—literally another culture, that extension of community.

LONDON: You've said that your connection to the natural world is also your connection to yourself. Do you think that's true for everybody?

WILLIAMS: We're animals, I think we forget that. I think there is an ancient archetypal memory that still exists within us. If we deny that, what is the cost? So I do think it's what binds us as human beings. I wonder, what is it to be human? Especially now that we are so urban. How do we remember our connection with place? What is the umbilical cord that roots us to that primal, instinctive, erotic place? Every time I walk to the edge of this continent and feel the sand beneath my feet, feel the seafoam move up my body, I think, "Ah, yes, evolution." [laughs] You know, it's there, we just forget.

I worry, Scott, that we are a people in a process of great transition and we are forgetting what we are connected to. We are losing our frame of reference. Pelicans pass by and we hardly know who they are, we don't know their stories. Again, at what price? I think it's leading us to a place of inconsolable loneliness. That's what I mean by "an unspoken hunger." It's a hunger that cannot be quelled by material things. It's a hunger that cannot be quelled by the constant denial. I think that the only thing that can bring us into a place of fullness is being out in the land with *other*. Then we remember where the source of our power lies.

LONDON: One of your great gifts as a writer is your ability to translate your experience of nature into words. Yet nature seems to inspire in us not words but silence—after all, that is one of the most profound reasons for living close to nature, to get beyond words. Do you find that sometimes the words get in the way?

WILLIAMS: That is so true, and I love what you just said about silence going beyond words. And, who knows, hopefully there will come a time when I have no words, when I can honor and hold that kind of stillness that I so need, crave, and desire in the natural world. I think you are absolutely right. Isn't that intimacy? When you are with a landscape or a human being where there is no need to speak, but simply to listen, to perceive, to feel. And I worry . . . (I think I must be worried all the time—maybe that is the other side of joy, you know, holding that line of the full range of emotions.) But we are losing our sense of silence in the world.

My husband, Brooke, and I were in the San Juan Mountains in Colorado. We were at almost 13,000 feet. I cannot imagine being in a place where there was greater silence, a deeper silence. But this peculiar sound, when the sun would set, occurred which was almost like these . . . the only way I can describe it to you is, it was like there was a turbine, a motor. I'm not talking UFOs here, I'm saying it was this very disturbing, low-grade noise that was almost coming up from the valley floor. And we were miles away from any towns or cities. And this is a frequent story that is being told in the American West right now. I know people have been hearing this bizarre low-frequency noise—it's not a benevolent sound, it's a very disturbing sound. I know friends who have been hearing it in Taos, New Mexico. A writer-friend of mine, Linda Hogan, a Chickasaw poet, has been hearing it around her home. And also in Utah. And I wonder what this sound is. Is it the sound of an industrialized society that is in the process of going mad?

So, I wonder about silence. Also about darkness. I love the idea that city lights are a "conspiracy" against higher thoughts. If we can no longer see the stars, then where can our thoughts travel to? So, I think there is much to preserve—not just landscape, but the qualities that are inherent in landscape, in wild places: silence, darkness.

LONDON: We tend to take very extreme views of nature in America. We see it as ours to do whatever we please with, or, conversely, as something to rope off and protect from human intervention. Do you think we will ever learn to coexist with nature in a way that benefits both?

WILLIAMS: I believe it is possible, and I think we have powerful role-models among us in the American West. Certainly the Hopis, a timeless civilization that understands sustainability and what that means about living in harmony, in tandem with the natural world. We have much to learn from them, and they will survive us, I feel certain about that. When you look at the Pueblo communities along the Rio Grande, when you talk to the Navajo people, the Ute people, and certainly the native peoples of California who still have their communities intact, it is what they have always known: that we are not apart from nature but a part of it.

LONDON: But we don't have much of a history of living in tune with nature.

WILLIAMS: You are absolutely right, for us as Anglos who are very new to this landscape, we don't have a history yet. I look at Los Angeles and I ask myself,

How can this ever be sustainable? And what are we contributing to that? Because we are all complicit. None of us is without blame. It's so difficult and it's so overwhelming and I think we have to make small choices in our own lives that can loom large collectively. But I worry. I think it's about capitalism, consumerism, our consumptive nature as a species approaching the 21st century. I certainly don't have the answers.

LONDON: How do we address this in our personal lives?

WILLIAMS: I think that it's too much to take on the world. It's too much to take on Los Angeles. All I can do is to go back home to the canyon where we live and ask the kinds of questions that can make a difference in our neighborhoods. How do we want to govern ourselves? How do we want to regulate development. We've just started an Emigration Canyon watershed council. We had our first meeting in our living room last week. And what was our goal? Simply to talk to each other, because there is a huge rift between those people in the canyon who want more development, those people in the canyon who want less, and the way that we are bound on this issue is the water—how much water we have. So I think that water is a tremendous organizing principle. Maybe that is one of the places, particularly in the arid West, we can begin thinking about these things.

LONDON: Trying to find common ground.

WILLIAMS: Absolutely. And also respecting each other's differences and then figuring out how we can proceed given those different points of view.

LONDON: With all the talk about the ecological crisis we are facing now, environmental policies seem to be losing ground. How is it that such a big gap has developed between what we say we value on the one hand and what we legislate on the other?

WILLIAMS: I feel we have to begin standing our ground in the places we love. I think that we have to demand that concern for the land, concern for the Earth, and this extension of community that we've been speaking of, is not marginal—in the same way that women's rights are not marginal, in the same way that rights for children are not marginal. There is no separation between the health of human beings and the health of the land. It is all part of a compassionate view of the world. How we take that view and match it with what we see in Congress with the decimations of the Endangered Species Act, the Clean Air Act, the Clean Water Act, child care . . . I think it's an outrage. You and I have spoken about what we can do as citizens, what we can do as a responsive citizenry, and this is where we have to shatter our complacency and become "active souls," as Thoreau

58

puts it, and be prepared to engage in *awareness*—that personal struggle between our grief and our sorrow. But I don't think we have any choice.

When I met Breyten Breytenbach, the South African poet, in Mexico—it was a symposium on landscape and culture—we were talking about this revolution, this evolution of the spirit. As you know, he is an extraordinary poet who wrote *True Confessions of an Albino Terrorist* and had been involved for years in the anti-apartheid movement, was imprisoned for seven, and he knows the shadow of the active soul. I remember asking him, "What can we do if we are interested in this revolution, this evolution of the spirit?" And he looked at me, dead-eye center, and he said, "You Americans, you have mastered the art of living with the unacceptable."

I think we have to stand up against what is unacceptable, and to push the boundaries and reclaim a more humane way of being in the world, so that we can extend our compassionate intelligence and begin to work with a strengthened will and imagination that can take us into the future.

LONDON: Terry, thank you very much.

WILLIAMS: Scott, thank you for taking us on this journey of ideas. It's a gift to be able to share this time with you and with your audience.

Terry Tempest Williams and Ona Siporin

A Conversation

Ona Siporin, *Western American Literature*, 1996

William Stafford once wrote:

> Justice will take us millions of intricate moves.

The intricate moves of Terry Tempest Williams in her efforts towards environmental justice are to turn the kaleidoscope ninety degrees, to listen to a shell (Pieces of White Shell), *to translate the calligraphy of herons in flight* (An Unspoken Hunger), *to name the snows* (The Secret Language of Snow), *and to trace the rapid unraveling of the lives of the women in her family* (Refuge). *Time spent with Williams reveals a woman whose intriguing power, determination, and ambition remain half-obscured by seeming contradictions.*

In late April of this year, at the request of Western American Literature, *I drove up canyon out of Salt Lake and introduced myself at Terry's door. She showed me into a living room where we sat by the windows and talked. I wanted to hear how Terry would situate herself. Perhaps it should seem obvious. She is the naturalist-in-residence at the Utah Museum of Natural History in Salt Lake City, has a master's degree in environmental*

Ona Siporin, "Terry Tempest Williams and Ona Siporin: A Conversation," *Western American Literature* 31, no. 2 (August 1996): 99–113. Reprinted by permission.

education, and has won the Southwest Book Award. In her many works it is clear that her
concerns are with the Great Basin and the deserts.

Still, I wondered how she would define her own place of enchantment. She started
slowly:

". . . I think of a triangle, and one of the points of the triangle, probably the
central point, would be Great Salt Lake, the Bear River Bird Refuge—a landscape
of my childhood associated with my family, my grandmother in particular. The
long-legged birds, great blue herons, avocets, stilts, ibis, shoveler, teal . . . the
names evoke the presence. To the south, [the point] would be somewhere on the
Colorado Plateau in the confluence of those canyons between Canyonlands and
Escalante. The red rocks—[it's like] being inside of an animal—the stillness there
. . . With the desert it's about heat, it's exposure. It's very much of the body. With
Great Salt Lake it's the whole notion that nothing is as it appears. The breaking
down of mythologies, even my own . . . Also, whenever you're out at the lake you
inevitably face Salt Lake City, so in a way it's the tension between a domesticated
life and a wild one. And then the point north would be in the Yellowstone plateau,
in the Tetons, in Yellowstone, and that would be a place of enchantment that includes animals: grizzlies, moose, elk, weasel, trumpeter swans. So that's a storied
landscape with Other. And that would be the triangle that I stand in . . ."

I asked her if it was the triangle she always intended to stand in.

"I can't ever imagine leaving Utah. It has such a wonderful radius . . . five
hours north, you're in Yellowstone and Jackson Hole . . . and five hours south
we're in the Colorado Plateau . . . It's interesting though—the one landscape I
have not written about is the landscape north and that might be the most private
and potent landscape of all for me. It's where I have written all my books; it's
where I feel a very strong sense of community . . . our family always spent the sum-
mers in Jackson Hole. And it's also where I think I was mentored—at the Teton
Science School—and where those ideas in terms of the land ethic were really born
in me."

"What changes are you seeing?"

"The changes I've seen in the Yellowstone Plateau, Great Salt Lake, and in the
Colorado Plateau are the changes we're all seeing in the American West. Certainly,
it's much more inhabited. In many ways the threats are greater, in terms of extractive industries that are always looming over the Kaiparowits Plateau. Or whether
it's the wilderness bill that was brought to the American people by the Utah delegation that [had] inadequate acreage and inadequate protection. Whether it's

AMAX out at Great Salt Lake and the draining of the lake. The idea of diking and damming it to the point where it's a fresh water lake at the peril of the birds, or whether it's up in the Yellowstone plateau [where] you've got the New World gold mine . . . all these lands are at risk . . . and that's one of the things that fuels my work as a writer. Not so much as a polemic, I hope, but writing out of a sense of loss, a sense of grief and a sense of joy, because I think passion encompasses that full spectrum of joy and sorrow. That passion creates engagement. And I think that all we can ask as writers is for engagement in our life and on the page."

"If you were giving advice to someone, not a writer, who wanted to make a personal effort for the environment, what would you say to them? Where would you guide [them]?" I asked her.

"To wherever they live. I think it's that idea that it may be that the most radical action you can commit is to stay home. And it's in that context that we become radical because we, we are digging root, we are staying put, we are making a commitment to place. And it is in that context that we begin to learn the names of things. In this country it would be pronghorn antelope, it would be black-tailed jackrabbit, you know, the avocets and the stilts, the sage, greasewood. So you begin to have a fierce sense of Other. And our notion of community is extended to include all life forms—plants, animals, rocks, rivers, and human beings. I think that out of that poetics of place a politics of place arises that is not radical or conservative, [but] is . . . an empathetic response."

"How does it manifest itself?"

"You care, you start caring about it. You see the river that's polluted and you want to do something about it. If you see a wetland that's being drained, you enlist your neighbors and figure out how that might, that land might be purchased or a conservation easement might happen. If a neighbor's barn burns down, you re-build it. Those kinds of community actions that are neighbor to neighbor. Again, it's not an abstraction . . . it's real work with real people with real intention. And I think it's ultimately about love . . . I believe that this renaissance in the West is about recreating community, defining what it is and it may be that in the end it does become defined through watersheds—state boundaries dissolve and we do find a regional approach to who we are and where we live and that our lives will be defined accordingly. I think that would be very exciting.

" . . . [An] interesting experience has been, my husband Brooke and I were involved with the President's Council on Sustainable Development—the region-al team—and the team went to various watersheds around the West and simply called together members of the community and listened to their stories, and their stories were all defined around particular watersheds . . . It was fascinating because people had very different points of view, came from very different backgrounds, but when it was aligned around water, there was a commonality . . . they all had stakes to hold. And so, the conversations shifted and they had to find some creative solutions, not to say there weren't moments of high levels of contentiousness, but I love it that that's the kind of thinking we're doing. I think the future will rest in small scale economies, local communities organized around watersheds and natural boundaries, not political boundaries."

Terry had lit a candle on the table next to us before we started talking. I understood this as a ritual act, though I wasn't sure what it meant to her. It was another of those "intricate moves" I was trying to figure out. Her stance on the land and environment comes through with grace and clarity, but I was also interested in her life as a writer and in her personal life: "There are times," I began, "when I am reading your work that I think there is this understated sarcasm or cynicism . . . a darkness underneath, an anger . . . remember when you walked up to those guys in the pickup . . . Do you know what I mean? You walked right up beside them and just put your middle finger right in their faces . . ."

"You make me blush," she laughed, "and maybe as women we know, we recognize, that in each other. I was reading Virginia Woolf's essay. It's a wonderful talk that she gave—I think it's in January 1931—at a society of professional women in London, and she was asked to talk about what it means to be a writer. And she ends up talking about how a writer has two tasks: one is to kill the angel in the house—which I love. She takes that from the Victorian poem, 'Angel in the House.'[1] I love how she talks about that. I don't have the direct quote, but when she says [something like] 'whenever I would sit down to my page, I would see her wings, the shadow of her wings over the paper and then she would whisper into my ear: be good, be pure, be kind, be deceitful' . . . um, and she goes on to say: 'I grabbed her by the throat and I killed her.' And I thought: 'How many times do we have to kill that angel in the house before we can begin to tell the truth on the page?' You know, the voice that says, 'be kind, be pure, don't question,' and I can feel that angel over my shoulder constantly . . . She has immeasurable lives, but I think particularly coming out of Mormon culture and growing up—as children you were to be literally seen, not heard. I think the voice of the feminine was not valued and so I think in a way, every time I pick up my pen, I feel I am engaged in some act of betrayal, every time I speak I feel that I am breaking taboo . . . And so

---

1.   The address referred to is Woolf's "Professions for Women," which was given at the Women's Service League in 1931 and published in Woolf's 1942 collection *The Death of the Moth and Other Essays.*

I think when you say that there's this darkness underlying my work or this, what I would call, sort of . . . trickster energy . . . I think that's very real.

". . . [T]he second aspect of Virginia Woolf's charge as writers [is that] we have to speak out of the body. The French deconstructionist, Cixous, says, 'We must learn to speak the language we speak when there is no one there to correct us.' Or Claudine Herrman in her book *The Tongue Snatchers* says we must take back the mother tongue. The French verb *voler* means either to take flight or to steal. To fly or to steal—that's largely what women have chosen to do when confronted with certain issues. We leave or we steal the dominant language, and what I think the French are telling us, admonishing us, is to say: 'What is the Mother Tongue?' How do we speak out of the truth of our own experiences or out of the body to really write with an authority that comes out of the marrow of our bones?"

"What's your specific approach to the environment as a woman? Or your specific power?"

"I don't know what my specific power is. I don't know what my approach as a woman is. I know the things that concern me, and the things that concern me are relationships. Women, health, and the environment—no separation. So that the essay 'The Clan of One-Breasted Women' was a seminal moment for me because suddenly, you know, I had been watching the women in my family die, one by one, and then to have that dream of that flash of light in the night in the desert over and over and over again, you know, illuminating buttes and mesas, and then to tell my father over dinner about that dream and having him say, 'You *did* see it.' 'Saw what?' 'The flash. The bomb. I thought you knew that. It was a common occurrence in the '50s.' And then he tells me the story of, you know, driving from California to Utah, approaching Las Vegas, you know, just before dawn, and seeing that cloud, pulling over. He thought an oil tanker . . . had blown up. And within minutes that light ash landed on the car. I think it was at that moment—talk about the power of story—that I realized the deceit I'd been living under. Children in the American Southwest drinking contaminated milk from contaminated cows, even the breasts of our mothers, members of the Clan of One-Breasted Women. The fact that the land, the health of the land, the health of the women in the land are all related . . . that is how I approach environmental issues. It's not an abstraction. Wilderness is not an abstraction, it's not an idea, it's a place. And in Utah we know it by name whether it's the Escalante canyons, whether it's Kaiparowits Plateau. In the same way, the health of the Earth is the health of its inhabitants. So, when I've watched nine women in my family all have mastectomies, seven are dead, I think that's an indictment on the health of our planet."

"Does what has happened to you and your family . . . allow you room for optimism?"

"I don't think about optimism. And I think I don't trust hope, because . . . hope is attached to what we desire and what we desire is usually selfish. I do believe in faith. I love Galliano when he talks about the fugitive faith, the faith that we've allowed to run away from ourselves. I have deep faith. I have deep faith in the power of individuals and the power of the community to make changes. I think that's why I feel so strongly about grass-roots activism, the response of citizens. And I have faith in the human imagination to alter its course . . . My optimism . . . is in my actions, and that's what I trust . . . and yet the paradox, the irony . . . is that when you live a deliberate life, a daily life—in a way, that is a gesture for the future."

My mind wandered to the action of writing. "You know, Kenzuboro Oe [the 1994 Nobel Prize winner for literature] said we cannot write true nonfiction, we always write fiction and sometimes we're able to arrive at the truth. I want to know what you think he means by that."

"I think his book, *Hiroshima Notes*, is one of the most powerful manifestations of a thinking mind overlaying a heinous act that I have ever read, and I think he clarifies this statement in his own text—that anytime we overlay our memory over our past experience it becomes a fiction . . . our memory is a fiction, so I'm not sure there is such a thing as pure nonfiction because it's all colored by memory, colored by perceptions, colored by our own biases whatever they might be . . . When we're creating essays, or we're writing books classified as nonfiction, the structure that we choose also creates a fiction. In other words, how we choose to tell the story, I think, affects the story that is told."

"What does that mean for the readers . . . How do they know how to trust us?"

"I think the component of all art—literature, nonfiction—that allows the writer the leeway to not let "the truth get in the way of the truth" is structure. [I]t gives us that kind of flexibility to create a story, to create an atmosphere so that the reader can settle in and be bathed in images, bathed in ideas. To me that is infinitely more trustworthy than if we were simply reporting, because [in structuring story] the writer does the work of distillation, creating an atmosphere in which truth can be revealed. That, in my mind, is what creative nonfiction is. If we were to be specific—is, for example, the story *Refuge* true? Yes, it's all true, and the structure is a structure based on chronology. The organization would be the various lake levels and the birds within those various levels of the Bear River Migratory Bird Refuge. Did I take liberties? I think the liberties I took were choosing what not to tell. In a way it reminds me of the Grand Canyon. To me what's most compelling about the Grand Canyon is what has been removed, eroded, washed away, rather than what remains. So it's the negative space that allows the reader to enter in on their own terms so that it's not a crowded text."

"What don't you tell?" It was a question I had been wanting to ask.

"What don't I tell? I think it's the difference between what is personal and what is private. I think we can tell when we've entered into a private domain on the page where we start feeling uncomfortable, where there is no context. Where the personal, I think, opens the door to the universal. I am also very careful if I am writing about my family; there are things I would never . . . betray [because] that is their story, not mine, to tell."

"That's a hard one to call."

"It is. You don't know what will be offensive to your family; oftentimes it's the small things, not the large things. So, I think the question that there is no such thing as nonfiction, I think anytime we enlist the memory, because memory is rooted in the imagination and the perceptions, the so-called truth can always be questioned."

"People always ask me when I'm telling stories, or anyway it's a common question, people will say: 'Is that a true story?' And I say, 'Yes it is, but it isn't . . .'"

". . . in the realm of art and the imagination, it is true . . . And it isn't a lie . . . In the realm of art anything is possible and probable and allows us those leaps of the imagination, those acts of faith that ultimately transform us and the culture that we're a part of . . . which goes back to . . . the power of the mind itself to tell stories— if we have the capacity or the patience to listen. [Like] when you were standing in Hovenweep [and] the story came up through the soles of your feet. Yes?"

I had told Terry about creating a story about an Anasazi woman and her children for the Museum of Natural History. It had been necessary for me to go to the land in order to find the story. "Well, maybe not so much through the soles of my feet, but it came certainly from the land . . . I was walking, I was just walking along the trail . . . and I was looking at the architecture and looking. I was with my children—my children have a lot to do with my writing—and it was like being transported to another space and realizing that the connection from the present to the historical has to do with things like [this]: I was just a woman walking along that trail. That's all there was to it . . . nothing unusual . . . nothing new. I was just a woman, like many women, who had walked that trail, and then of course I was the woman who was walking with her two children [and so, the story]. I could not have written it from Logan. I had to be on the land where it would have happened, and [once I was], it rose."

She paused for a moment. "I remember as a child, [my grandfather] said every word that is spoken remains audible in the universe . . . and I love that—so any

66

story that has been told still circulates among us . . . And with the land, I think that when we are sitting on the land, walking in the land, like you say, there are stories there that can be retrieved, both from the distant past [and] maybe even from the future. It's interesting to think about."

"What do you think is going on with western writing now—how would you characterize the state of western writing, whether in environmental or other terms, fiction or nonfiction?"

". . . I think of my father who I love and he'll ask me a question and I'll start to tell him a story and he'll say [snapping fingers] 'bottom line.' I don't want bottom line. I don't want achievements, I want stories.

"I think what we're seeing in the American West right now, as we approach the 21st century . . . is that the West is filling up—[even] as huge as these open spaces are . . . and I think we, as Westerners, are questioning assumptions on every level. Public lands—whether it's the appropriation of water rights—what does that mean? What does that mean in terms of wildernesses, large wildernesses, what does that mean in terms of wildness within our own communities, what does that mean in terms of development, second, third, fourth homes in the American West? . . . I think [this] could be viewed as a very chaotic time. But I think that out of this chaos and out of a [seeming] polarity, when we hear, when we read in the papers, of environmentalists versus ranchers, developers versus conservationists, rural communities versus urban communities—it's all a shorthand to say that we are in flux, that we are rethinking who we are and where we live and how we want to be.

"So I do find that it's a time of creativity both in terms of public policy and community action and literature, [and] I think the literature is reflecting what the populace is living. Much of the literature that is coming out of the West is based on loss."

"What are you thinking of?"

"[Well] look at Teresa Jordan's *Riding the White Horse Home*. I think that's an example of the shifting ranch culture. Her family lost the ranch—where do they pick up from there? Or Leslie Marmon Silko's *Ceremony*—what is the place of Native people at this point? Alienation. Sovereignty. Jim Galvin's *The Meadow*. It's fiction; it's nonfiction; who can say? The landscape is the primary character and the human beings really move in and out of that landscape almost like weather. Bill Kittredge's *Hole in the Sky*—I think there's an example of a man who comes from one culture and ultimately moves into another and asks the question: What stories do we tell that evoke a sense of place? And perhaps the old stories don't work for us anymore. So it's a shattering of the mythologies, the mythology of the cowboy, of the rugged individualist, of using the land simply for one's economy.

67

So I think that it's a very exciting time. It could be said that we're engaged in a renaissance. If that is so, I think it's only because we're engaged in a renaissance of our relationship to place."

"And where does your work fit in with the people you've mentioned?"

"I think it's hard to see oneself in context because you see yourself from the inside out. I know where my priorities are, I think, and my passions, my questions, and that they center around issues of family, and culture, and relationship to place. So I'm aware of my biases, which are gender, geography, and culture. I am a Mormon woman writing out of the Great Basin, the Colorado Plateau. It's the lens out of which I see . . . I'm also concerned with issues of spirituality because in many ways I think if the old stories aren't working for us, if they have lost their blood, so to speak, I think our institutions have also lost their blood. And so where does that place us? How do we breathe life back into a religious language or a religious tradition as Anglo Americans? For instance, the myth of the cowboy in the American West that is so entrenched. I think it is not helpful in terms of our relationship to place. I think the mythology of the rugged individualist is exactly that, a myth. As Patty Limerick tells us, the West was founded on a sense of fierce cooperation, otherwise we wouldn't be here. The idea that it is a monoculture—I don't believe that either. I think the American West is an unbelievably complex set of cultures, from Hispanic to Native peoples to Mormon to Jewish to Italian . . . that's the history of our immigration. [And] out of these disparate voices there is a wholeness that is rising that is ultimately a literature of experience. It may be that the writers are creating the bridges on which we can move into a new era. The theologian John Cobb believes we are now moving into the next era, which he calls Earthism, where we will redefine our sense of place and our relationship to the Earth in a sustainable fashion. He says that usually it is a point of disaster or deep pain that propels us from one era into the next. I would suggest that we are already in a disaster: the deaths of other species, the loss of our forests. I think that we have forgotten the option of restraint and that it is no longer the survival of the fittest that is called for, but the survival of compassion."

"What does this mean in your work?"

"I think for me it's a time of listening, a time to go underground, and I don't know what it will yield, but I trust it. I think that anytime you go into a landscape of story or art, hopefully, the outcome will be a literature of compassion, something that causes us to pause and think about something in a different, fresh way. The power of story is that it bypasses rhetoric and pierces the heart. It goes into the cells."

"Do you feel like you've achieved at this point in your life what you wanted to achieve?"

"I've never wanted to achieve anything but to live, I mean, truly so. I never imagined myself as a writer. What I've always known is that I love the land, I love my family, and I love language, and I love stories—that's all part of the whole. So when you talk about achievement, I don't know how to respond to that."

"Well, think of it this way: If you could gather the whole nation together, what would you want to say to them? And do you feel like you're on the way to saying it?"

"You know what I'd love?"

"What?"

"If I had a chance to have the whole nation right here . . . I would love to ask what story comes to each person's mind in terms of a peak experience in nature, as a child. Or, a story of each person's relationship to where s/he lives. I mean, I think that would be so revealing in terms of where our hunger is, of what we're connected to, what we have forgotten in terms of our relations. That's what I would love . . . because I think it's only in the act of telling and receiving stories that we will be healed as a nation in terms of our relationship to place, where we can truly move with any sort of compassionate intelligence. In the telling of the stories we [would be] allowed to cry . . . to laugh . . . to be free. And right now I think there is this excruciating denial that is being played out through consumption, through distractions, you know, whether it's our love affair with the Internet [or something else]. Our transformation and our growth as individuals and as a people is through the intimacy of our relations, and that is most poignantly developed through story-telling. If you tell me a story, suddenly I become accountable for that knowledge and you and I are bonded forever."

We started to tell stories of the people we knew and their relationships to the environment and Terry came back round to her interest in creating a literature that reactivates a sense of the ancestral, a vision that includes a strong sense of the animal.

"I think it's that: a wild response. It's remembering what we're connected to."

"There seems to be a strong theme of education in your books; you're telling people about the natural world. People will look at the books and learn things about the Great Basin, and I wonder how much you feel like an educator?"

"I never thought about it in terms of the writing. I mean, certainly my background is in environmental education and cultural foundations. All I ever wanted to be in my life was a teacher. That was my great passion, and in many ways it still is. I think that is why I will forever be at the Museum of Natural History. Maybe it's my love affair with facts: the fact that tortoises can live to be over one hundred years old, the fact that their shells are made of hexagons. I've just been studying desert tortoises and I fell in love with this word *brumation*, the reptilian counterpart of hibernation. I love knowing that turkey vultures have a special acid in their urine, and when they excrete, instead of shooting out like with eagles, it runs down their legs, almost like an antiseptic so they can hang out in carcasses and still remain hygienically prepared. I just love facts, because I think the facts create the story, the facts create the form. There's a part of me—the mystical side of me—that only can exist because of the grounding in the sciences, which is what Albert Einstein was saying, that the true source of the mystical is in the science. So again, no separation, the imagination, the biological mind, it's all the same . . . I think, as a writer, what I want to understand are the relationships of all living things. You know, what relationship do we have to the birds, what relationship do birds have to the land, what relationship does the notion of health create on the page? . . . I believe writing is an act of consequence. If I'm writing an op-ed page for the *New York Times* on behalf of Utah Wilderness, then I do have something in mind for the reader. I want them to become aware of America's Redrock Wilderness Act. I want them to become aware that democracy wasn't served by Utah's delegation. And I would hope that they would become involved in citizen action. If I'm writing something like *Desert Quartet*, the intention is very different. With that book, I wanted to explore what it might mean to write out of the body and to create a narrative where it was of the flesh, and even ask the question, 'What might it mean to make love to the land?' Not in an expletive manner, but in a manner of reciprocity. That's a very different intention. The narrator in *Desert Quartet* is fictional. The narrator in *Refuge* is not."

"I knew there was a big difference between narrators in your pieces."

"I think each of my books has turned on a question. With *Pieces of White Shell* it was 'What stories do we tell that evoke a sense of place?' In many ways, the Navajo sent me back home. And with *Coyote's Canyon* it was 'Okay, do I have those stories within my own culture?' So there are seven stories that are white-robed a bit to give them a mythic cast. With *Refuge* it was 'How do we find refuge in change?' It was a question I was plagued with every day of my life during those seven years. And with *Unspoken Hunger*, I think those are essays that really talk about how a poetics of place translates to a politics of place. And if you look at 'The Village Watchman' about my uncle, it really is an essay about Other. It's in direct contrast to the piece called 'Testimony,' which was the testimony before our Congress on the Pacific Yew. You're talking to congressmen and they're up on risers, and it's hardly a democratic process. So, there are very different intentions in all of them . . ."

I thought about the essay "Testimony." To me, it is one of Terry Tempest Williams's most poignant pieces; it has a quality of quiet command and clarity. When the interview ended, I was not ready for it to end. There is more to this woman, I kept thinking, more to the woman who is ready to go off to Spain and who thinks about writing fiction:

"I'm obsessed right now with Spain, and I have no idea what that is about, none . . . a flight? . . . my desire to learn a new language? I don't know if it is that there is a country that understands the darkest of all passions. I don't know what it is, but there is this seed of Spain in me that is growing and I don't know if that's going to be a novel . . . or if it's just where my imagination is right now. I need some new ideas. I find that what I'm reading now has nothing to do with this country. I want to read Paz, I want to read . . . Wole Soyinka . . . they have not been afraid of suffering. We're so comfortable in this country and so it's been very interesting to take root in another country in a secret sort of way, as a foreigner where you don't cast a shadow, where you have no obligations and you're simply being human.

". . . I would love to write fiction. It would be such a relief because I'm so tired of having to expose myself. I look at the first-person pronoun "I" and I just get sick to my stomach. [In fiction] I would not have to be a slave to facts. I would love not to have to be accountable to my family. I would love the sheer delight of a novel, of fiction. I just don't know if I could."

It was time for me to go. We stepped onto the porch and Terry suddenly turned to me, "You've got to have a flower for the drive back." She rushed down to her flowerbed along the porch and around the side of the house, where she found a tulip in full and intense bloom. With a haste I could not understand, she twisted it from the ground and handed it to me, and I drove away with it on the seat beside me.

After all she had so articulately expressed, it was the lighted candle she had placed on the table beside us and this flower that I wondered about. I didn't know what they meant; they reminded me of the small acts we commit that we want to carry large meaning, like putting your hand on someone's shoulder when she's in pain. And I thought how sometimes I make those actions to someone else not just for the other person, but for myself too, because I am quietly desperate to make contact in a world full of contradictions.

I entered the city thinking of how Williams had said that she couldn't imagine leaving Utah, yet was obsessed with Spain, how the most radical act was staying home, yet she wanted to break out of her own genre and flee from her own land.

You could say this is a portrait of a woman who doesn't know what she wants. But I think not. In the tension between what Terry Tempest Williams has told us and what she has not told, between the life she lives and the life she dreams of living, there is a writer on the move. Given sustained courage she will go to those places she has never been. I hope she will take us with her.

A Conversation with Terry Tempest Williams

Jocelyn Bartkevicius and Mary Hussmann, *The Iowa Review, 1997*

On a cold spring day in central Iowa, the interviewers traveled with Terry Tempest Williams to the small town of Kalona, home to an Amish community. On the perimeter of that community, we had lunch at a home-style cafe and visited an antique store, a converted church where we discovered among the dry sinks, oak tables, tinker toys, depression glass, and familiar quilt patterns, a red and white Hopi-design quilt with such a history of being mistaken for a Nazi pattern, it was kept folded inside-out, on a lower shelf. Later, we visited writer Mary Swander at her home in a converted one room schoolhouse surrounded by Amish homesteads. We drove down dirt and stone roads, flying past school children in simple home-made pinafores and trousers, past horse-drawn buggies. After herbal tea overlooking the farm fields and broad sky at Mary's wall of windows, we visited sites from her poems and memoir—the Amish phone booth and the paddock with the one-eyed goat among them. We ended our day in Kalona with Mary at an Amish fabric and quilt store where we looked at display quilts and watched a woman and girl at work on a new quilt.

We talked with Terry that evening at The Iowa House on the Iowa River.

Jocelyn Bartkevicius and Mary Hussmann, "A Conversation with Terry Tempest Williams," *The Iowa Review* 27, no. 1 (Spring 1997): 1–23. Reprinted by permission.

A Conversation with Terry Tempest Williams

JOCELYN: Today in Kalona, at Mary Swander's house, you spoke of journeys to the interior of places, how, over time, seeing first-hand the way people live, your initial idea of a place is transformed. It's a transformation that obliterates all memory of a first impression or any preconceived expectation of that place.

So much of your writing centers on place, the fine nuances of place. In *An Unspoken Hunger*, you are being guided through a place, from the perimeter to the interior, just as we were today in Kalona. In *Pieces of White Shell* and *Refuge*, you open with the very feel of the place, the texture of sage on your fingers. Your latest book, *Desert Quartet*, moves even closer, into "an erotics of place," where touch becomes multi-layered, taking on an even greater significance. What is your relationship to place—both the familiar and the new? And how do guides fit in?

TERRY: I think each of us intuits a homeland, a landscape we naturally comprehend. We take those eyes with us wherever we go, whether to the farmlands of Iowa or the Plains of the Serengetti. I can tell you that my eyes are always first eternally rested on the Great Basin and the Colorado Plateau where I live and that when the landscape translates differently, I start looking for cues or images. When I came to Iowa, the first thing that struck me was the over-arching sky, this confidence of sky, this wide sky that moves unencumbered. I was thinking these clouds have nothing to butt up against except each other. In the American West that's not true, especially where I live. In Basin and Range country the clouds are much more tentative. They have to contend with mountains. With my beginner's eyes in the Midwest, it appears to be a landscape of subtleties, subtle things like the quality of light in Iowa is different. It seems more discreet or diffused or dispersed because again, there is so much sky.

One of the things that has touched me so deeply here is this vast expanse of landscape on all sides, north, south, east, west. There is almost a sense of the sea. I'm used to more of a border country closer, adjacent to mountains or deserts. So I think these differences all play into one's perceptions. And yet, there are always the commonalities. For example, going out to Cone's Marsh just an hour or so from Iowa City, one can see great blue herons, cinnamon teals, and white pelicans even in the Heartland. On the shores of Great Salt Lake, you can see these same species. These magnificent birds call us home wherever that may be. The ground beneath our feet is not so different.

A Voice in the Wilderness

You asked about guides. Certainly today, I think we saw an example of a wonderful guide, Mary Swander. A place. Going out to her one room schoolhouse, having her take us to the fabric store. Place becomes a personal landscape; I felt as though she gave us our entree into the Amish community, she is trustworthy and therefore we ride in on her coattails. My first guide here in Iowa was you, Mary, taking me to lunch, explaining your family in Waterloo, how you always want to go north, yet this is where you remain, talking about the value of weather, giving me clues as to what it means to live here. And then when we met three years ago, Jocelyn, knowing you were here in Iowa placed my imagination in Iowa as a possibility because you were bringing me stories. So, I think it's circular, it's almost like a kaleidoscope, you turn, you see, you turn again, you see differently.

MARY: We talk about the ways landscape affects and shapes culture, in that we can identify a western or southern sensibility, for example. Do you detect a midwestern sensibility?

TERRY: I haven't been here long enough yet, only 12 days. [Laughter] I do think, however, there is an over-riding American sensibility. For example, Americans are open and curious and we share a humor. Even though our humor varies regionally, much seems completely foreign to me because it's so domesticated. We can use the patchwork quilt metaphor of the Amish. Everywhere one looks, there is a different square, a pattern of tilled land, the designs of farmlands. It's not that way in the American West. In Utah, one can drive for miles (or walk for that matter), in dry, open terrain of sage or juniper with buttes and mesas on either side. Whether that translates to domesticated personalities vs. wild personalities, I don't know.

JOCELYN: So far you've spoken about place visually, as with the image of a kaleidoscope, which I love. You opened *An Unspoken Hunger* with that image. And yet in several of your books place is tactile, especially in your new book, *Desert Quartet*, where it's not only tactile, but erotic. It seems to me that you cross a border there, depart from what a lot of people feel safe talking about, depart from just using our eyes—we're such a visual culture—and move into touch. How important is touching a place? Do you feel that your writing is becoming more tactile?

TERRY: I think first we have to ask ourselves: How do we define erotic? Our culture has chosen to define erotic in very narrow terms, terms that largely describe pornography or voyeurism, the opposite of a relationship that asks for reciprocity. One of the things I was interested in with *Desert*

Quartet was to explore the use of language in its pure sense, to use the word "erotic" to intensify, to expand our view of Eros, to literally be in relationship on the page. When we're in relation, whether it is with a human being, with an animal, or with the desert, I think there is an exchange of the erotic impulse. We are engaged, we are vulnerable, we are both giving and receiving, we are fully present in that moment, and we are able to heighten our capacity for passion which I think is the full range of emotion, both the joy and sorrow that one feels when in wild country. To speak about Eros in a particular landscape is to acknowledge our capacity to love Other.

Another impulse: What does it mean to write out of the body? I wanted to play with that idea. What would it mean as a writer to bypass the intellect and feel the words before we understand them? That makes us uncomfortable. Not only, Jocelyn, do you say we're a visual culture, I think we're a very linear culture, very rational culture. So what happens when we write in a more organic form where it is circular, not linear, where it is tactile, not simply on the surface? Again, I think that makes us uncomfortable. Intimacy makes us uncomfortable, so there is another issue here; I really believe our lack of intimacy with the land has initiated a lack of intimacy with each other. So how do we cross these borders? How do we keep things fluid, not fixed, so we can begin to explore both our body and the body of the earth? No separation. Eros: nature, even our own.

MARY: What's been the reaction to *Desert Quartet*? It's very different from your other books in that it reads very much like a prose poem. It seems to arise out of a very intimate and lyric sensibility, not an intellectual one. I can see how that would make some readers uncomfortable.

TERRY: I don't know. Often the writer's the last to hear. I can tell you it has not been reviewed much, perhaps because people don't know what it is. It doesn't fit a particular genre. Is it fiction? Is it nonfiction? Poetry? Memoir? I wanted the book to be like a landscape one must enter on its own terms, I wanted the structure to mirror the desert. It is also a correspondence between Mary Frank, the artist, and myself, a correspondence through image and narrative. We were both exploring the erotic in very different ways, yet with convergences and confluences. We wanted *Desert Quartet* to be a marriage of text and image.

MARY: The four elements, earth, fire, air, and water, which are the chapter titles in *Desert Quartet* were first published in the *New England Review*.

75

A Voice in the Wilderness

In reading those versions I noticed that the "water" chapter was written from a "he" persona. In the book that persona is a woman. What happened there?

TERRY: Well, you've done your homework. Writing engages the creative process, metamorphosis; I change all the time. For *Desert Quartet* there were hundreds of drafts. It kept being a distillation, both of the idea that was holding the language together as well as the language itself. Here's the long version. When I was asked to be "essayist-at-large" at the *New England Review*, I thought it would be an intriguing assignment because I didn't know anyone in New England. I thought I was free to write in a way that I wasn't free to write within my own community, which is Mormon, at least in my imagination. I thought, This is perfect, I can write four essays, stories, about the erotic landscape set inside the Colorado Plateau. I can send them off to New England where there are lots of trees, where I don't know anyone who will read them, and I can play, experiment with both the internal as well as external landscape. The assignment actually created the structure of the four pieces, hence "quartet." "Desert" was the subject matter and also a subtext of "elements of love," which was the initial title. I wanted to explore what it means to live and love in the world with a broken heart, what it means to live with a divided heart. I wanted to explore these questions through metaphor, the land, itself. The initial structure differed from the final version. The first essay was "Earth" and it used the first person narrative. The second piece was "Fire," written through "she," then came "Water" which was "he," and finally "Air" written as "we." I wanted to explore each one of these sensibilities beginning with the personal, moving through the feminine and masculine and then ending with the collective. That is how they were originally published at the *New England Review*. After I had gone through this year's work, I showed the pieces to my editor at Pantheon. He read them and said, "Will you please do me a favor? As a gift to me, will you rewrite this in a first person narrative?" I said, "No, absolutely not, because the reader would believe I was the narrator." The other pronouns were self-protection. I was also thinking about the issues of masculine and feminine, singular and plural. He asked again. Finally I said, "I'll try it and yes, I'll send it to you for New Years."

When I started writing *Desert Quartet* in first person, the male configuration of the "water" section didn't work anymore. Something interesting happened. Writing it from the "I" perspective took me closer to

76

the truth of the story which became a story about a woman with frogs. It became simpler and more complex, at once, certainly less literal. I was forced to go deeper, dive deeper into the water where the bloodwork of the writer occurs. I realized that in our culture we have no protection when we choose to enlist a first person narrator because readers naturally assume it is you. The criticism is that it is solipsistic, self centered, indulgent: all of those things that make me want to run and hide under a rock forever. But I believe there is something larger at work, the "I" becomes the universal "I." In Japan they call creative nonfiction the "I" novel and everyone reads it as fiction. There's always the speculation that it could be personal, but because readers call it fiction they allow the writer to save face. I think that is a very gracious way to read,

JOCELYN: And you said that it deepened the work to speak in the "I" voice?

TERRY: Yes, I believe it did because I was forced to confront my own tensions, conflicts, passions, fears in a way that I didn't in the first published versions. I removed the masks and faced the elements themselves. It forced the language to be tighter—more restrained. I think the pieces then became more suggestive than literal. In that sense, ironically, it opened up the text to the subtleties of the desert itself. Often times we think when we use first person narrative, it closes the text, but I think once we have the courage to put "I" on the page we are free to work with the language and the ideas. Perhaps it is the difference between primary and secondary experience. I don't know.

JOCELYN: In writing *Desert Quartet* and its many drafts, you're not only expressing the land, the place, the self, and all our different personas, but also challenging the boundaries of genre. You write from—and for—so many communities: you're a scientist, a naturalist, you work in a museum. It seems to me that for a long time the tradition of nature writing was very similar to the tradition of science (as I understand it, that is): the self observes the other. The self remains detached and objective. Instead of going out and being in the land, being with the land, they seem to be voyeurs. You were talking before about our narrow definition of erotics as voyeurism . . . Have you come to writing as a scientist or do the two, writing and science, brew up together with you?

TERRY: I think it's about passion, whether it's passion for birds or passion for the connectedness of things, the embodiment of landscape, even our own bodies; whole, no separation. I think my first relationship to the natural world is as an animal. That's how we respond until we think it gets bred out of us. One of the first images I have as a very small child was sitting with my mother and grandmother on the beach in California and feeling the waves circle around us, even the foam around my legs, my body's impression on the sand. The sand shifts as we shift. Being there with my mother and grandmother on either side was very female, very porous, very tactile. I think about that image in our own evolutionary nature.

JOCELYN: How did that way of being not get bred out of you?

TERRY: Maybe it has, again, I don't know. I do, however, believe the culture I come from which is Mormon, is in many ways a magical religion. Magic has been part of the theology's evolution. I'm sure the Hierarchy would disagree with me on this, but our Church was founded by Joseph Smith, a 14 year old who had a vision. We were taught as children that we could have visions too. Add to this notion my family's love affair with the land where most of our time together was spent outside, and I became a prolific daydreamer. To imagine over a landscape came quite naturally. The natural world was the spiritual world. There were many times when I'd pretend to be sick just so I could stay home and watch birds in our back yard. I knew that there was something there and I knew that my grandmother—you talk about guides, she was always there with the field guide in her hand, always there with binoculars—understood those yearnings. And so it was a spiritual experience being in nature, it was a safe experience because we were largely with family, it was an intellectual experience because we were learning the names of things, were learning what was related to what, and what we might see, and it was fun. It never stopped being fun for me, so it's a simple response. And it was most always in a context of love and respect for the land and for each other.

MARY: Do you ever feel any tension between your two identities—your scientific, naturalist self and your writerly self? Have you melded those two identities?

TERRY: I can see my own evolution when I look at the books I've written. For example, the first book I wrote was *The Secret Language of Snow* with Ted Major, an ecologist who started the Teton Science School. That book is a dialogue between science and the perception of language. The book takes 12 Kobuk Eskimo words for snow—you know how we always hear there's a hundred words for snow?—and elucidates these words in terms of boreal ecology. For example, the word, "pukak" translates to mean "sugar snow" or "snow that can cause an avalanche." Skiers understand this snow as "depth hoar" or "snow that is created by a large temperature gradient."

A Conversation with Terry Tempest Williams

Another example is "Api" or "snow on the ground." "Siqoq" translates to "swirling snow." One word creates an environmental image. The keen perception of the Kobuk People have helped illuminate the winter for scientists who study snow. I wrote the poetry at the beginning of each chapter, Ted provided much of the information, then I worked with the text in terms of language. It was a real education, to see what bores, what excites. To see how language and a sense of lyricism can lighten the density of scientific facts so that the reader can move through them easily and with pleasure was a great apprenticeship. I also learned how difficult it is to write for children. It is a rigorous exercise in clarity and precision. Nothing can be taken for granted.

Then came *Between Cattails*, another book for children, which is a celebration of my childhood obsession with the Bear River Migratory Bird Refuge, dedicated to my grandmother, Mimi. It was the first place where I fell in love with birds. Again, I spent a year studying about marsh ecology since I wanted the text to be factually accurate. I also wanted it to sing like the marsh sings, so it was another exercise in figuring how to braid these different voices—the scientific and the lyrical. The next book, *Pieces of White Shell*, explores Navajo mythology. It asks the question what stories do we tell that evoke a sense of place? I was starting to feel that somehow the stories science gives us aren't enough. I needed something more. In many ways the Navajo culture, the children in particular, sent me back to my own culture, Mormon. That's where a creative fusion really started to take place—in a crisis situation—my mother was dying, the bird refuge was flooding and I saw two stories—how could I bridge them together?

JOCELYN: Two stories that needed to be told?

TERRY: The two stories that I was living, which in many ways were the two minds I was inhabiting. There were times when I thought I was completely schizophrenic, that I was living in two worlds. What pulls the scientific mind and literary minds together? Through the Navajo apprenticeship, I realized it was story, but I was looking at story from a distanced, exterior point of view. With *Refuge*, there was no distance whatsoever, and there were moments when I thought I was going mad. One particular moment is vivid: I had been to a family reunion, mother had been dead maybe six months and one of my great aunts said, "So what are you doing?" I said, "I'm trying to tell the story of the rise of Great Salt Lake and the death of my mother." She looked at me and walked away. I thought, Am I going

79

crazy? Is there no correspondence here? I remember that night. I came home and got out a childhood easel that Mimi, my grandmother, had given me. It was the biggest paper I had, I found two black magic markers and with one hand wrote: "Bird Refuge," and with the other hand wrote, "Mother," then circled them, then wrote "Great Salt Lake," under Bird Refuge and "Cancer" under Mother. I realized that the only thing holding them together was the narrator, so I drew two lines and wrote "narrator" and circled it, stood back and realized I had created an image of the female reproductive system. At that point, I understood what I was really acknowledging—it wasn't the scientific mind or the poetic mind, but the feminine mind that I wanted to embrace. That was the language that I wanted to liberate. I had a visual map I could now trust.

JOCELYN: On other occasions, you've talked about Claudine Herrmann's *The Tongue Snatchers*. I think you once told me a story about speaking at a board meeting and having the book right in front of you, looking at the picture on the cover so you could continue to speak a woman's voice.

TERRY: Yes. An extraordinary storyteller, Laura Simms, told me I had to read *The Tongue Snatchers*, so I found it at Strand's and read it on the train from New York to DC. I was on my way to the Governing Council meeting of The Wilderness Society, as male as you can imagine. I had it in my purse in the boardroom and I knew we were going to be discussing some difficult topics so I thought it might make things interesting to put it at the center of the table. I was sitting in the middle and I sort of inched the book up. On the cover is a woman screaming with her tongue being ripped out. I wish you could have seen some of the looks on the men's faces around the table. I'm not sure it made any difference in terms of how we talked about things, but it reminded me of a healthy form of indignation, that as women, we need to sit at any table mindful of what it means to be silent. Our silence is also our voice and our voice is also our silence. It depends on what a particular situation demands. On these occasions, we become shape shifters. Claudine Herrmann, Hélène Cixous, Clarice Lispecter, and Chandralaka from India, these women give me tremendous courage.

JOCELYN: Did you start reading more works by those women after having read Herrmann's book?

TERRY: Yes, many of the French writers have influenced me. I don't think you can read *Desert Quartet* without feeling their presence. I think we find our own evolution through the evolution of text.

A Conversation with Terry Tempest Williams

JOCELYN: Having read French feminists, and thinking about their concept of writing through the body, do you consciously interrogate the category of nature writing? Is that something you are interested in doing? Do you read male nature writers and think they're way off somewhere else and you consciously want to move such writing into the body?

TERRY: I'm not comfortable with the genre itself. I mean, what is nature writing? When I think about the writers I love: Virginia Woolf, Emily Dickinson, Walt Whitman, Melville—it goes beyond gender. They are writers whose language is the embodiment of the natural world, of those primal forces that create "the lightning region of the soul" on the page. To me that is so-called nature writing; but to many others, it wouldn't be classified as such. I'm interested in revolutionary language. I'm interested in revolutionary texts. In many ways I find writers such as the South African poet, Breyten Breytenbach, the Chinese poet, Bei Dao, and Federico Garcia Lorca asking the questions of our time rooted in both culture and place. I just finished Auden's *The Prolific and the Devourer*. He also addresses the tension between a poetics of place and a politics of place. I just reread Virginia Woolf's *The Waves*. What a riveting piece of "nature writing." The oscillations of human conversation mirror the waves themselves. The power of physical metaphors illuminates and magnifies the psychological landscape. Again, no separation. To read Lispector's *Apprenticeship* or *The Hour of the Star*, Coetzee's *Waiting for the Barbarians*, *The Letters of Emily Dickinson*, or the French poet, Bonnefoy, is to read the world whole and holy. Jeannette Winterson and Carole Maso also inspire me because they find their own forms that honor the integrity of their voice. These are some of the places where I find my inspiration. There are writers within the genre of natural history that I do think are creating revolutionary books in revolutionary times, writers like Edward Abbey, Barry Lopez, Linda Hogan, Simon Ortiz, Charles Bowden, Anne Carson and Rick Bass. But I would not call them exclusively "nature writers" either.

MARY: In a review of your collection, *An Unspoken Hunger*, John Mitchell said that one of your major themes was that environmental action is a creation of women. I wondered if you thought that was accurate—that women act as intermediaries between the earth and human conduct.

TERRY: Again, I think that's too easy; I don't feel comfortable with these kinds of labels. They narrow our scope, confine our imagination to think beyond boundaries and borders. Although I'm very interested in feminist

81

language, and the feminine critique and eco-feminism as an intellectual exercise, I find that in many ways that kind of writing, like so much of the writing coming out of the academy, is removed from the body. When I hear, yes, women are the caretakers of the earth, I think yes, in many ways we are but no, we cannot solely be seen in that nurturing role. It is limiting and ultimately unfair to both men and women. It is all very complicated. What is our biology and what is our conditioning?

JOCELYN: "Caretakers of the earth . . ." Isn't that just foisting things off again on women?

TERRY: Of course. Susan Griffin writes brilliantly about this subject in her books, *Woman and Nature* and *Eros and Everyday Life*. As women, we are tied to the earth through the cycles of our own bodies, whether it is through menarche or giving birth. I do believe we tend to see the world in more holistic terms, the patterns and connections that weave humanity together. But why—is another matter. Is this an "essentialist" point of view? I can only speak out of my bias, which is female, but I must tell you, I am primarily interested in the human response. We each have to speak out of our own authenticity whatever that is. And I believe we do it most powerfully through story. Story bypasses rhetoric and pierces the heart. We feel it. We don't have to argue over the semantics. Women and nature: It is also about politics. It is true that when we look at grass roots activists and activism, where good work has been done on behalf of the land in urban and rural landscapes, and in preservation of the wild, we most certainly see women on the front lines. Wangari Maathai in Kenya who organized the Greenbelt Movement, Lois Gibbs who exposed the Love Canal in upstate New York, and Rachel Carson, who had an extraordinary effect on how we view pesticides with her book, *Silent Spring*, the list could go on and on. And when you look at leadership positions in grassroots organizations, they are largely held by women. But that is not mirrored on the national level. There, we see a more corporate model adopted by environmental organizations such as The Wilderness Society, Audubon, National Wildlife Federation. Hopefully we will see the predominance of male leadership change. It doesn't matter whether we are talking about literary genres or the concerns of women, we would do well to paint a wide landscape that does not constrict our thinking. This is the work of the imagination and imagination is always about possibilities.

MARY: I often think genre is more a matter of marketing than anything else. Your work resists easy categorization but your books seem to be put into

arbitrary slots—nature writing, women's issues, new age, western literature, to name a few. Does that bother you?

TERRY: I don't think about it. Perhaps that's for others to think about, like those
in publishing or in the realm of the academy. I stand back and smile, or I
simply shrug my shoulders. That's not where I live as a writer and it's not
what possesses me. What concerns me most are the questions. What stories we tell that evoke a sense of place, or how one finds refuge in change,
or what it means to make love to the land with ultimate reciprocity. That's
what I'm interested in. I don't think a writer can really concern herself
with what the critique or categorization is or she becomes paralyzed.

I remember being at a symposium where academics were discussing
my work. It was terrifying. A writer works from the inside out and on that
level how can one have a critical point of view? On another level, a writer
has lived with the writing and worked with it from all different angles and
perspectives. One knows the secrets woven into each sentence, the alchemy
inherent in craft. A male professor at the symposium gave an exhaustive
discussion/critique of *Desert Quartet* explaining everything I had done and
why, and then he turned to me and said, "Your response?" After a bit of
silence, I said hesitantly, "With all due respect, nothing you say is familiar
to me and no, that was not my intention." As I began to explain what my
process was, what my intention was, he turned to the audience largely made
up of graduate students and said, "It's so much easier when they're dead."

Or there's the professor, bless his heart, who did his dissertation on
not *Refuge* per se, but the cover of *Refuge*. He said it was so obvious to
him that I had created this erotic image on the cover of the paperback,
so that when turned horizontally, one would clearly see the female sex
organs—the vulva, labia and clitoris—and that this was the exterior of the
body politic. I was speechless.

JOCELYN: It seems to me that your journey as a writer has been blessedly outside of the academy, more so than many writers' journeys. I say blessedly
because I have mixed feelings about working inside of that community
and that's why I'm very interested in your path as a writer. It seems so
internal—you're asking questions that genuinely interest you and so often you're collaborating so that it's not just your own internal question,
but something of a community question or a question you're asking with
somebody else.

TERRY: If we say we are an organism, we are an animal and if we are a good mam-
mal, then somehow, we are perceiving on some level what other members

83

of our species or family or community are thinking and feeling, so that our individual impulses in many ways become collective impulses. Recognizing that the most personal of feelings may in fact, be most general, enables us as writers to take greater risks. That's why I love collaboration because in a way one plus one equals three, that creative third. It's not a consensus, but a communal response, and therefore may be closer to the truth, whatever "truth" might be. I don't see collaboration as a compromise, rather a widening of the artistic circle.

JOCELYN: It's interesting how collaboration transforms your work in *Desert Quartet* which is the only work of yours that I've seen in print separately and then transformed as you were talking about earlier with Mary, and revised, yes, but also—what seems like it would be a simple matter—placed beside paintings. The writing seems to become another genre. It's as if the two of you are collaborating and also your work is collaborating.

TERRY: Collaborating with Mary Frank on *Desert Quartet* was an exciting process and an exhaustive one . . . There were exterior tensions because we were both artists and had our own visions and yet we both knew that we were committed to this "third thing." It's like a marriage or a relationship, it's the relationship that you're in the service of—in our case it was the exploration of the erotic landscape. We went through eighty-some journals of Mary's drawings. It was fascinating to see her visual mind. I have so much respect for the intensity of her work, her life. She is fearless. When she read the text, she had some very difficult questions for me that I didn't want to answer and she would not proceed as a collaborator until I had dealt with them.

JOCELYN: Can you give an example?

TERRY: I could give several but I would like to keep them private. What I can tell you is that her wisdom, her honesty inspired me, pushed me, in ways I might not have chosen to go alone. She is sixty-two years old. I'm forty years old. She has lived a vastly different life than I have and yet both of us share so much of the world, similar sensibilities and aesthetics. She absolutely demanded that I go back into the text and either be more explicit or remove certain passages. She really made me look at my deepest fears. I think I stretched her in other ways, physically, pushing her to create a book where nothing is random. We worked very hard to try and make the book as seamless as possible. If we choose to use a turkey vulture on the page then those fingers near the fingers of flames matter even though someone might say what in the world does a turkey vulture have to do with fire and passion. But when the narrator is saying, "once again I allow myself to be ravished," here is that image. Or the notion of the bat hanging down or the woman who is literally touching herself—"a fast finger that does not tire," both what a woman experiences in loving her own body, and what the rhythm of the river provides that is beyond any human comprehension in terms of movement. Not only were we translating personal ideas to collaborative ideas, but we also had to translate them to a commercial realm where we were working with a publisher, an editor, and a designer, asking for a certain size, for a certain type of paper, for a certain fluidity on the pages, even color—making a book enlists a sense of trust and community and belief that what you are all creating is an object of beauty.

MARY: Perhaps in one sense all your work is collaborative. You have a relationship with landscape that seems collaborative, certainly reciprocal. As far back as your first book, *Pieces of White Shell*, you collaborated with the Navajo culture in some way, exploring those stories and myths, yet making them your own, making them speak in a larger context.

TERRY: The children were my teachers. The great hubris of that book was that in the beginning, I thought I was going to create an environmental education curriculum for Navajo children. I was on the Reservation all of thirty seconds before I said, No, I don't think so, and threw the curriculum out the window. Finally, in desperation as the children and I sat in the classroom, I took out a pouch I had attached to my belt and started passing around the various contents: rocks, sand, sage, a bouquet of feathers bound by yarn, deer skin. Each one of the objects became an ember, a story that ignited the children's imaginations and allowed them to speak. They were sharing their stories and in the process I was able to find my own. Somewhere in that cultural exchange we met on the shared grounds of our humanity, the trust once again, of our own relations.

MARY: There seems to be a kinship between Navajo storytelling and the Mormonism you describe—that kind of willingness to believe in the unbelievable. It was as if you had to travel to the Four Corners in the American Southwest in order to look at your own culture.

TERRY: Yes, it is true, the Navajo culture sent me back home to my own. There are similarities, a strong family structure reinforced through generational storytelling, a keen belief in the power of healing, but there are also marked differences. I had to come to terms with the fact that in Mormon culture, or any Christian religion for that matter, we are taught that

85

human beings have dominion over the land. This is one of the things that has led to my own estrangement from orthodoxy. Most Indigenous People do not view their relationship toward the Earth this way. They see themselves as a part of nature with a sense of kinship extended to all forms of life. These differences in philosophy loom large in our actions toward nature and how we view ourselves as human beings. As we approach the twenty-first century, I think another hubris we carry is that we think we are beyond landscape. For example, when nature writing is discussed, it's often viewed as soft or sentimental. We continue to see landscape or our relationship to nature as optional. The criticism of environmental writing—that it's not mindful of class, that it's an extravagance—is a critique of our own minds in terms of how we view our relationship to landscape. To speak about nature is to ultimately address issues of health, justice, and sovereignty. Nature writing in the pure sense is not cynical. It can be a literature of hope and faith and how we might move within our communities to heal our severed relations. When we look at postmodern fiction, so much of it is deeply cynical. Here are two trends in American literature on absolutely divergent paths.

JOCELYN: Maybe that's why students are sometimes resentful at first when we talk about going out into the land to write what they see.

TERRY: I know I encountered this type of reaction in the beginning from the students here in the nonfiction program at The University of Iowa. But as they ventured out into the wetlands and walked along the river, I watched their minds open. Before too long, they were pouring over field guides and developing their own sense of biological literacy. The students found that by heightening their awareness to the natural world, something was sparked in their writing, as well. This is not to say that writing about landscape is an epiphany around every corner. That kind of writing drives me crazy. But to see landscape as a complex set of principles, metaphors, and social considerations that are germane to this point in time. I think about Octavio Paz when he says that if we're interested in a revolution, an evolution of the spirit, it requires both love and criticism, that it is a writer's obligation to critique his or her own society or community. By the same token, how do we continue to keep our sense of compassion whole so that we don't become solipsistic, so that we don't become nihilistic and contribute not only to the passing of all other species, but even our own soul?

JOCELYN: In *Desert Quartet*, did you and Mary Frank both go out into the same landscape?

A Conversation with Terry Tempest Williams

TERRY: No, Mary had been out west during the course of our collaboration. She and her husband traveled to Arizona and the Four Corners region. She knew the country I was writing about from her own point of view. Curiously enough, right after I had finished writing *Desert Quartet*, I became involved with fellow citizens in a massive campaign to stop a dreadful wilderness bill, HR 1475 and S 884, the Utah Public Land Management Act of 1995. This was a curious juxtaposition in my own life. On one hand, I was completely immersed in the idea of Eros and nature, writing out of the body, wanting in some way to respond to the beauty of these sacred lands of the Colorado Plateau through language. And then on the other hand, I was asking, What can we do to stop this legislation? As a writer how can I be of use? So much of my writing of the last two years has been of a political nature whether it was writing a letter to Congress or an essay for *Audubon* magazine simply outlining the issues. I think each of us takes our turn within community and my number came up on this one. So, on one hand I was revising the essay of "Water" and on the other hand, literally, I was writing an op-ed piece for the *New York Times* regarding Utah wilderness. These are the kinds of confluences we experience as writers and yet they were both the same thing—a love of land. A response to home.

JOCELYN: Do you speak in different voices? One would seem very politically focused, the op-ed voice. I heard you on National Public Radio on that same issue where you were speaking to the reporter as you walked on the land. And then the writing in *Desert Quartet* is so poetic, it's like a series of prose poems. Does that feel like the same voice to you when you move from community to community and setting to setting?

TERRY: It's complicated, and as always, nothing is as it appears. It would be easy to say that the political voice is found in the *New York Times* op-ed piece, and that the poetic voice lives inside *Desert Quartet*, but I actually think that *Desert Quartet* is a far more political piece of writing. I remember talking to a librarian friend of mine about texts, and I started to read to her the *New York Times* op-ed piece because I wanted her opinion about something and I couldn't even get through it, the language bored me so. Because I was trying to explain to her what we were engaged in regarding Utah's wildlands, I ended up sharing with her the story from *Desert Quartet* about the frogs. That was where the motion was, the emotion. The irony lies in the fact that more people would have read the *New York Times* piece than will ever read *Desert Quartet*. So, again, I think it's about

87

shape shifting, about assessing what the occasion demands. How can we as writers serve the culture in a long term sense and in a short term sense? I had felt that my family was under siege; I responded. It's immediate. One is held accountable. It was the only weapon I had against my senators Orrin Hatch, Bob Bennett and my representatives Jim Hanson and Enid Greene Waldholz, among them. Would they understand *Desert Quartet*?

MARY: In your collection, *An Unspoken Hunger*, there's an essay in which you take newspaper clippings about the Gulf War and insert them into the narrative about going to a nuclear testing protest with your uncle, the ex-state senator with the guns in his car. What made that essay so effective was that by putting those disparate statements from our culture together, you made another sort of collaboration, a whole new piece in which the sum is greater than the parts.

TERRY: We live in an era with so many variables. Maybe everyone thinks that the time they live in is heightened, but I do believe we face unique circumstances, if nothing else, the dwindling of the Earth's resources and an increasing population should bring us to our knees. There are huge disparities all around us. Take today for example; we're in a car, with jets overhead and an Amish carriage on our right. We visit an antique store delicately looking at quilts that are hand stitched and find ourselves practically in tears as we see our childhood before us, whether it's fiesta glass or tinker toys. On the other hand, there's fast food down the street, we are pressed for time, there will be a dozen e-mail messages to respond to when we get back to the university. Talk about a crazy quilt—who can make sense of this? All we can do as writers, as human beings, is pull the pieces together and see what pattern emerges.

MARY: I was reading that at the turn of the century, as society became more urban and industrial, there was simultaneously a great nostalgia for a sort of romanticized English countryside version of landscape. It struck me that the more things change, the more things stay the same. There must be something missing in our relationship with landscape that makes us keep repeating these patterns of environmental destruction and nostalgia for what we're destroying.

TERRY: I think we are in a transitional time and perhaps this is heightened by the approaching millennium, which is largely symbolic if nothing else. I've been thinking about that, about this business of millennialism—what happened in the 16th to 17th century, from the Middle Ages to the Renaissance. What's happening now. It's interesting that John Cobb, a theological historian at Carleton College, says that at the turn of the century the world was being focused through the lens of Nationalism. And that Nationalism played itself out in the most horrific way with World War II, with Nazi Germany and Hiroshima. We saw that Nationalism was no longer useful, and that the only thing that could take us out of Nationalism into the next era was Economism, the big build up. Now we are seeing the same pattern again; Economism is no longer useful. Cobb says that often one moves from one era to the next through great pain. He mentions the Holocaust as an example and wonders what type of holocaust will move us out of Economism. I know that's a very sensitive word, but I feel we're already seeing it in the form of environmental degradation. Our own forests, our deserts, our waters, whole species disappearing at a tremendous rate—where will that take us? Cobb thinks it will deliver us to Earthism—a sense of an extended community, and that we will be forced, if we are to survive, to live more cooperatively, on a much smaller scale in terms of sustainability. I think that's a very idyllic point of view, but an evocative one. I would like to believe him. As we discussed earlier, we are living in an unprecedented time because of diminished resources and the terrifying pressures of population that we have never seen before.

MARY: Well some of us are, but some of us just don't seem to get it.

TERRY: I think that comes back to our obsession with our own species. That we aren't willing to extend our compassion outwardly, whether it's a Judeo-Christian ethic or whether it's an American ethic who can say, but we are deeply, deeply solipsistic.

JOCELYN: There's such a resistance to the idea that we're animals, and I love that in *Desert Quartet* you write the animal body. You're in your animal body.

TERRY: Mary Oliver writes, "There's really only one question: How to love this world?" I love that. Perhaps the second question is the one asked by Breyten Breytenbach, "The real revolutionary question is: What about the other?" I think in this next century we are going to be forced to think about the Other in much more compassionate and meaningful ways, practical ways. And not out of altruistic impulses, but for our own survival. Could we even say "for the love of God?" Perhaps it is no longer in our evolutionary interest to think in terms of the survival of the fittest, but rather, the survival of compassion.

JOCELYN: And you see that happening more through writing, through being in the land and breaking down that boundary of separateness.

A Voice in the Wilderness

TERRY: That's certainly the impulse that I write out of. What would it mean now to write sustainable prose?

MARY: What is sustainable prose?

TERRY: I honestly don't know, I am simply asking the question. If that's where we're moving as a species, if that's what we need to start thinking about—how to live in sustainable communities, how to create sustainable economies that don't exploit the land and the people but rather extend our compassion and imagination to foster new cooperative solutions, then wouldn't that be an interesting structure to overlay narrative? We are really talking about the need for new stories in our culture, stories that allow us to reconsider our lives.

MARY: You often write about the importance of story—certainly for us as individuals, but also for communities. I find that really interesting to think about—how cultures are shaped by the stories that are told. For example, the American story of expansion and exploitation. Maybe it's time to change the stories we're telling.

TERRY: Exactly. Maybe that is one of the impulses we are seeing in memoir—the old stories don't work for us anymore and we're desperately trying to find the stories within the truth of our own lives. Maybe that is also the impulse driving creative nonfiction right now, life today is so surreal, fiction no longer serves us or satisfies us in the same way. Or maybe it is as it has always been. We are simply hungry for good stories, fiction or nonfiction. Story is the umbilical cord between the past, present and future; it keeps things known. Story becomes the conscience of the community, it belongs to everyone. When we think about what it means to be human, it is always answered or explained through story.

MARY: And you've said that the most personal stories are the most universal in the way they reach beyond themselves to illustrate larger truths.

TERRY: There was an article in the *New York Times Magazine* about the growing trend of changing one's religion. Catholics become Muslims, Muslims become Buddhists and Buddhists become Christians. Religion has always been one of the most powerful stories within our own families, passed on from generation to generation. If we are letting go of that story then it makes sense we have to create another. What will it be? I don't think we know it. So in that sense, maybe all of our texts are experimental right now because we've lost our universal symbolic language. I was interested in reading a Davenport-Hines biography on W. H. Auden. One of the reasons Auden returned to Christianity was because of the symbolic language. There was a common point of communion in which he could write to his perceived audience. I think it could be argued that today there is no overriding symbolic language that holds us together, but I do think the diversity of expression and ideas we are seeing right now is and will be ultimately positive.

JOCELYN: Is this the importance, do you think, of collaboration? Because, as you are talking about the importance of stories, I find myself thinking back to Milan Kundera, in *The Book of Laughter and Forgetting*, I think, who writes of ostriches crowding in and appearing to mouth words, and it's a moment when a character sees that all the people tell their own stories just to tell them—nobody listens to the others' stories. In collaboration, you're telling your story with another artist and listening. As you pointed out before, the two stories create a third story. So, it isn't just telling, it's hearing as well.

TERRY: One of the things we continue to learn from Native Peoples is that stories are our medicine bundles. I feel that way about our poems, our essays, our fictions. That it is the artist who carries the burden of the storyteller. Terrence Des Pres speaks of "a prose of witness" that relies on the imagination to arrive at the heart of the matter. I believe this is our task as writers to respond to the world as we see it, feel it, and dare to ask the questions that will not allow us to sleep. Imagination. Attention to details. Making the connections. "Art—right words to station the mind and hold the heart ready."

JOCELYN: What are you working on now?

TERRY: At this particular moment, nothing and it feels delicious. It is time for me to go underground and listen.

MARY: But you wrote a new piece this very week!

TERRY: I did, but that comes out of the dailiness of life. The students here inspired me. I saw them taking such risks and working so hard on their essays. I wanted to work alongside them. We carry stories with us. Don't you think? And there has been this particular story that has been possessing me. It's about my family's construction business that was shut down for 18 months due to federal regulations regarding the desert tortoise. This was the same tortoise my husband and I were working to protect as an endangered species in St. George, Utah. I was thinking how we are all endangered species. My father, an endangered species. My father whom I will list as a threatened species, threatened by his emotional nature, threatened by my emotional nature. These are sentence fragments that have inhabited my mind. I think we're always holding on to sentences until they finally surface. To write an essay takes time, weeks, months, even years, as the various strands weave themselves together and then suddenly, you begin to see it as a full-bodied piece that demands to be brought to the page. To write an essay is to be in the service of an idea. But in terms of a project that will consume me as *Refuge* did, as *Desert Quartet* did, I don't know what that will be. I need to stay home, be still. I trust the silence and the questions that will move me into the next mysterious terrain. As I said, it's time to listen and go underground to hear what the roots are saying.

Talking to Terry Tempest Williams

About Writing, the Environment, and Being a Mormon

Tom Lynch, *Desert Exposure*, 1999

Terry Tempest Williams is a naturalist and writer from Utah. Her book Refuge: An Unnatural History of Family and Place, *which documents the rise and fall of the Great Salt Lake in the mid-1980s as well as the impact of fallout-induced cancer on the women of her family, became an almost instant classic in the literature of nature. She has collaborated in editing a forthcoming anthology,* New Genesis: A Mormon Reader on Land and Community. *She is also the author of* Pieces of White Shell, Coyote's Canyon, Desert Quartet, *and* An Unspoken Hunger, *as well as several children's books. For many years she worked as Naturalist-in-Residence at the Utah Museum of Natural History, and she recently served as the Shirley Sutton Thomas Visiting Professor of English at the University of Utah.*

Throughout her work, Terry Tempest Williams interweaves family, story, landscape, and the more-than-human world, exploring how human communities relate for good and ill with the natural world. She is one of the most graceful yet forceful voices for the preservation of wilderness areas.

Terry Tempest Williams will be in Las Cruces as part of this year's Border Book Festival (March 7-14). She will be reading with Barry Lopez . . .

Tom Lynch, "Talking to Terry Tempest Williams about Nature, the Environment, and Being a Mormon," *Desert Exposure*, March 1999, 18. Reprinted by permission.

A Voice in the Wilderness

In conjunction with her visit to Las Cruces, Terry Tempest Williams was interviewed by Tom Lynch. Tom teaches Southwestern Literature at New Mexico State University. He publishes both scholarly and creative work on the relationship between people and the natural world.

TL: When I heard about the theme of this year's Border Book Festival, Our Bodies / Our Earth, I immediately thought of your work, Terry. As much as anyone's, your writing seems to connect the human body with the more-than-human natural world. Why is this connection so important to you?

TTW: How can we not align our bodies with the Earth? We are made of the same stuff, so to speak: water, minerals, our blood like a river flowing inside our veins. To imagine ourselves as something outside of the Earth, foreign, removed, separate, strikes me as one of the reasons our collective relationship to the natural world and other creatures has been severed. I believe our health and the health of the land are intrinsically tied.

I've witnessed this as "hibakusha" (the Japanese word for 'explosion-affected people'), downwinders, and the predominance of cancer in our family due in large part, I believe, to the fallout in Utah from nuclear testing of the 1950's and 60's. To see ourselves as part of the Earth and its community, not apart from it as Robinson Jeffers writes, to me can be an act of humility and awareness.

TL: Your work is part of what seems to be a renaissance in the genre of nature writing. Why do you think this renaissance is occuring, if you think it is?

TTW: I think there has always been a strong tradition in American letters of place-based literature, literature that sees landscape as character. Look at Melville, Thoreau, Emerson, Dickinson, Whitman of the nineteenth century and in this century, Mary Austin writing about the desert, Willa Cather writing about the prairies, Hemingway, Faulkner, Steinbeck honoring the land in their novels and short stories. The list goes on and on, poets, too. W.S. Merwin, Galway Kinnell, Adrienne Rich.

Is this to be called "nature writing?" If there is a "renaissance" in the genre as you suggest with contemporary writers particularly in the American West, perhaps it is because we are chronicling the losses of the exploitation we are seeing, that we are trying to grapple with "an ethic of place" and what that means to our communities in all their diversity.

TL: What influence, if any, do you think such writing is having on the larger public debates about environmental matters?

TTW: Writers who see the land for its wisdom such as Aldo Leopold, *A Sand County Almanac*, and Rachel Carson, *Silent Spring*, made an enormous contribution to public awareness, even policy changes in the government agencies and the establishment of NEPA and the EPA. Writers such as Edward Abbey and Wallace Stegner, I know for myself, inspired my own thinking about place, alongside Peter Matthiessen, Simon Ortiz, Barry Lopez, and Denise Levertov.

      The diversity of writers today who are not afraid to articulate the truth of our lives, the depth of our humanity, writers such as Denise Chavez, Benjamin Saenz, Chuck Bowden, Gary Nabham, Susan Tweit, Tony Nelson, Linda Hogan, Naomi Shihab Nye, Pico Iyer, Rachel Bagby, too many to name, are giving us a new language to see the world with, new stories born out of individual landscapes that enable us to see the world whole. And these writings in all their eloquence are also political.

TL: I suppose it is fair to say that most people do not equate Mormon culture with environmentalism. Yet you are very forthright in being both a Mormon and an environmentalist. What do you see as the connection between the two?

TTW: It is true, many people would say "Mormon environmentalist" is an oxymoron, but that is only because of the stereotype and veneer that is attached to the religion. Our history is a history of community created in the name of belief.

      If you go back and look at the teachings of Brigham Young, his journals and sermons, they are filled with very strong notions of sustainability. Early brethren of the Mormon Church gave rousing speeches on the perils of overgrazing and the misappropriation of water in the desert.

      Unfortunately, much of this ethic has been lost as the Mormon Church has entered modernity. Like so many other facets of American culture it has assumed a corporate and consumptive stance with an emphasis on growth and business. But I believe there is change inside the membership of the Church of Jesus Christ of Latter-day-Saints.

      Bill Smart, another Mormon, and I put together an anthology of Mormon essays that celebrate community and landscape, with Gibbs Smith, a Utah publisher. We asked around 40 members of the Church in good standing, if they would write a piece about how their spiritual views have enhanced their views of nature, or conversely, how nature has added to their sense of Mormon theology. What emerged was an evocative testament *New Genesis: A Mormon Reader on Land and Community*, a very diverse (and I must say surprising in its content), collection of wide-ranging ideas, that we hope will be a touchstone for other Mormons to contemplate their relationship to place.

It could be said that the environmental movement in the past has been a political movement. I believe it is becoming a spiritual one. Native peoples have always known this. It is my hope that my own people within the Mormon culture will remember what our own roots are to the American West and the responsibility that comes with settlement.

TL: Ann Zwinger has said she doesn't go out into nature as a woman. Yet your gender seems to be a very important part of your work. Why?

TTW: Each of us writes out of our own biases. I am a Mormon woman who grew up in the Great Basin and now lives in the Colorado Plateau. These are the lenses of culture, gender, and geography that I see out of. Of course, we are all human beings, but it seems to me there is an honesty to state where it is we come from and how our perceptions have been shaped. The fun part, the difficult part, is then to shatter them and see the world from different points of view.

TL: You have been a strong supporter of the preservation of wilderness in Utah. Can you briefly explain why?

TTW: I have been a strong supporter of wilderness preservation in Utah because it feels like these lands deserve protection from the continued rape of the West. That is not to say that I do not have respect for the extractive industry in my state, I do. But I believe some lands are truly special, say the word, "sacred," even—that because of their importance biologically speaking to the migration corridors of animals, the habitat necessary for threatened and delicate species of plants, and the spiritual values they hold for society and inspire: silence, awe, beauty, majesty—that these lands have their own sovereignty that deserves to be honored and defended by the law.

I know it is very popular these days in some parts of the Academy to say that "wilderness" is simply a human construct, that wilderness has become irrelevant before it has become resolved. We do not have language that adequately conveys what wildness means, but I do not believe we can "deconstruct" nature. This notion strikes me as a form of intellectual arrogance. Personally, I feel grateful to the national park ideal, places of pilgrimage within North America that allow the public to engage with the natural world. I am grateful to those who enacted the 1964 Wilderness

Act and the other pieces of revolutionary legislation that maintain a sense of the commons: clean air and water.

Wilderness reminds us of restraint, that is a difficult and contentious idea for our society that defines itself on growth and consumption. There is no question this is "an American idea" but until we can come to a sustainable vision where we do not exploit everything in sight, it's the best we can do—our challenge is how to create sustainable lives and sustainable communities in a dance with wildness. I believe that is what we are working toward in the American West and it is not easy. In fact, it is a long and arduous and at times, difficult process, one that requires a good deal of listening and patience and compassion. I keep thinking of Stegner when he said, "We need a society to match the scenery."

TL: One of your early books, *Pieces of White Shell*, is set in the Navajo nation. What did you learn from the Navajo? How did your experience with them influence your direction as a writer?

TTW: One of the things I learned from the Diné when I taught on the Navajo Reservation was the power of stories inherent in the land. It made me wonder as Anglos, what stories we tell that evoke a sense of place, of landscape and community. Again, we have much to learn from Indian people and the long-time Hispanic families who have inhabited these regions in the West for centuries about what it means to live in place.

TL: I recall hearing you read from a manuscript version of *Desert Quartet: An Erotic Landscape* at a conference in Salt Lake City a few years back. At the time, you seemed nervous about writing frankly about the erotics of landscape. It seems a risky thing to write about. Has the reaction to the book justified your nervousness, or has it been favorably received? Why did you choose to write about this topic?

TTW: You ask about *Desert Quartet* and why I wrote that book. I think every writer struggles with various questions and tries to make peace with those questions, those longings through their art, their craft. I am interested in the notion of love and why we are so fearful of intimacy, with each other and with the land. I wanted to explore the idea of the erotic, not as it is defined by my culture as pornographic and exploitive, but rather what it might mean to engage in a relationship of reciprocity. I wanted to try and write out of the body, not out of the head. I wanted to create a circular text, not a linear one. I wanted to play with the elemental movements of Earth, Fire, Water, and Air, and bow to the desert, a landscape I love. I wanted to see if I could create on the page a dialogue with the heart-open wildness.

A Voice in the Wilderness

TL: I think a lot of nature writers struggle with the issue of audience. It is easy to write to the converted, to those who read environmental publications and who seek out nature writing. But there is also a great need to reach people who would never seek out this sort of writing, to do the hard work of conversion, as it were. How do you see yourself negotiating this problem?

TTW: As a writer, I honestly don't think much about "negotiating the problem" of audience. As I said earlier, I write out of my questions. Hopefully, if we write out of our humanity, our vulnerable nature, then some chord is struck with a reader and we touch on the page. I know that is why I read, to find those parts of myself in a story that I can not turn away from. The writers that move me are the ones who create beauty and truth out of their sufferings, their yearnings, their discoveries. It is what I call the patience of words born out of the search.

TL: Have you been to southern New Mexico before? If so, where? What was your impression?

TTW: I was in Las Cruces for the first time, I believe in the spring of 1996, at the invitation of Antonya Nelson and Robert Boswell through the University. I was able to meet with some of the students in the Creative Writing Program and gave a reading on campus that night. It was a wonderful experience. I had the very strong sense of camaraderie between the faculty and students and the community in general. That night there was a party and I was able to visit with dear friends such as Denise Chavez and Susan Tweit.

Tony took me for a wonderful walk around the plaza and town of Mesilla. It was such a rich blend of Indian and Hispanic cultures, a flavor too, of borderlands. My memory of that day with her is sheer magic. The landscape was very familiar to me. A few years earlier, my father and I had done some hiking in the mountains near El Paso. I love the feel of arid country and the miracle of water when found. It was also a haven for raptors, their shadows brushing over us midday.

I am so excited to be able to be part of the Border Book Festival, to be part of this wondrous community in Las Cruces that exhibits this kind of wholeness. This is a very special place. One day, I hope I can travel down to parts of Chihuahua where my grandmother was born. She was part of the Mormon underground whose family practiced polygamy. She would always tell me stories of how beautiful it was and what she remembered as a child growing up in northern Chihuahua. I know there are a lot of my relatives still living there.

TL: What projects are you currently involved with?

TTW: I am currently working on a book called *Leap*, set in Spain, that I have been working on unknowingly for the past seven years. Hopefully, it will be out next spring, but I work slowly, so who knows.

     And after that, I honestly want to get to know this place where we are living. My dream is to have an occupation of simply watching light.

     My husband, Brooke, and I have just moved from Salt Lake City to a small community in the redrock country of Southern Utah. It feels wonderful to be in a quieter, wilder place. We love Salt Lake and have lived there all our lives, but the pace and the distractions of urban growth were taking their toll on us. We were ready for a new adventure and much of Brooke's work is working with rural communities in Utah and issues surrounding sustainability, so it feels right.

     Much of the town of two hundred people that we now live in is Mormon. I am home-schooling some of the high school kids that are our neighbors and I am loving all they are teaching me.

TL: In your line of work it is easy, I would think, to get depressed, to focus on all that has been lost. What gives you hope?

TTW: You ask what gives me hope. Two words: forgiveness and restoration.

Testimony, Refuge, and the Sense of Place

A Conversation with Terry Tempest Williams

David Thomas Sumner, *Weber Studies*, 1999/2003

Terry Tempest Williams is a "placed" person. A fifth-generation Utahn, she weaves the history, people, landscape, plants, and animals, of Utah and the West into her work—work for which she has received national attention.

Having grown up in Utah, Williams has had a lifetime interest in the natural world that surrounds her. This is apparent in her education and work. She holds a B.A. in English and an M.A. in environmental education from the University of Utah and has worked as a teacher at Navajo Reservation in Montezuma Creek, Utah, and as naturalist in residence at the Utah Museum of Natural History. She has also served as the Shirley Sutton Thomas Visiting Professor of English at her alma mater.

Williams has authored a long list of books as varied as the Mormon tea, Rabbit brush, and sage of the Colorado Plateau; yet, like these plants, her books all spring from the same arid western soil. Her books include Pieces of White Shell: A Journey to Navajo Land; Coyote's Canyon; Refuge: An Unnatural History of Family and Place; An

David Thomas Sumner, "*Testimony, Refuge,* and the Sense of Place—A Conversation with Terry Tempest Williams," *Weber Studies* 19, no. 3 (Spring–Summer 2003). Reprinted by permission. This interview was originally conducted in September of 1999 and included in David Thomas Sumner, "Speaking a Word for Nature: The Ethical Rhetoric of American Nature Writing," (Ph.D. diss., University of Oregon, 2000). The version published in 2003 in *Weber Studies* and reprinted here was slightly revised.

Unspoken Hunger: Stories from the Field; Testimony: Writers in Defense of the Wilderness *(edited with Stephen Trimble);* Leap; *and* Red.

Williams has also received many awards including the Children's Science Book Award from the New York Academy of Sciences; she was named one of the "Utne 100 Visionaries" by the Utne Reader; *she is a Rachel Carson Honor Roll inductee. Williams received a Lannan Literary Fellowship, a Guggenheim Foundation Fellowship, and the "Spirit of the West" award from Mountain-Plains Booksellers Association.*

Williams lives with her husband, Brooke, in Castle Valley, Utah, near the Colorado River.

DTS: Are there collections similar to *Testimony?*

TTW: First of all, David, I would like to say how heartbroken I am about the death of Neila Seshachari.[1] She was a beacon of light and wisdom for all of us who knew and loved her. I cannot think of *Weber Studies* without paying my respects to her memory, the time and affection she brought to this journal.

In answer to your question, yes, there are several collections that have been inspired by *Testimony.* It has been very moving to see this simple form adopted by other regions in need of voices speaking on behalf of conservation. The most recent one is called *Arctic Refuge* compiled by Hank Lentfer and Carolyn Servid from Sitka, Alaska. It elucidates the fragile and enduring beauty of the Arctic National Wildlife Refuge. It was distributed to Congress in anticipation of the Bush-Cheney Energy Bill and their desire to drill for oil there.

There have also been chapbooks created for Petroglyphs National Monument in New Mexico, the Boundary Waters in Minnesota, the Blackfoot River in Montana, and I believe there was one made in Florida. Rick Bass has just published a collection of essays on behalf of the Yaak, and there was also a fine collection on the Tongass National Forest.

The Bolsa Chica Land Trust in southern California has also put together a book with writings by local people on why these wetlands of the Bolsa Chica Ecological Preserve should be protected from the ravages of development. Those people are an astonishing group of activists in Huntington Beach, California, who have preserved over 800 acres, a sliver of endangered

---

1.   Neila Seshachari (1934-2002) was a professor of English at Weber State University and the longtime editor of *Weber Studies.*

marshlands between the Pacific Coast Highway and huge oil wells and billion-dollar developments. The initial projection by the developer was 4,700 homes, and the Land Trust has negotiated that number down to 1,000. This is one example of what a few committed and imaginative people can do to protect their own valley. Very inspiring, against all odds.

DTS: (The conversation then shifts to my and Terry's relationship with Mormonism. I mentioned that she seems to be walking a line that refuses the orthodoxy but that also refuses to give up on the culture and the people.)

TTW: I am convinced there is a broader vision within Mormonism. There is something beautiful and meaningful here on the edges of this "American religion," as Harold Bloom has called it. I do not believe that a fundamental viewpoint is all that is available to members of the Church of Jesus Christ of Latter-day Saints.

I was reading the Dalai Lama's book, *Ethics for the Next Millennium*. He writes that it is a very dangerous premise to suppose there is only one true religion. He says, "I am not advocating Tibetan Buddhism. I am simply sharing my desire to speak about compassion." While growing up, how many times, I thought to myself, had we heard that Mormon phrase: "This is the only true church?" Something inside of me, very early on, just kept saying no.

DTS: The world is too big.

TTW: Exactly. And what about our own family members who are not LDS? Does that mean my beloved grandfather does not go to heaven? These were my thoughts as a child. I remember thinking, "Well, I doubt I'll make it to the Celestial Kingdom, but that's okay because how could anything be more beautiful than this Earth?" [The Celestial Kingdom is the highest in the three-tiered Mormon heaven, reserved for the most righteous. The Terrestrial Kingdom is the middle level, reserved for good people who did not recognize the truth of Mormonism. The Telestial Kingdom is to be on earth and like earthly existence in many ways.]

DTS: (We return to our conversation about *Testimony*). First of all, could you tell me how *Testimony* all came together?

TTW: It was a collaboration with Stephen Trimble. The atmosphere we were working in was very contentious—politically. It was 1995. You are familiar with the issues surrounding the Utah Wilderness Bill, right?

DTS: Yes, I testified before the panel you were on at the Indian Walk-In Center in Salt Lake City, down by the old Derk's Field.

TTW: Wasn't that an amazing night, David? That was truly one of those mo-
       ments in time I will never forget. It went on until—what? Two in the
       morning? That's the kind of thing that could never happen in an "official"
       hearing before Congress, nor in any local or state government. It was a
       kind of deep democracy inspired and carried out by "the people."

       Some quick background: After the 1994 Republican sweep in the
       elections, the Utah Congressional delegation, led by Jim Hansen and
       Orrin Hatch, announced it was going to come up with a Utah wilderness
       bill, once and for all. Hansen and Hatch believed they had the political
       power to get what they wanted. To Governor Leavitt's credit, he did say
       they had to open it up to a public process. This was in January 1995. For
       the next five months local hearings were held in every county that had
       proposed wilderness in it. We were told that the voice and will of the
       people were heard. And then, in June, Hansen and Hatch presented the
       1995 Utah Public Lands Management Act.

DTS: Right, and they proposed only 1.8 million acres out of the 22 million
       acres of available BLM lands.

TTW: That's correct. It was a slap in the face of democracy. Over 70 percent of
       the people in Utah wanted more wilderness, not less, most advocating for
       the Citizen's Proposal which at the time was asking for 5.7 million acres
       of wilderness.

       Those of us within the conservation community were outraged. It
       felt like an enormous betrayal of public trust in the name of our public
       lands. We immediately went into a defensive posture. I was on the board
       of the Southern Utah Wilderness Alliance, and we were having intense
       discussions on strategies and how to launch a full-fledged campaign on
       behalf of America's Redrock Wilderness.

       Privately, I kept thinking, "What can I do as a citizen? What can I do
       as a writer?"

       That is why we went into the citizen's hearings, as a protest to the
       way we were being shut out of formal discussions with our own delega-
       tion. That's why we had the meeting at the Indian Walk-In Center.

DTS: Right, I tried to testify in several places but was not allowed.

TTW: It was unbelievable. You wonder what kind of a democracy we really live
       in, especially now, in the post-9/11 world in which we find ourselves. But
       I refuse to be too cynical. I do believe we still have a voice in this country
       and that numbers do count. A bedrock democracy requires rigorous and
       relentless participation.

The next day, after the citizen's hearings, were the formal Congressional Subcommittee Hearings in Cedar City. The whole point of the hearings the night before was to glean testimonies from people that could then be relayed to Representative Hansen. I was asked to deliver those testimonies in person. I remember staying up all night transcribing the beautiful words of people such as yourself. The challenge was to put something down that was meaningful and succinct. We had five minutes to speak.

We flew down to Cedar City, and the process began. There were three panels: the political panel, the extractive industry panel, and the conservation panel. We would testify last. Congressman Jim Hansen and his colleagues sat on a riser above us. I remember how his glasses were perched on the end of his nose, how when I began to speak he was shuffling his papers, yawning, coughing, anything to show his boredom and displeasure. I was half-way through reading the citizen's testimonies—speaking on behalf of those who were at the Indian Walk-In Center the night before. He wasn't even listening—that was clear. Finally, I stopped mid-sentence and said something to the effect, "Congressman Hansen, I have been a resident of Utah all of my life. Is there anything I could say to you that will in some way alter your perspective so that you might consider wilderness in another way?"

What I remember is how he leaned over his elbows and looked down on me over the tops of his glasses and said simply, "I'm sorry, Ms. Williams, there is something about your voice I cannot hear." It was chilling—personal. I don't think he was referring to the quality of the microphone. And then, it was over.

I'll never forget that moment. To me, it became a metaphor, a symbolic representation of our delegation's inability—no, refusal—to hear what we were trying to say about wildness.

But you keep at it, day-after-day, even in the face of opposition and public opinion. What choice do we have when it comes to the preservation of the land? So often, someone will come up to me and say, "Why don't you find another story? How many times can you say the same thing over and over?" What I would like to say is how can we divorce ourselves from life, from nature which is the very stuff of life? We are the embodiment of both the domestic and the wild. One informs the other.

After the hearing in Cedar City, I wrote an op-ed piece for the *New York Times*, entitled "Open For Business," outlining the atrocity of this bill sponsored by the Utah Congressional delegation. I wanted to expose in a national forum why the Utah Public Lands Management Act of 1995 was a radical betrayal of our public lands, lands that do not just "belong" to Utahans, but to all Americans.

The campaign for America's Redrock Wilderness led by SUWA was in high gear. In July there was a hearing before the Senate in Washington. Again, there were three panels. Senators Hatch and Bennett both testified. The conservation panel, once again, was last. I was fortunate enough to be invited by the environmental community to testify alongside Bill Smart, a Mormon in good standing, for years an editor of the *Deseret News*, and a member on the board of the Grand Canyon Trust. Bill is an incredibly thoughtful and wise man. Phillip Bimstein, the mayor of Springville, Utah, also testified, as did Ray Wheeler, a man who knows Utah wilderness as well as anyone. He is a writer and photographer who has devoted his life to its preservation.

The panel on industry had finished its testimony—representatives ranging from the Farm Bureau to the oil and gas companies. The conservation committee was next. Mayor Phillip Bimstein was the first to speak. Halfway through his sentiments, Senator Larry Craig, a Republican from Idaho, chair of the Senate Committee on Natural Resources, stood up and said out loud, "This one is yours, Senator Hatfield." Hatfield was a lame duck from the state of Oregon. Craig continued, "Will you come and take this—? I have an appointment." Phillip had to stop his testimony while this "changing of the gavel" occurred, and then Senator Hatfield said, "Your time is up—next!"

It was so rude and ill-mannered. For the rest of the hearing, Senator Hatfield just sat there and read other papers during our testimonies. Basically, we ended up speaking to the wall and for the Congressional Record.

We all left completely disheartened and discouraged. It was hard not to ask, "What is the point?" No wonder America has become so cynical of government and the political process.

When I returned home, Steve [Trimble] and I met for coffee. Our conversation circled around what we could do as writers. I remember thinking, "Perhaps Congress can't hear one voice, but maybe they can hear a community of voices." Earlier that winter, Steve and I had talked about the possibility of a little chapbook on behalf of Utah Wilderness. If my memory serves me, Steve said, "Perhaps now is the time. We can do this." That was the spark that lit the fire for us to write an impassioned letter to our friends that simply began with the sentence: "We need your help." The letter went on to say, "Here's the political situation we are up against. We know you love Utah's wild country. Will you please write the most eloquent, beautiful piece you have ever written? We cannot pay you, and we need your essay in three weeks." Something like that. And in three weeks, we had twenty-plus pieces of writing from all over the American landscape, essays as heartfelt as anything we had ever read.

DTS: And you got heavy-hitters.

TTW: I suppose you could look at it that way. For us it was a circle of friends, our community of writers who were committed to language and landscape. Steve and I were genuinely moved by the response. You don't know the strength of any community until you ask for help in times of need.

The roster of writers included John McPhee, author of *Basin and Range*; Charles Wilkinson, one of the leading experts on water law in the West; Barry Lopez, Bill Kittredge, Ann Zwinger, Richard Shelton, all powerful voices within American letters. Karen Shepherd, who was serving as a congresswoman at the time, contributed. Mardy Murie, who along with her husband, Olaus Murie, helped craft the 1964 Wilderness Act, allowed us to publish a piece of hers regarding wilderness—she turns 100 this year. The other end of the spectrum, age-wise, was Rick Bass, a potent writer and wilderness advocate who was in his thirties at the time. We asked the distinguished writer and lover of Utah, Tom Watkins, if he would consider writing a foreword to place this gesture in an historical context, which he did.

From there, we sought a designer, again a friend of ours, Trent Alvey, who graciously agreed to work on this project. He agreed to do it *pro bono*. We found funding from the Cummins Foundation for $6,000, a local foundation sponsored by Annette and Ian Cummins, great supporters of conservation efforts here in Utah. This paid for the printing costs of one thousand chapbooks.

Steve and I had the pleasure of putting these essays together in a sequence we felt was the most powerful progression of their ideas. We had to work quickly. We knew the biographies were important to show the standing and reputations of the writers involved. We wanted signatures from each of the writers to add solidarity and depth. I recall the flurry and frenzy of all the writers faxing their signatures to us so we could incorporate them into the design, adding power and presence to the book. I remember the thrill of receiving Scott Momaday's signature. That signature was a piece of art—so beautiful is his script. We were so excited, feeling the momentum of it all. Good work is a stay against despair. We included a map and list of all the proposed wilderness areas. We picked out individual pictograph designs for each writer. The whole chapbook is full of secrets—I will tell you that—stories tied to each writer, the unspoken connections that bind us together. Again, our work must be fun as well as meaningful. Steve and I had a ball creating *Testimony*, even though—you must know—we were a bit crazy with the speed and rapidity of this project. We basically had a bit more than two weeks to put it all together.

It is important to note that the Southern Utah Wilderness Alliance had a critical role in teaching us—helping us to place *Testimony* in the halls of Congress. Again, this is the power of collaboration, one community supporting and helping another. Mike Matz, who was director at the time, was an incredible help, and without the brilliance and political savvy of Cindy Shogan, who was SUWA's congressional liaison in Washington, *Testimony* would never have found its way into the hands of our lawmakers. Dozens of volunteers helped distribute the chapbooks on the Hill.

In mid-September, Steve and I went to Washington. We had the thousand copies of *Testimony* mailed ahead of us. We held a press conference on the Triangle, next to the U.S. Capitol. Tom Watkins spoke. He was also working for The Wilderness Society at the time. Congressman Maurice Hinchey, sponsor of HR 1500, America's Redrock Wilderness Bill (the bill today is HR 1613; Congressman Hansen had it changed to dilute its familiarity), was present. Congressman Bruce Vento from Minnesota, another sponsor of the bill, was also present. They publicly accepted copies of *Testimony* and also spoke on its behalf, creating the sense that this was, in fact, a literary bill being brought to the halls of Congress by American writers. They said they would carry these words to their colleagues with the view of wilderness as a gift to all Americans. Senator Russ Feingold was also in attendance and vowed he would carry *Testimony* to the floor of the Senate.

After the press conference, a reporter from the *Washington Post* came up to Steve and me—did Steve tell you this story?

DTS: No.

TTW: Well, anyway, Steve and I were standing to the side, and the reporter walked up to us with his pad and pen, saying, "What a waste of time—." I said, "Excuse me?" I couldn't believe what I was hearing. He said, "What fools you are. Do you have any idea how much paper gets passed around Congress? You are so naive. This will never see the light of day."

I was ready to punch this guy. Forgive me, I know that doesn't speak well of me. Fortunately, Steve had much more presence of mind. He stood there very calmly and said to the reporter, "Writing is always an act of faith."

Copies of *Testimony* were, in fact, passed throughout Congress and to the media. I was personally able to take a copy to Mrs. Clinton and also presented one to the President. We had one placed in the hands of Vice President Gore and key members of the administration, such as Katie McGinty, John Leshy, and George Frampton.

It's hard to say what the impact of *Testimony* was, but as you know, the bill never got to the floor in the House. This was all part of a larger campaign to protect wilderness in Utah. There were so many people working together from so many different fronts. Again, that is the power and strength of community and collaboration.

In March of 1996, the Utah Public Lands Management Act of 1995 finally found its way to the Senate floor. The Senate went into a filibuster. As you know, a filibuster is about taking up time. What is needed is words to take up that time. Senator Bill Bradley from New Jersey stood up and said, "With all due respect, Senators Hatch and Bennett, these wildlands belong to all Americans, and I would like to read from one of my constituents, John McPhee: "Basin, Range, Basin, Range . . ." At that moment, *Testimony* was entered into the Congressional Record. It was followed by other senators reading from *Testimony* throughout the filibuster. The bill eventually died.

Six months later, on September 18, 1996, largely due to the strength of the environmental community and the political atmosphere surrounding the 1996 presidential election, President Clinton designated the Grand Staircase-Escalante National Monument, protecting two million acres of wildlands in Utah. Afterwards, President Clinton held up a paperback copy of *Testimony*, just published by Milkweed Press for a mass market distribution, and said, "This made a difference."

DTS: So he held up a copy of *Testimony?*

TTW: He did. There was a small luncheon held outside on the rim of the Grand Canyon after the formal ceremony. Bruce Babbitt, Mike Matz, president of SUWA, Robert Redford, Charles Wilkinson, and I were among those in attendance. It was very moving to hear the President's words. One usually never really knows the tangible effects of literature.

DTS: Right, this is not exactly a measurable thing.

TTW: I remember reading a comment from Mother Teresa when a reporter had come to visit her in India. The reporter asked, "How can you continue with so much failure all around you?—All this death!" She looked at him and said, "This is not about success. This is about being thankful."

This is how I feel about wilderness.

DTS: Those are great stories.

TTW: We all carry great stories, especially in the name of community. May I share one more?

One of the falsehoods that emerged from this contentious debate over Utah wilderness in 1995 was the polarity that you could be Mormon, Republican, and anti-wilderness; or you could be non-Mormon, Democrat, pro-wilderness—but you could not be Mormon and for wilderness. (I suppose you could be non-Mormon, Democrat and anti-wilderness, as well.) Anyway, these were the assumptions being portrayed by our political leaders and the press.

After the Senate hearing in July of 1995, Bill Smart and I were so disgusted with the process and the lack of respect given to citizens, along with the careless comments being made publicly, that "Mormons did not want wilderness," which we knew was not true, that we wanted to do something to dispel these myths. Again, that question: "What can we do—? What can we do together?"

Once home, we met with the publisher Gibbs Smith, another member of the Church of Jesus Christ of Latter-day Saints, and decided to put together an anthology of LDS writers asking the question, "What role has wildness or nature played in your beliefs as a Mormon?" Or conversely, "What role has Mormonism played in your view of nature?"

We solicited around forty different Mormon voices. Most of them were not writers but members in good standing from diverse backgrounds. The essays were as personal and varied as the contributors themselves: ranging from Salt Lake Mayor Ted Wilson's narrative on climbing the granite walls of Little Cottonwood Canyon in the Wasatch Mountains, to Larry Clarkson's sensual relationship to the sea, to Hugh Nibley's critique of air pollution as a sin against God, to Dorothy Solomon's memoir of growing up in a polygamist household, comforted by nature.

The anthology *New Genesis: A Mormon Reader on Land and Community* was published in the fall of 1998. It has given members of the Church cover, so-to-speak, to acknowledge their love of the land. I know this book is being used as a text at Brigham Young University. If nothing else, this collection acts as another point of discussion where we can begin to talk about an ethic of place as we try to "create a society to match a scenery," as Wallace Stegner has admonished us to do in his book *The Sound of Mountain Water*.

DTS: I want to ask you a few theoretical questions about nature writing. First of all, are you comfortable with the term "nature writing"?

TTW: I don't really know what that is. And I think what it does is run the risk of compartmentalizing, marginalizing and saying that that is all that's here. And I think the term is detrimental for the land. It marginlizes the land as something extra, instead of something integral to what we are doing. And I think, as Barry Lopez has eloquently said, and Stegner too, this is a literature of hope. It is also a literature of loss. I think that at the end of this century we are coming to grips with our mistakes and the prices we have paid. And I can only speak to my own experience, but to me this kind of writing that you see throughout the American literary tradition—whether it is Melville, or Dickinson, or Whitman, or Mary Austin, Willa Cather, Aldo Leopold, Steinbeck, or Hemingway—is a form of nature writing. I mean, let's talk about nature writers. What about Hemingway—*The Green Hills of Africa*, his sense of landscape, *The Nick Adams Stories*, all of those? I think it is an American question: "What is the correspondence between wilderness and the human spirit?" And I think that at this point in time, especially in the late 20th century, we seriously need to question and critique the values that have led us astray at our own peril. For me, the revelation in *Refuge* was when I realized my mother's health and the health of the desert were the same story. Our body, the body of the earth—there is no separation.

DTS: There is this moment in *Refuge* that I really find interesting. In *Desert Solitaire*, Ed Abbey comes to the desert believing that the universe does not care for the individual, and he leaves the desert after this Havasu experience saying, "The universe may not care for the individual, and this heartbreaking beauty is going to be here whether there is a heart to break or not, but the individual cares about the individuals, and we are important to ourselves and to each other, and that itself is an important discovery."

As I read *Refuge*, and I am coming at it from Abbey, I almost see you coming at the same problem, but from the opposite direction. What I mean is that it seems that instead of coming at it like Ed Abbey, already thinking the universe is indifferent, you come at it from our Mormon tradition which tells us the universe does care about us, but when we go out in the world we have to face this realization that there is indifference there. And there is this moment in *Refuge* where you talk about how being able to accept change and indifference is really the route to healing. You seem to be addressing the same problem, but from a different tradition, so you come at it in a different way.

TTW: I see what you are saying. We never see our own work from the outside because we write from the inside. It is that paradox. That is why the Great Salt Lake is so fascinating—this huge body of water that no one can drink. In this universe that we feel is embraced through our tradition, there is this cold indifference. And it is in the detachment that I think the healing occurs—that you are part of something so much larger. You feel the vastness and the smallness.

DTS: You say that you are uncomfortable with the term nature writing—as am I, as are most—but I have yet to come across a term that works. It is the kind of nonfiction that involves landscape that seems to be this really important part of American letters right now.

TTW: Perhaps that is your challenge as a scholar. I don't know what it is I do. I write about the questions that keep me up at night. In *Pieces of White Shell*, the question is "What stories do you tell to give a sense of place?" With *Refuge*, it is "How do we find refuge in change?" With *Leap*, it is "How do we breathe life into the orthodoxies that we are a part of?" It's the questions that propel me. I don't know what categories they are put in. To me, that is the work of the scholar and the academy. In all honesty, I don't pay much attention to it. It is interesting to me, but that's not how I see my work. I have found my books in everything from occult, to feminist studies, to nature writing, to essays, to—who knows? I think the only thing I haven't found them in is whimsy. Again, it is our propensity to categorize the world. And I think if anything comes out of this literature it is that the world cannot be categorized. It is seeing the world as whole, even holy. It is being mindful of the relations that sustain us. The fragmented world we are part of can only be healed and brought together through this kind of ecological mind.

DTS: Meaning?

TTW: When Gregory Bateson talks about "steps to an ecology of mind," I think that's what this literature is addressing.

DTS: There seems to be this special relationship within nonfiction that is interested in the landscape and empirical observation. One of the things that makes *Refuge* speak is that it is clear you know birds. It is clear you have some knowledge. If you were faking that, it would lend a hollowness and become a framing device rather than an integral part of the narrative. So my question is what is the relationship between writing about the natural

111

world and observing well and accurately? And what do you see as your obligation to the reader to have some integrity in that observation?

TTW: To me, writing is about how we see. The writers I want to read teach me how to see—see the world differently. In my writing there is no separation between how I observe the world and how I write the world. We write through our eyes. We write through our body. We write out of what we know. I guess I don't know how to answer that.

DTS: Well, let me take another tack. Because it is literature—and one of the great things about literature is that it is able to organize facts in a way to help us see things differently and to embody truth in a different way from other forms of communication—there is leeway. But literature that addresses the natural world is a really special hybrid. So, do you feel an obligation as a person who's writing about landscape to make sure you are within a certain empirical reality?

TTW: The integrity comes through the power of realization and what you see and how you convey that story. I remember I was terrified about writing *Refuge*. The first draft was called *The Bird Letters of Beverly Bliss*. It was fictional because I thought I was safer—I wouldn't have to expose. But then, as I was moving through it, I thought the world too remarkable, the world too miraculous not to tell the truth. If that book had been turned into fiction, into a novel—even though the structure is novelistic—I don't think it would carry the same weight because it would have to be imagined—where the fact is that it was true.

For me, I work on a very intuitive level—a very physical level. I was spending time with the birds; I was spending time with my mother. I didn't ask myself whether or not these two parallel stories worked together. At that time it simply was the truth of my life. I thought I was writing this book about the Bear River Bird Refuge, and I didn't realize that there was this correspondence, until, really, after my mother had died. I was at a family reunion—you'll appreciate this—and hundreds of people, and my Aunt Bea . . .

DTS: I have an Aunt Bea. [Laughter]

TTW: Well, you will relate to this. She is a total Mormon woman, totally stalwart, and she asked, "Terry, what are you doing with yourself?" (And then, she quickly looks at my stomach, wondering when I am going to have a baby.) And I said, "Aunt Bea, I'm writing a book." And she said, "On what?" And I said, "On the rise of Great Salt Lake and the death of my mother." And she looked at me as if I had gone utterly mad, and she walked away. I remember driving home, and I was so discouraged, thinking: "What am I thinking? Maybe I am going mad." And I had this easel downstairs; it was actually

Mimi's. I just went down, and I thought, "What am I doing?" I hadn't really questioned it—it was so internal. I took two Magic Markers, and I wrote "Bird Refuge," you know, and "Mother." And I had "Great Salt Lake," "Cancer," because these were all my resources— "Mormon Church." And I circled them, and I stood back and said, "What is holding these together?" I thought, "The narrator—how I see." So I put "Narrator" and drew two lines and stood back and realized what I had drawn was a map of the female reproductive system. And I thought, "This is what I know in here." And the price of withholding that creativity is what I saw my mother and grandmother go through. At that moment I thought, "I can do this."

I then literally picked up the manuscript, and—I think I was in my nightgown—I pulled on my Levis and cowboy boots and tore down to Kinkos. It was two or three in the morning. I started shuffling madly through the manuscript on the counter: "Refuge— Refuge— Mother— Mother— Mother— Birds— Birds— Birds." I saw it more clearly, and I took all of the section on mother and the family illness, and I told the guy behind the counter, "I want you to put this on the brightest color you have—turquoise or whatever." As I was waiting, in walks Mark Strand, former poet laureate of the United States and former University of Utah professor. And I was thinking, "Oh no, please don't hand me back my bright blue manuscript—not while Mark is here." But the guy says, "Here you go, Terry." And Mark just looks at me and says, "You writing for Hallmark these days?" And I looked at him and said, "Mark, are there days when you just don't think you can write one more word?" At that point, he just said, "Every single day." And, then, I knew I could go on.

So I took the manuscript and drove back up the canyon and started shuffling again. And I was thinking, "This is too intense. It needs more space. This, this, and this have too many birds—it needs more connection." And that's really how the balancing came. This is all to say that for me what holds the integrity of a book and of a vision is the structure. And at the very end there has to be something deeper that holds it together. It is not enough to have the birds as the headlines of the chapters, even though they are metaphorical. I was in my office in the museum and had the hydronomy charts. And I realized that the connection was the lake level. And when I charted the lake's levels for all of those months, I realized that, honestly, the lake level corresponded identically with the emotional levels. I mean, you can't make that up. And that is the faith I have in what it means to live in "place." I absolutely believe in that.

113

And, to me, that is the integrity of a literature of place—it is not a contrivance. It's simply paying attention to where we are at any given point in time, at any point in space. We must be willing to understand. I mean, those things happen. They really do. And that story could happen—it happens over and over again. I mean, you know, there really was an owl. My father is the biggest unbeliever on the planet, and I will never forget when we heard that owl. I don't know. Maybe there isn't any meaning in life, but we can create our own meaning. And that, to me, is my definition of faith.

DTS: In other words, taking hold of what we have here.

TTW: It is more than that. It is what you were saying. We don't need another world—we don't need the Celestial Kingdom. It is right here—right now. What does that say about us if we cannot see it?

DTS: And if we cannot preserve it and live well in it.

TTW: That's right. That, to me, is what writing is about—having to speak to place—having to speak to faith—having to speak to the darkest part of ourselves and embrace our own paradoxical nature. We see this paradox over and over again in the natural world: It is violent. It is tender. It is beautiful. It is awe—it is full of awe. It is all of this, and it is this kind of complexity that I think creates a sense of peace—a settling of the soul. And, ultimately, more than anything, it gives birth to compassion.

DTS: One more thing. Getting back to *Testimony*. It seems to me that the title itself is very important, in many ways, to that collection.

TTW: David, as one familiar with Mormon culture, you know exactly where the title of *Testimony* came from—from the Mormon practice of a monthly testimony meeting where members of the congregation share their personal spiritual experiences with one another in the sanctity of this communal ritual. Few people have recognized this connection. Perhaps this was the most subtle of secrets held within this little chapbook. But Mormon people recognized the connection. People like Congressman Jim Hansen, Senator Orrin Hatch, and Senator Bob Bennett certainly recognized it. You and I sat through those testimony meetings—still do. We listen to our friends and family share the open chambers of their hearts. You and I can remember that quickening of the Spirit, the desire to speak what we believe to be true and worthy of sharing—yes, this is exactly where the title of *Testimony* comes from. It is a gesture of gratitude and humility in the name of community.

The Transformative Power of Art

An Interview with Terry Tempest Williams

Michael Toms, *New Dimensions Radio Show, 2000*

We live in the midst of the sacred and the profane, light and darkness, conscious and unconscious, life and death, visible and invisible worlds sometimes meshing, sometimes col- liding, always moving us towards the mystery, ever deeper. And we wonder as we wander. This is our journey on this edition of New Dimensions, as we explore the relevance of a 15th-century artistic masterpiece to the world and time we presently inhabit with our guest, Terry Tempest Williams.

Terry Tempest Williams, former Naturalist-in-Residence of the Utah Museum of Natural History, is the recipient of a Lannan Literary Fellowship and a Guggenheim Fellowship. She's the author of Refuge, An Unspoken Hunger, Desert Quartet, *and* Leap. *Join us for the next hour as we explore the wilderness world and the wondrous world of Terry Tempest Williams. My name is Michael Toms; I'll be your host. Welcome to* New Dimensions.

Michael Toms, "The Transformative Power of Art," New Dimensions radio interview, June 29, 2000, program 2821. Produced by New Dimensions World Broadcasting Network. Used by permission.

A Voice in the Wilderness

MT: Terry, welcome.

TTW: Thank you, Michael. It's wonderful to be with you.

MT: Nice to be with you too.

TTW: Happy birthday! May I say that?

MT: Oh sure, thanks. Thanks very much. A 15th-century Hieronymus Bosch painting—how did that happen?

TTW: It's a good question. Brooke and I decided we needed a vacation. It was 1993, shortly after I had finished writing *Refuge*, which was about the rise of Great Salt Lake and the death of my mother from ovarian cancer. I think that anyone who has had the privilege of being with a loved one when they die, in those last moments when the breathing is becoming more shallow and when you see that transition from life to death, finds that dogma is shattered and spirituality rises. And in that moment, I was confronted with the real question: what do I believe? I think that was the question that carried me into Spain. We wanted to go to a country that I perceived as unafraid of death. We had frequent flyers—nothing romantic about that—and I was interested in Federico Garcia Lorca's concept of *duende*, the raw power of the earth, that which threatens to create art.

    Anyway, we landed in Madrid. We could hardly wait to go to the great art museum, Museo del Prado. We were wandering through the galleries in awe of Velásquez's *Las Meninas*, the elongated saints of El Greco, the Dark Paintings of Goya, we turned, and there we were, confronted with *El jardín de las delicias*, *The Garden of Earthly Delights*, by Hieronymus Bosch. At that moment, I realized I knew the painting, or at least part of it: the panels of Paradise and Hell. My grandmother had thumbtacked these prints above the bed where we slept as children. What I didn't know, Michael, was the whole center panel, the panel of earthly delights; I never knew that existed. The body, the body of the triptych, my body—and a seven-year search ensued.

MT: So you wrote a whole book about this search and this journey. Do you recall the feelings you had when you saw the painting?

TTW: I do! I remember the colors vividly. I think that, as children, the art that we are raised with seeps into our blood stream. It becomes part of our DNA. In the left panel, there was Christ in his pink robe, in the Garden of Eden, with his left hand on Eve's right wrist taking her pulse. Adam is sitting below that wild pink fountain with the owl inside. There are giraffes, elephants, unicorns, three-headed birds, and then, on the right panel, the panel of Hell, there is that bone-white, hollowed man looking over his shoulder with the cavern inside, the ladder moving up with all sorts of terrifying creatures, that woman stretched across almost like a human sacrifice along the strings of the harp, the pig in the right-hand corner dressed as a nun, the fires, the flames, the ears, the cannon of ears with the knife resting on top—terrifying images. Those images came rushing back to me. And then I saw that center panel, this wild menagerie of cavorting, human beings, thousands of them, naked, in connection with Eros. The council of birds, people sitting on the backs of mallards, a couple making love inside a mussel shell, the cavalcade of horses, bulls, deers, and bears with men riding them, circling the pool of women balancing berries on their heads—just wild. I couldn't believe it. Literally, one day in the Prado turned into three weeks in the Prado turned into seven years going back and forth.

MT: So you became known as "the woman who watches."

TTW: The woman who stares at Bosch. It's true! I think the guards thought I was completely mad. I remember one day I had been bird watching in Parque de Retiro, behind the Prado, the beautiful park in the center of Madrid. It was hot, a perfect time to go in and spend time in the landscape of Bosch. I walked in. I had binoculars still dangling from my neck and a field guide in hand. I sat down in this cradle chair in the intimacy of the Bosch room, and without much thought, I saw birds in the painting, I picked up my binoculars and started watching them. I don't know how much time I'd spent in the landscape of El Bosco, but when I pulled the binoculars down, I saw the guards shaking their heads to each other.

MT: That's cute. The painting is very large, is it not?

TTW: It is. It's like a large window that one looks through. It's 220 by 195 centimeters; that translates to about 8 feet by 6 feet.

MT: And it's a triptych. There are three separate panels.

TTW: That's right. And, traditionally, these were traveling altarpieces—portable altarpieces. And, if you think of a cupboard, you have the two outside doors. In this instance of *The Garden of Earthly Delights* it's a round bubble in terms of blacks, greys, and greens—some art historians say the third day of creation. You open it up like cupboard doors and then, again, you are just shocked with the explosion of colors, primary colors: reds, yellows, blues, pinks, greens, golds. It's a wild landscape.

MT: He painted this painting, in the year 1500, eight years after Columbus found America, right?

TTW: Right.

MT: But the world didn't really know, and I can't imagine Bosch really knowing, that the world was round.

TTW: It's really interesting. It was prior to Magellan's circumnavigation as well. And there were so many times, Michael, I thought, "was Hieronymus Bosch painting from the future?" How did he know? What was intuition, what was instinct, what was extraordinary observation on his part? He rendered 35 species of birds perfectly. I think you make a good point about Columbus's voyage to the Americas. Imagine the encyclopedic knowledge that was coming back to Spain at that time. Hieronymus Bosch was a Flemish painter, part of the Low Countries under the rule of Spain, but I think that there is this interesting juxtaposition in his work between what is real and what is imagined. I also think it's important to note that Hieronymus Bosch was painting on the cusp of the Reformation, and I don't think it's too much of a leap to suggest that, five hundred years later, we may be on the cusp of another reformation, call it an Ecological Reformation.

MT: Certainly it seems to be a spiritual reformation as well in that more and more people—I just keep reading things like Gallup Polls and Harris Polls—are looking for meaning and purpose in their work, in their life, and there's this hunger, this quest—particularly in the West, particularly in the United States—this quest that's kind of a direct response to our materialist culture.

TTW: Exactly! I wondered this many times watching the painting, the landscape of Hieronymus Bosch. What were they thinking of in 1500, coming out of the Middle Ages, moving into the Renaissance? What was their hunger? And in that way, spiritually, and now ecologically—and again, how do we separate the two—I don't think five hundred years separate us.

MT: And I don't think Bosch was accepted quite readily in his time, was he?

TTW: You know, we know very little about Hieronymus Bosch. There are those who thought he was a heretic; there are those who thought he was a real true believer. I think it's fascinating to note that *The Garden of Earthly Delights*, this triptych, hung in the private quarters of Philip II's bedroom. What does that mean?

MT: He was King of Spain?

TTW: The most pious of Spanish kings who led the Second Spanish Inquisition. He was the grandson of Ferdinand and Isabella, the son of Charles V, ruler of Spain during the time when they said "the sun never set on Spanish Empire."

Was it a direct rendering of Christianity, Paradise, Earth, where we succumb to lust and then pay for our bloody sins, as they say, in Hell? Or was Hieronymus Bosch making a statement against Catholic Spain? I think the pig in the nun's habit can't be too positive in the corner of Hell. I was also interested in the fact that there's a little owl in the pink fountain in the eye that looks like a pupil. I identified it as Tengmalm's Owl, which is known for its rapid musical phrasing of "poo-poo-poo," and I wonder, were there Medieval ornithologists that caught Hieronymus Bosch's sardonic humor?

There are also other art historians, Fraenger among them, who believe that this was an altarpiece for a religious sect known as the Adamites. Another art historian, Laurenda Dixon, claims that this is a map of alchemy with all sorts of alchemical images: the large fountains, the vessels, the bubbles. So there is a wide gamut of interpretation.

MT: I think, in your research, you found that Hieronymus Bosch himself belonged to an association of men that worshipped Mary.

TTW: Yes, Our Lady of Lourdes.

MT: And there are all these images of women who look like Mary in the painting—and also Aphrodite—all there.

TTW: Right, and I think that's one of the things that gave me courage to really follow my own imagination, inspired by Bosch's, because we don't know what the painting means. All we can know is how we respond. And I do believe in the transformative power of art—the power of art to change our lives. The question came into my mind over and over again: can a painting be a prayer? Can wilderness be a prayer? What happens when the boundaries of a painting blur? What happens when the boundaries of wilderness blur?

MT: Yes, really. And all the cherries in the painting . . .

TTW: There are hundreds of cherries. I just love them. And again, it's just lip-luscious in that center panel. It made me laugh because, in Utah, the cherry is our state fruit. In my research I found that the cherries in Medieval days symbolized female genitalia. And I thought, "I doubt that the Utah legislators consciously knew that—maybe unconsciously."

MT: It always comes out, doesn't it?

TTW: It does.

MT: You can't hide it. You can't keep the unconscious down; it's going to out somewhere.

TTW: I know. And maybe again, that's why we keep responding through the centuries to the wild imagination of El Bosco, as the Spanish call him:

his distinct personal iconography, his symbols that both translate to the collective as well as the personal.

[music break]

MT: I'm speaking with Terry Tempest Williams, the author of a book entitled *Leap*, which almost defies words to describe it. It's really a personal journey, it's storytelling, it's history, it's mythology, it's dreams, it's visions, and it's an account of her experience of living out her vision of the painting of Hieronymus Bosch that she found in the Prado Museum in Madrid. And the title of the painting again?—You can say it so well.

TTW: *El jardín de las delicias.*

MT: Which means?

TTW: *The Garden of Earthly Delights.*

MT: Yes.

TTW: And it really was falling in love with the painting. I think *Leap* is a book of questions, Michael. Another aspect that bled through the painting—as I thought about the cusp of the Reformation and Bosch's critique, perhaps, of Catholicism—had to do with my own tradition, which is Mormon. What happens when our institutions no longer feed us? And I don't think this is specific to Mormonism, but any -ism, really—Catholicism, Mormonism, Judaism, even Buddhism. How do we create a living faith, a faith that is alive yet one that honors the traditions, the seeds of tradition, that have been planted?

MT: Mormonism has always been fascinating to me because, having been raised a Catholic, I heard about the Mormons when I was going to Catholic school—not always in the most positive light, I have to say—but I was always fascinated. Who are these people? Because what was told to me was that this was the only religion that had not broken off from the streaming that Catholicism says goes back to Jesus, right? And it was Luther that came along, and then you had Protestantism. But the Mormon religion was not part of that stream; it kind of emerged spontaneously through Joseph Smith.

TTW: Right.

MT: Right. Joseph Smith had the vision of the angel Moroney?

TTW: Angel Moroni.

MT: Moroni.

TTW: Right.

MT: And then he was given tablets—tablets or books?

TTW: The golden plates.

120

MT: Golden plates, which no one knows where they are.

TTW: It's . . . it's a wild religion, and maybe that's why it came up again in this wild painting of Hieronymus Bosch during my meditations. The Mormons will tell you that Joseph Smith was part of the restoration of the gospel of Jesus Christ. And I was fascinated because it has occurred to me that here is a religion—Harold Bloom calls it an American religion, born out of American soil in the post-Revolutionary era—I thought, if ever there has been a religion that has been born out of the Earth it should be Mormonism. It is founded literally on golden plates culled out of Hill Cummorah. And here is a religion born out of questions, a religion born out of personal revelation—Joseph Smith asking which church was the true church, kneeling in a sacred grove of trees, and then having a vision, and, later, having a vision of these golden plates containing sacred texts. So that foundation is laid in this book. And I wonder how a religion that really has deep mystical roots, ties to hermetic tradition, even alchemy— the mystical vision of Joseph Smith moving to the communal vision of Brigham Young, the Mormon exodus into the Salt Lake Valley in 1847 when he rose and said "This is the place"—how have we gone from the mythical to the communal to the corporate vision of Mormon Inc., which we saw a couple of years ago on the cover of *Time* magazine. That's one of the questions that I raise, and again, how can we move back to that more personal place of revelation?

MT: I think also of the great gift of the Mormons in their emphasis on ancestry, on where we came from, and on our own personal lineage. That has helped people all over the world discover their ancestors in ways that would not have been possible had it not been for the Mormons' focus on that particular dimension.

TTW: Right, and our sense of history, forward and back. So again, these were some of the questions brought up, inspired by this painting that really asks us to think about what we believe and about our own personal mythology, as well as a collective one.

MT: Now weaving in and out of your book *Leap* is this constant return to your connection to the Earth and the land and the wild and of course this painting—I can't imagine a painting that could be wilder.

TTW: It's true. And I love the scale of birds and animals in relationship to human beings, particularly in the center panel. I think that's a statement in and of itself in terms of scale and proportion. What do the birds have to teach us? How would our lives be different if we were listening to the

121

wisdom of other beings, other species? And then you look at the right panel of Hell and that proportion is skewed. It's almost like the animals have now turned on human beings as we turned on them, so there's a lot of interesting ecological questions that come through in this painting.

MT: And this was at a time, I think, when Bosch was living, when there was great hunting going on of animals.

TTW: Right, and animals were very much a part of the symbolic life of human beings. This panel painting grew out of the tradition of illuminated manuscripts, Books of Hours, and it's almost as though Hieronymus Bosch took the animals in the marginalia and brought them into full focus, into the centerpiece of a painting.

MT: Yes, yes. But I think one of the aspects of Europe that I'm always struck by when I visit Europe is that you don't see wildlife. Wildlife is very minimal because it's all gone.

TTW: And I think that's one of the things that sent me back home. I would be looking at this surreal landscape of El Bosco, and then I would go home and read the headlines in newspapers, and it was hard to tell what was real and what was imagined. You know, Frankenstein food with Bt-corn affecting monarchs, DNA taken from fireflies injected into the ears of the mice so that their ears glow. I think about the tons of nuclear waste sitting on the banks of the Colorado River, uranium tailings, so on and so forth. We have our own litany of horror that is a companion piece to Hieronymus Bosch's images of Hell.

MT: One of the really interesting stories that you wrote about in *Leap* was the experience you had of riding in an airplane with somebody from P&G.

TTW: That's right, Proctor & Gamble. It was, I'm sure, the longest plane ride of his trip, but we were stuck on the tarmac for two hours, and it was actually quite funny, you know how you don't talk to people on planes. Usually people respect one another's privacies, but we started talking, and he said, "So what do you do?" And I said, "Well, I'm a writer." And he said, "Really, what kind?" And I said, "Well, I write about the environment." Long pause. "What do you do?" "Well, I work for a corporation." "Really, which one?" "Proctor & Gamble." Long pause. And then he looked at me and said, "So you're one of them," and I looked at him and said, "So you're one of them, is it as bad as they say?" And then we had a fascinating conversation for the next two hours.

MT: Yes, it was fascinating. It's a great story. It really has so much. Give us just a little flavor of it.

TTW: Well, it was interesting. This man was from Germany but had impeccable English. His grandmother took him out of Germany toward the end of World War II because she was not comfortable with her husband's politics. That's all he would say. He moved to England; he said you had to have an impeccable accent or you were beaten up.

MT: Right. If you didn't learn English pretty fast you were in trouble.

TTW: Can you imagine after the Blitz? And he never lived in a place long enough to vote, and that was an interesting discussion where he said, "You're not naïve enough to believe that a vote matters?" And I remember saying, "Perhaps I'm too much of an American to believe that it does matter." And then he really did start talking about the truth of his own life. He was on his second marriage, he didn't know his older kids, there was no respect for wisdom, he was a man in his late fifties, he was sick of the word "innovation."

MT: The younger generation was catching up . . .

TTW: He said, "I have footprints on my back if I don't keep up with them." And then he said, "But what am I supposed to do?" And then when it got into that place of discomfort, then he just looked at me and said, "Clean, clean, clean, clean—that's what Proctor & Gamble does."

MT: He also made the comment about how the management at the top or the people running the company—there's no way to change it.

TTW: That's right. He said, "What are we supposed to do, it's out of our hands," and they said, "Out of our hands but you are the CEOs, you are the vice president." And he said, "There isn't one of us sitting around that table that believes we have any control over this." Pretty terrifying.

MT: Yes, it's indicative of what has happened to many corporations in our culture; they have become entities unto themselves.

TTW: And yet this deeply human man was lamenting the loss of his own private life, having no sense of place, and yet just saying, "You know, your teeth are clean, aren't they?

MT: We clean the world, we keep the world clean.

TTW: And he said to me, "How many times have you gone to corporations with your hands open with asking for money for your causes?" And I said to him, "More times than I care to admit." So we're all complicit in this very complex world, and I think that's what was intriguing to me about this triptych. So often we get caught up in our own dualities—this or that, black or white, urban/wild, conservative/liberal, whereas I think that Bosch's genius was saying there is a real world, a beautiful world, an

MT: ambiguous world, a world of discovery and curiosity that is the center panel, the middle path.

MT: It reminds me of that conversation that you were having with the cattle rancher, somewhere, I think, in Utah.

TTW: Right, Escalante.

MT: Yeah, and he took his hand and swept it across the horizon and said, "What's that?"

TTW: Yes. "Wilderness. Why do we need to designate it as such?" So *Leap* is a book of questions. All these ambiguous issues: How do we live a life of greater intention? What does it mean to be human? Again, what do we believe, and how do we make peace with our own contradictory nature?

MT: And you said yourself, that you're a person of extremes, always living in extremes, and the middle path is . . .

TTW: It's terrifying to me.

MT: It's a terrifying one, yes.

TTW: And yet, maybe it's just because I'm in the middle of my life and a woman almost 45. This is where the beauty is, in Hieronymus Bosch's triptych, *The Garden of Earthly Delights*. I want to live in that middle panel. I want to live in that place of joy and love and openness.

MT: Where do you live now?

TTW: We live in Castle Valley, Utah, which is just outside of Moab. And Michael, I can honestly tell you, I believe that Hieronymus Bosch moved me from a place of orthodoxy, even Salt Lake City, to a place of freedom in Castle Valley, Utah. I could no longer live with the split within myself of living in the city yet really being married to the wild. And I think both Brooke and I, after 25 years of marriage, really wanted to live in a place of beauty so that we could live in the garden, so to speak, and it's made an extraordinary difference in terms of settling our souls. And again I have to say that I believe in the transformative power of art, the restorative power of art, even the restorative power of wildness.

MT: Yes. And the line blurs and the definitions blur when we start thinking, "What is art?" Really, in some ways, it is everything.

TTW: It is. And again, no separation. There's a discussion in the book where I'm looking at an installation by the British artist Damien Hirst, and I ask the question, "Can wilderness be an art installation?"

MT: I'm speaking with Terry Tempest Williams, author of *Leap*. My name is Michael Toms, you're listening to New Dimensions.

[music break]

124

MT: There is a line that recurs in *Leap*: "The place where I was born is now a prison."

TTW: That is literally true. I was actually born in Corona, California, just outside of Riverside. On my 40th birthday our family gathered together at Capistrano Beach as we've done for years and years, 30 years as a family, and my father said, "Would you like to see where you were born?" and I said, "Of course." It was the March Air Force Base. And as we drove to the hospital where I was born, I saw that it is now a prison, and the house where I was born is now the parking lot of a bank. And the orange groves are now subdivisions. I think that's a story very common to my generation.

MT: Yes, it is. Yes, very true.

TTW: How do we find hope in the midst of despair? I think that was one of the questions that I was wrestling with, and Hell was not an easy place to be, I can tell you, in writing this book. And I think about Hélène Cixous when she says that the only book worth writing is the book that threatens to kill us. And there were times, Michael, I felt that. But in the horizon of Hieronymus Bosch's Hell, there are passages of light, pathways of light, and I think we can move through there and find that place of joy, but only if we dare to go as deep as we dare. I think that it's only in really confronting our own fears, our own darkest selves, personally, collectively, that we can hold grief and move it into a place of love.

MT: I'm reminded of your account of meeting the tiger shark in the Monterey Aquarium and then meeting the tiger shark in formaldehyde in the Brooklyn Museum. When I read that passage in the book I was reminded of Rilke's poem, "The Panther."

TTW: Yes, that's a great poem. I love that poem, don't you?

MT: Yes.

TTW: Yes, it's in our embrace of darkness that we really can feel the light, and that isn't a cliché. And I think that, if we live without embracing the dark, without looking eye to eye with the black panther, then we remain in a state of denial. And, to me denial is what leaves us stuck in Hell.

I think that, more and more our frame of reference is becoming smaller and smaller. How many of us really do spend time in wild places, open places? And I think that open minds are in a direct relationship to open country. And I think that there's the metaphorical world, there's the symbolic world, there's the world of the artist, and there's also the physical world—and we still have wilderness on this planet. We still have large tracts of wilderness in the American West, and I keep hoping that there

125

will be a day when we have laws that protect them. I wish we didn't have to separate wilderness as something we have to designate as a people. But unfortunately we do. And I think that our challenge now is to discover how we as human beings can find those bleed-through zones, the buffer zones, so that our villages, our cities, have a graceful movement into wild country, so that there aren't these boundaries that separate us from the world we're a part of.

MT: Yes. Going back to Mormonism, I was interested that you made references in *Leap* to Mary Magdalene. I think of Mormonism as a patriarchal religion, I may be mistaken about that . . .

TTW: I don't think you're mistaken.

MT: Okay, good.

TTW: I hope it's changing. As the women in the Mormon Church change, the Church will change. But you're right, the hierarchy is male.

MT: So you were writing about Mary Magdalene. She was at the foot of the cross with Jesus. And then, something I never knew, I learned in your book: she went to Rome. Tell us that story.

TTW: She went to Rome and somehow got an audience with Caesar. She basically said, "Christ did rise in the resurrection," and he said, "No, that cannot be true. Christ could no more rise from the dead than the egg that you hold in your hand could turn to blood." And the egg that she held in her hand turned into blood. That is the story, and I find it deeply moving, whether it's metaphor or whether it's real. Again, the eggs that one sees in the center panel, I think, represent that notion of rebirth. And if you look at the center panel of Hieronymus Bosch, right in the heart of the whole triptych, Michael, is an egg balanced perfectly on a man's head. And that's where the image of Mary Magdalene came to me. And it was interesting in the research to find her own pilgrimage to Rome, Caesar, etc., even the egg turning to blood.

MT: Yes, I think that even in the mystical streaming of the Catholic Church there's all this evidence that, in the early stages of the Church, women were much more prominent than the later Church acknowledged.

TTW: I think we see that with the feminine, even the Virgin Mary. And in Mormonism you do not see that kind of honoring of Mary or Mary Magdalene. You see the honoring of the mothers in the homes in individual Mormon households, but there is no question that the men hold the priesthood. And I hope this is something that, in the future, will be changed. I think the truth is that, in households everywhere, you're working toward a

126

MT: partnership of the masculine and the feminine, male/female, husband/wife, whatever partnerships we're in—that balance.

MT: I'm speaking with Terry Tempest Williams, author of *Leap*. My name is Michael Toms, you're listening to New Dimensions.

[music break]

MT: I'm speaking with Terry Tempest Williams, author of *Refuge* and a book entitled *Leap*. We're talking about Terry's leap from a painting by Bosch to a book entitled *Leap*, and the story is really a leap in many, many ways; it's a wonderful leap, actually.

TTW: You know, I love the line from the poet Federico Garcia Lorca, for he says, "we must follow the vein of our own blood." And so often, I think that, in terms of our own private obsessions, we don't chose them; they choose us. I would never have known on that morning in 1993, standing before *The Garden of Earthly Delights*, that this was the direction my life would take for the next seven years. I really did fall in love with the painting, and it really did seize my heart and turn me upside down, inside out, to see the world in a new way, and I love the restorative power of art.

I think one of the most amazing things, Michael—and this is where you and I were saying it's why I love nonfiction—is that you couldn't write this in a novel; no one would believe you. May I share a story with you about my father?

MT: Yes, please.

TTW: I come from a family where I literally have to listen to Rush Limbaugh to find out what they're thinking, and my father is the Marlboro man without the cigarette. We were at a family dinner, and he was saying, "I don't know where you're going. You say you're going to Spain, you say you're going to watch a painting, but quite frankly I don't even believe the painting exists. I think you're over there doing something else." I said, "Dad, come with me," and he said, "I'd love to, I'd love to see this painting for myself." So we figured out a time we could go, we boarded the plane, we landed in Madrid, I was worried about my father, who was getting older, so I said, "Dad would you like to go to the hotel and rest?" "No, I want to go see Bosch." We went into the museum with our luggage, the guards now truly thought I was crazy, and I said, "Dad, do you want to see Velásquez?"—"No." "El Greco?"—"No, no, I want to see Bosch." We were moving through the gallery and I thought, "finally I can have a spiritual experience with my father." We turned the corner and I said, "Dad, here it . . ."

The painting was gone.

He couldn't believe it. "Where's the painting?" I'm speechless. I said, "Dad, I don't know, it was here last year, it was here during at the end of Franco's Spanish Civil War, I don't know where it is." Then he said, "Well I'm going to go find out!" He left. I couldn't believe it. He came back with the guide, Juan Manuel, and said, "Please explain to my daughter where this painting is." There was a little postcard that I saw behind Plexiglas that said "*restoracion*." To make a long story shorter, my dad doesn't hear very well and he certainly doesn't understand the Spanish accent very well, so Juan Manuel tried to describe the painting to my father—keep in mind that the card was four inches by three inches—and he pointed to the center panel.

MT: Your father was asking about something in the center panel.

TTW: Yes, he was saying, "What is this?" Juan Manuel said, "Right here you see the Pool of Adultery," and my father said, "What?" He said, "The Pool of Adultery." My father said, "I'm sorry I cannot hear you, the pool of what?" And he said, "LEWINSKI!" and my father said, "Oh, I get it, the pool of adultery!" By now we have a very large crowd gathered around this small postcard. I think it was at that point my father fell in love with art. My father never did see the painting, but he did see Velásquez and Goya and El Greco.

MT: He had to see the other paintings, I guess.

TTW: And I remember he said, "Terry, I'm so sorry I didn't get to see your painting." My father flew back to Salt Lake City; I stayed. And I was able to find out what happened to the painting. It was in the bowels of the Prado, behind closed doors, being restored after five hundred years by two extraordinary women: the Dávila sisters, Theresa, and Rocío—and again, that changed my life. I walked in, and here was this triptych, unframed, unhinged, raw, bare, and they were able to show me through their X-rays how many times Bosch changed his mind in all the various gestures and subjects, and through chemistry studies what the pigmentation was. But in the end, I'll never forget, Theresa said—and these are the preeminent restorers of 15th and 16th century paintings in the Prado—she said, "In the end, the restoration of painting is a spiritual process. El Bosco tells us what to do. We have to listen to the painting; the painting tells us what to do." And then after many days with them, they handed me a white cloth doused in what they call "artist spirit" and invited me to wipe a portion of the face of the center panel clean. And it was at that moment that Theresa said, "Hieronymus Bosch put his finger on the wound." So then the question can be asked, "What is the wound?" May I share with you another passage?

MT: Yes.

TTW: [reading]

> Hieronymus Bosch put his finger on the wound. What is the wound? Our wound, separation from the Sacred, the pain of our isolation, may this be the open door that leads us to the table of restoration, may we sit around the table, may we break bread around the table, may we stand on top of the table, may we turn the table over and dance, leap, leap for joy, all this in the gesture of conserving a painting, conserving a landscape, conserving a spirit, our own restored spirits once lost, now found, Paradise found, right here, on this beautiful blue planet called Earth.

MT: That's a great question.

TTW: In looking at what they did to restore this painting—and it's now back in the Prado, no longer hanging as a butterfly suspended, but rather supported by the foundation that it now can be the altarpiece it was meant to be—but I was thinking: conserving a painting, conserving a landscape, that maybe our task in this new era of restoration of the natural world will require a reversal of our sensibilities. It will require listening in a way that we never knew possible. What is it that the land wants? What is it that the land knows? What is it that the land needs?

MT: I think it was in the section of the book where you were writing about Philip II, whom you were talking about earlier in our conversation, where Teresa de Ávila was visiting him and remarked about how incredible a listener he was?

TTW: Yes.

MT: And then you started writing about wonder?

TTW: Yes.

MT: And listening. Could you talk a little bit about wonder.

TTW: Philip II was really an amazing character in history. He's largely portrayed as a very dark figure, because of his association with the Inquisition, rightfully so. The other side—because we always know there are dark and light, positive and negative—he was an absolute lover of the natural world, curiosities, esoteric literature. His library was probably the most expansive library known to man at that time. All matter of mathematics,

129

science, astronomy, astrology, alchemy, all of it—and I think that incredible sense of wonder is born out of longing. It was Philip II who had the New World mapped, who had every province of Spain mapped. So I think it's the wondering, the wandering, that creates its own alchemy of the imagination as well as the intellect.

MT: So it's really the questions, not the answers.

TTW: I think so, yes, the mysteries. Again, Rilke—it's the questions that keep us alive, that crack us open, break us open to see the world in a new way, that promise us a new way of seeing, a new way of being. I think that, if we ask the question, the awareness follows.

MT: So what's lighting you up right now? You've written this book; it is really behind you. So what's lighting you up now?

TTW: What's lighting me up now, Michael? Open time, open space, just being home, being in the desert, learning what it means to live in an erosional landscape. It's deeply, deeply humbling, and I'm just so excited to be open to the possibilities of learning about what it means to live in a new place.

MT: And taking time. It's so important to take time, isn't it?

TTW: More and more I find that is the issue: how to create time, how to create buffers around us so that we are doing nothing. I think that may be our biggest disease right now—the disease of busyness. With all these modern conveniences that are supposed to be time-savers, I think we've never had less time. So I think creating open space, time to do nothing, time to love, time to be, time to dream, to think, to walk, is its own act of civil disobedience.

MT: That's great. So you're hopeful about the future, are you?

TTW: I am hopeful, are you?

MT: Yes, absolutely.

TTW: I just feel, as I was saying when I was thinking about Hieronymus Bosch painting on the cusp of the Reformation, that I really believe that five hundred years later we're on the cusp of another reformation, an ecological reformation, a spiritual reformation, where there is going to be a reversal of everything we've known possible, an upheaval of all our institutions, political, religious, spiritual, judicial—and I can't wait to see what arises out of this.

MT: May it be so. May all of our aspirations be fulfilled.

TTW: May it be so. Thank you so much, Michael.

Lighting the Match

An Interview with Terry Tempest Williams

Susie Caldwell, *Whole Terrain, 2001*

In many ways, the idea for this issue of Whole Terrain *was born the day I heard Terry Tempest Williams read from her most recent book* Leap. *She ascribed the inspiration for her book's title to W. H. Auden's poem, "Leap Before You Look." "I love the way this poem embraces the idea of risk," she explained, "particularly his last line, 'Our dreams of safety must disappear. To leap before we look, to follow our intuitions, this is the pathway to change.'"*

The author of eight books, including Refuge *and* An Unspoken Hunger, *Terry Tempest Williams is a woman of tireless passion. She has testified twice before the United States Congress regarding issues of women's health and the environmental links associated with cancer. She has also been a committed advocate for the protection of wild lands, including the redrock canyons of southern Utah.*

Ms. Williams is a strong believer in the importance of play and creativity in advocacy, and writes about both in Leap, *an exploration of Hieronymus Bosch's 15th century masterpiece* El jardín de las delicias. *Her book takes readers into the world of Bosch's triptych, through "Paradise," "Hell," and "The Garden of Earthly Delights," as the author*

"Lighting the Match" originally appeared in the 2000–2001 issue of *Whole Terrain*, an annual journal of reflective environmental practice published by the Environmental Studies Department at Antioch New England Graduate School. Reprinted by permission.

discovers the connections between each panel of the painting, and her life. At one point, she finds herself staring at the painting through binoculars, counting the species of birds depicted. "Hieronymus Bosch was an extraordinary observer of nature," she says, "His renderings of birds, plants, and animals express a joy of the natural world that is more than merely symbolic. Bosch's sense of scale places human beings alongside animals as equal partners."

A fifth-generation Mormon, Terry Tempest Williams grew up in Salt Lake City, Utah. She now lives in Castle Valley, Utah, with her husband, Brooke Williams.

SC: In *Leap*, as in all of your work, there is a sense that you are deliberately inviting paradox, as if you are trying to dissolve the opposites society imposes on us. Is this important to you?

TTW: Life is paradox, there is nothing to invite. There is the life of the imagination. There is play. There is Trickster energy. Contradictions. That's one of the reasons I fell in love with Hieronymus Bosch, and why I became possessed by *El jardín de las delicias*. Here is an imagination so huge, so wide, so subversive, that on one hand, his triptych could hang in the private quarters of the most pious Spanish King, Phillip II, who led the Second Spanish Inquisition and the Counter Reformation. On the other hand, according to some art historians, it may have been an altarpiece for the Adamite sect who worshipped the body, who thought the act of making love was its own kind of prayer. Was Hieronymus Bosch able to speak to both religious believers and so-called "heretics" of the Catholic Church? Was his iconography so original it could be interpreted in a myriad of ways? Perhaps that is the role of the artist. Hieronymus Bosch gave me the courage to trust and follow my own imagination.

SC: Is it imagination that helps us hold to our center, to our core?

TTW: I believe it is. The world moves through us. We can never know what is next, and more and more I keep thinking something is carrying us, dreaming us.

        When I walked into the Prado Museum in 1993, I could never have known that would lead me to a seven-year meditation on a painting. I could never have known where that painting would have carried me, but I trusted it. I was in love, and how do you turn away from that? Is it disruptive? Absolutely. At times you feel like you're going mad, but what choice do we have? To turn away from our own growth. And the only things I trust are growth and change; one mirrors the other, one supports the other.

SC: That reminds me of W. S. Merwin's poem, "Gift":

132

I have to trust what was given to me

if I am to trust anything . . .

I have to hold it up in my hands as my ribs hold up my heart

I have to let it open its wings and fly among the gifts of the unknown

TTW: I love Merwin's poetic wisdom. To trust what we are given. To trust the unknown. What is real and what is imagined? Even the river near my home looks constant, but it fluctuates every day. One day it's green, one day it's blood-red, one day it's brown, one day there's ice on it. It's constantly changing, shifting.

Are we so different? And again, isn't that the nature of play? To keep motion in our lives? The humor, the wickedness of turning a situation upside down, inside out, standing on our head, seeing the world from a different point of view, that's what the Trickster knows and embodies.

SC: Yet, we are terrified of that side of ourselves because it is often too unpredictable, too dark. Is that what you were thinking about when you wrote the section "Hell," in *Leap*?

TTW: I kept thinking, What does it mean to stand inside darkness? What does it mean to allow yourself to travel through Hell? You don't see anything for a good long while, but then your eyes adjust, and different senses take over. It is a shot through the dark. Having the courage to stay with it, to stay in it. It has its own beauty. I was always raised that the goal is to be happy. I don't believe that. I think the question is not 'how do we be happy?' but 'how do we embrace change?' To me, part of that transformation takes place in the dark.

SC: Can you give me an example of a transformative moment that came out of darkness?

TTW: When I visited Terezín, a holding station where Jews were confined before being transported to Auschwitz, I was struck by the indomitable spirit that remains, largely through the art that was created in the most heinous, dire circumstances. The irony is that the Nazis supported the artistic impulse because it was useful as part of their propaganda campaign. When the Red Cross would come to see Terezín, the Nazis would say: "Look at our model concentration camp! The children are writing poetry, we have opera, we have music."

In spite of the propaganda, what they couldn't have known was that the art was creating an emotional resistance that helped keep the people both physically and spiritually alive. An opera was created for the children called *Brundivar*, which translates to "Evil Insect" (a metaphor for Hitler). The children sang this opera with their full bodies, with sweet voices of innocence and promise, and it played continuously, even though the actors were changing as the children would die, as the musicians were transported, the music kept going, the opera kept going. The spirit of the people was not only being maintained, but enlivened, even in the shadow of death.

The courage to tell the truth through art is, I believe, a radical form of play. It is a testament to the transformative power of art, the transcendent power of art. The teacher who was behind the poetry of the children was taken to Auschwitz and killed, but her suitcase remained with four thousand manuscripts. Those are the acts of courage. Call it art, call it play, call it spiritual resistance. I think it's all part of the same impulse. It's not being immobilized by the dark, but finding instead that creative spark inside—a strike moment, a match illuminated through an act of friction.

SC: Is that what play is? Finding light in the dark?

TTW: It's the act of lighting the match. That's what play is, that's what art is, that's what the act of writing is. It's full of illumination, and it's always going to be changing and flickering, even on the cavernous walls of Altamira.

SC: If we are in a time of darkness ecologically, why isn't there more art or more play in the environmental movement?

TTW: It could be said that this is a hellish moment on earth environmentally, but I don't choose to see it that way. We are definitely disconnected. We know the litany of horrors: the deprivation of resources, the level of consumption . . . I could go on and on. My grandfather would always say, "I'm as low as a snake's belly." So what do we do to pick ourselves up from the realities of the world that we live in? I believe it is through art that we can find our lifeline.

I think there is tremendous artistic power in the environmental movement right now. Look at Peter Schulman of the Bread and Puppet theatre, an environmental theatre of resistance and social change. Look at the artists around the world that are doing extraordinary installations— Kiki Smith, Andy Goldsworthy, Walton Ford, Lynn Hull, for example. Greta Schmidt, a woman who gathered sacred mud from a particular site in Greece, brought it to Philappi, where it is alleged that the apostle Paul first came to Europe to tell of Christ. She was able to receive permission from the Minister of Culture in Greece to perform a dance in this sacred mud in the midst of these ruins. It was a gesture to the earth. Julia Butterfly Hill is another example. Her act of tree sitting is its own form of art. These wild acts matter.

I think there are tremendous individual and collective gestures going on. I do not think art is frivolous. I do not think that play is inconsequential. I think it adds to that collective strike moment where the match is lit inside the cave.

SC: Why does play matter?

TTW: In *Leap*, I talk about Seisdedos, one of the early conservators of *El jardín de las delicias*. In 1936, when Franco was bombing Madrid in the midst of the Spanish Civil War, Seisdedos was in his office in the Prado restoring a 15th century painting, and he was thinking, "What am I doing, what does this matter that I am restoring a painting when my fellow countrymen are on the street dying?" And then he remembers the doctors who are in the laboratory trying to find a cure for a disease that will ultimately save lives, and he realizes that even in the process of restoring a painting, he is restoring the soul through the healing power of art. And I think that's what art does, and literature, dance, theatre, and music: it lifts the blinders from our eyes so that we can see the world fresh again.

I truly believe in the power of the imagination to move us through this place of crisis. If Hieronymus Bosch was painting on the cusp of the Counter Reformation in 1500, and here we are 500 years later in the year 2000, I don't think it's too much of a leap to suggest that we are in the presence of an Ecological Reformation that will have as profound an effect on consciousness as the Renaissance did, following the Middle Ages.

I find it incredibly exciting that out of our chaos, there may be a new sensibility emerging—one that will require an upheaval of institutions as we know them: political, judicial, religious and educational. I know that Thomas Berry, in his latest book, *The Good Work*, talks about us entering the Ecozoic Era. We are in a tremendous period of transition, and I think if we can embrace the idea of sacrifice and compassion, and include the Other, the non-human communities, then we can move into this era of restoration of the spirit and the land. I think we can enter the world with a sharper sense of the Sacred, and certainly a deeper politics—where there is no separation between our internal landscape and the external one.

SC: There is a moment in *Leap* when you feel yourself pull away from the Mormon Church. It happens during a celebration of the church's history when several thousand missionaries stream in the stadium, carrying torches. Has carrying the torch of activism ever felt like missionary work?

TTW: It's a great question. The older I get, the less I know, and the less sure I am of my so-called 'positions' in the world. One of the things that's been so humbling in our recent move to southern Utah is the feeling that environmentalism, even wilderness, is no longer an abstraction. We're seeing how people *are* making their living off the land, trying to live in semblance with the land. It's not black or white, conservative or liberal, it's not the panels of "Paradise" and "Hell" in Bosch's painting, but rather the middle panel, "The Garden of Earthly Delights," that place of discovery and complexity. I don't believe there is one true church. I don't believe there is one solution for living in a sustainable way on the planet. I think it's a mosaic, like all the various tableaux in Bosch's middle panel: one group eating berries, another embracing an owl, a group flailing inside a mushroom, a couple making love in a bubble, others climbing towers. I think we need this, that, and all of it.

Yes, there is a time and a place for wilderness. As much as possible. Yes, there's a time for land trusts. There's a time where, of course, you have to have logging, and mineral extraction, but how do you do this so that it's not at the expense of something else? I don't believe in the fast, set divisions. I think it's a question of how we create this matrix where human beings are part of the Earth, not separate. I think it's a woven tapestry that is complicated, demanding everything and more of us. That's why deep acts of play and engagement of the imagination are important, offering us maps that the rational mind cannot envision.

I think the questions have to be asked, "Why do we diminish the arts in our culture? Why do we diminish acts of play as frivolous, or environmentalism as elitist or optional?" It's the very stuff that saves our lives.

Wild Mercy

and

Restoring the Dialogue

Reflections on 9/11

Michael Toms, *A Time for Choices* Radio Show, 2001 and 2002

In the months following the devastating bombings of the World Trade Center Towers on September 11, 2001, Terry Tempest Williams—along with dozens of other writers, artists, activists, religious figures, community leaders—participated in A Time for Choices, *a series of brief interviews with Michael Toms of New Dimensions Radio. These crucial interviews focused the voices of some of the country's most powerful and passionate voices on the rapidly changing world that the bombings—and the subsequent choices of American and world leaders—created. Terry's first interview in this series, "Wild Mercy," was aired in September 25, 2001, just two weeks after the bombings. The second, "Restoring the Dialogue," was aired four months later on January 10, 2002.*

Michael Toms, "Wild Mercy," September 25, 2001, program 2891, and "Restoring the Dialogue," January 10, 2002, program 2913, interviews on the New Dimensions Radio *A Time for Choices* series. Produced by New Dimensions World Broadcasting Network. Used by permission.

Wild Mercy

TTW: I was in Washington, D.C., with a group of photographers and writers celebrating a new exhibit called, ironically, *In Response to Place* and sponsored by the Nature Conservancy. At that time there must have been six or seven photographers and myself sitting around a table. These were photographers who normally haven't cast their gaze toward wild places: Sally Mann, Mary Ellen Mark, Richard Misrach, Lynn Davis—powerful visionaries through their cameras. We were talking about the enduring grace of landscape as we were signing books, when we heard, like the rest of America and the world, that the Twin Towers had been struck. We stopped. We couldn't believe it, and we were paralyzed by the thought. We didn't have the images before us, just the pictures in our minds. We kept on signing books. It didn't register. I think we were in shock.

Moments later, a security guard came in and said, "You need to evacuate, the Pentagon's been struck, and we have reason to believe the White House is next. Run!" And, again, paralyzed, we finally stood up and fled. I remember holding Richard Misrach's hand as we ran out on to the street. We could see people running across the lawn of the White House, people exiting the Executive Office Building, and I remember looking up at the sky, thinking, "What's happening?" I could see a plume of smoke rising from the direction of the Pentagon. The next thing I remember, Michael, is being crammed into a cab with everyone and the cab driver turning around very calmly and saying, "And just where would you like to go?"

MT: Yes.

TTW: And, at that moment, I think we all realized that there is no place to go. We're here, and the American landscape has changed.

MT: Forever.

TTW: Yes.

MT: So, as you have reflected on the events since September 11, what do you see now? What reflections have you had? What wisdom have you gleaned for yourself?

TTW: You know, Michael, I think we're still in the process of sorting this through, don't you?

MT: I do.

TTW: And I think it's going to take a long, long time for us to realize how this has entered our bloodstream. I was fascinated by a small piece published

in the *New York Times* on the Friday following the attacks. It was just
called "Seismic Shift." Did you see that?

MT: I didn't see it.

TTW: It was fascinating. It was both a metaphor for and a reality of what we
have experienced in these last two weeks and of what we will continue to
experience in the uncertainty of the days to come, standing in the center of change. Basically what the article said is that this event registered
in the Earth. According to the Columbia University Lamont-Doherty
Earth Observatory in New York, the bombings registered seismic activity.

It went on to say that the first seismic register occurred at 8:46, followed by another 18 minutes later, followed by a third, this one a bit
stronger and more sustained. At 9:59, another occurred, and 29 minutes
after that, the final pulse registered in the Earth. John Armbruster, one of
the scientists at the observatory, said, "An earthquake is something that
gets out of the earth and into a building. But this event, unprecedented in
my eyes, began with the building, and the subsequent effect leaked into
the Earth." A seismic shift, even a shift in consciousness—that's the image
I keep holding on to. There was no place, not even the Earth, that did not
register this event. And I guess, Michael, the question I keep wrapping
myself around is, "Who has the strength to see this wave of destruction as
a wave of renewal?"

MT: Yes. We hear, certain voices, selective voices, rising up out of the din that
we're hearing in the media, which seem to advocate moving militarily
with some kind of response, whatever that turns out to be. But, rising
through the din, there are other voices. I think of Barbra Lee, the Oakland Democrat who was the one no-vote on the resolution authorizing
the president to use military force in response to the attacks—and of the
cries coming out against these voices, accusing them of being unpatriotic,
of not being with the program. You are someone who, over many years,
has been a lone voice on ecological issues and have suffered these kinds of
arrows. What do you have to say about this at this time?

TTW: I'm so grateful for Barbra Lee. Because of her I felt that, in the midst of
this—again I want to say, forgive me, manic patriotism—we did have one
voice that registered dissent, one legislator who wanted to slow down, to
be reflective, to not sign over all of our powers to one human being.

When I was wandering the streets of Washington I met a woman
from Costa Rica who, almost in a mantra, kept saying over and over and

over again, *"La paz de la gente es la paz de la Madre Tierra"*—The peace of the people is the peace of Mother Earth. And I think that we have never needed those sentiments more. I was also thinking about Pablo Neruda in his *Book of Questions*—it's the questions that give me comfort—when he says, *"¿Quién da los nombres y los números al inocente innumerable?*—Who assigns names and numbers to the innumerable innocent?

I just keep thinking that we have forgotten the option of restraint—that it's no longer the survival of the fittest, but the survival of compassion that matters. And I do think that the coming days are going to require strength, courage, and a gathering together for those of us who define patriotism in another way—not just as waving flags, but also as standing our ground in the places we love and continuing to honor the Earth and its wild places. So when I hear Frank Murkowski, the senator from Alaska, say on that very day of the attacks that it is no longer under discussion whether or not we will drill in the Arctic; we will drill in the name of national security, I want to say, "This is still a democracy. And we still are people of conversation and dialogue, and nothing can take the place of this kind of bedrock democracy. Bad policy is bad policy."

MT: Yes. I think of Mayor Giuliani, who has been pretty much acclaimed as a hero—and in many ways is—in some of the actions that he took as mayor of New York in the aftermath of September 11. At the same time, I heard him say that the price of freedom is obedience and order. And a remark like that is a little scary to me.

TTW: It's interesting, when I was finally ready to go back home after the attacks, Washington, D.C., was a total police state: F-16s flying low, SWAT teams dressed in black on top of the White House, ID checks around every corner. It was really unnerving to one's soul, to say the least, on top of the grief that we were all experiencing. Anyway, a cab arrived at four in the morning, and I thought, "Finally I get to go home to the West." A gentleman opened the door. He walked around, it was dark, his head was bowed, he looked up and said, "I am from Afghanistan. Perhaps you would feel safer in a different car." And I just burst into tears, and he burst into tears; we just held each other, and during that 45 minute drive to Dulles, his mother called twice, begging him to not be in his cab, and he said, "I have to feed my children." It is these kinds of stories that are still floating through my bloodstream.

MT: Yes.

TTW: But back to what you were saying about blind obedience, we had a gathering in Jackson Hole, Wyoming. One of the participants was a Danish woman named Inga Kurtz—an amazing woman who harbored hundreds of Jews in her home because she felt that it was the right thing to do. We asked her, as one of our elders, "What do you have to share with us—we've never been here before in this country." She said, "What I would say is this: beware of mob mentality. Beware of this blind obedience in the name of patriotism that ultimately takes our lives." And she said, "That's what I fear most, and it can take over in seconds. Hold on to your instincts, hold on to your liberty, and just continue to stay in that place of reflection and resolve." And I thought that was really interesting from someone in her eighties who had been in her own war and made courageous decisions.

MT: Terry, thanks for taking the time to be with us.

TTW: Michael, could I close with one paragraph?

MT: You may.

TTW: This is called "Wild Mercy":

> The eyes of the future are looking back at us and they are praying for us to see beyond our own time. They are kneeling with hands clasped that we might act with restraint, that we might leave room for the life that is destined to come. To protect what is wild is to protect what is gentle. Perhaps the uncertainty we fear is the pause between our own heartbeats, the silent space that says we live only by grace. Wild mercy is in our hands.

MT: Terry, can you tell us the source of that?

TTW: That paragraph is from *Red: Passion and Patience in the Desert.*

MT: Terry, thanks, once again, for being with us—I appreciate your taking the time to do this.

Restoring the Dialogue

MT: So here we are in 2002, Terry, and we've gone on for four months since 9/11. What do you see at this time, in this place, at this point?

TTW: What do I see? I can tell you what I saw today. It was a gift of a day. This morning I saw a buck and a doe, two deer, mating, early. That was thrilling. I saw an ermine, pure white from the winter, in the woodshed, and I saw a black widow that I thought was dead; I reached down with a piece of paper to take her outside, and she came back to life from a state of dormancy. So I see the rhythms of the Earth continuing, and that's what I hope for our own species as well—only I hope that they're more enlightened ones.

A Voice in the Wilderness

MT: Some listeners might not be sure where you live. Where do you live?

TTW: We live in the Red Rock desert of Southern Utah, and right now we have snow on the red rocks with the red sand bleeding through. And I've been thinking, here it is, the middle of January, and the meadowlarks are singing. I find that an incredibly restorative note.

I did go to Ground Zero, Michael, in December, with my niece Diane, who turned 12. She wanted to see Ground Zero. She did not see the images on television—she was away at camp in Utah. And I always take my nieces to New York City on their 12th birthday as a rite of passage, so that they know there's a larger world beyond Salt Lake City. And I was deeply moved by what we saw, and perhaps most importantly, by what we felt. There was a tremendous sense of quiet and unity. The politics seemed to be burned away there, and what you felt was literally a portal of souls. It was very, very powerful.

MT: So, it is hallowed ground.

TTW: It certainly felt that way to us.

Here's something that I have found interesting. A friend of mine, Laura Simms, who is a storyteller living in Manhattan, made the decision that she would spend the year going into the public schools and telling stories to the children. She felt that telling stories could be a form of healing. And she very carefully picked a repertoire of stories that, she felt, were full of hope and healing. When she got to the schools, she began telling these stories, and they were quite light. And the children said, "No, we don't want those stories. Scare us. Tell us a scary story." And the teachers said, "No no, don't—these children are in too much pain." But Laura trusted the children's requests. She proceeded, in this one school in particular, to tell them as frightening a story as she could think of, and the children absolutely loved it. It was as though they wanted to sit in the center of their fear and know that, at the end of the story, they would survive. I thought that was very, very instructive.

MT: Yes, really. So what about yourself? What do you see 2002 as a year to do?

TTW: I feel it's a year to listen. I feel it's a year to be brave. I was reading William Faulkner, some of the essays and speeches that he delivered. And there was a sentence where he said, "Never be afraid. Never be afraid to raise your voice for honesty and truth and compassion, against injustice and lying and greed. You will change the earth." That's what is, I think, at the center of my heart. I want to be able to listen. I want to be able to be brave. I want to be able to act in ways that might make a difference—as small and as large as those may be.

MT: Terry, when you went to Ground Zero, what did your 12-year-old niece think? What was her perception?

TTW: It was interesting, Michael. I think we always fear for our children, and we want to protect them and create a context so that they can be held in their own understanding. But I'm always struck by how they stand fully in their own truth without our guidance.

There's a gallery in SoHo with a special exhibit, a photographic exhibit called *Here Is New York: A Democracy of Photographs*. After we had been to Ground Zero, we went in and saw this array of images by professional photographers, by tourists, by residents of New York, by children—the whole gamut. The photographs are literally being hung, taped, thumbtacked, clothespinned on wires across the ceiling, on the floor, on the walls, everywhere. And you look at these images and you ask yourself, "Which one speaks to me?" And if you choose to take an image home, for 25 dollars, the money goes to the Children's Fund. And I said to Diane, after we had been to Ground Zero, "You may select an image that you can share with your family at home." And there were remarkable images—everything from what looked like a nuclear winter, to fireman holding each other, to flowers and offerings left at the sites, to birds, to a child sitting in a center of a peace rally holding a candle—everything. And Diane picked, without much hesitation, the image of a plane crashing into one of the towers, the second plane. And I was really startled by that because it really was the most graphic, the most horrific, the most terrifying of all the images. And I said, "Diane, why are you picking that image?" And she said, "Because I don't want to forget."

MT: That's a good reason. Very profound.

TTW: I think that the other thing Diane took back with her were the stories. She was listening to the stories that people were telling at Ground Zero. A woman, a young woman there with her mother, was telling her what it was like to escape. A fireman there with his son was talking about the friends he had lost. Just listening to the stories that people were telling was very powerful for Diane—again, to bear witness. And the image I took home was Diane standing in front of a banner that said "COURAGE." And I think that's where we stand now. How do we choose to define courage?

MT: Yes, that's a good question. Terry, as you were traveling around, going to Maine, going to New York, going back to Utah, how was it to travel?

What did you see, feel, and hear while you were going through airports and traveling on planes?

TTW: You know, Michael, looking back over the fall, what struck me was that, from September 11 until October 7—that period before we started to bomb Afghanistan—we were really living in a grace period that I had never experienced it before. It was a time of possibility and contemplation. We could ask, "Are we large enough to do nothing? Do we have it in us to act with restraint and compassion?" It was a time of consideration, it was a time of discussion, and it was a time of prayer. I remember being in the Seattle airport on the Sunday that we started to bomb Afghanistan. As I watched President Bush informing us that air strikes had begun, I felt like we had another shattering moment, another fissure, if you will, in the landscape that we were inhabiting in this country. And after that everything changed. I felt like things went back into the atmosphere of fear rather than the atmosphere of hope.

MT: I think that's a good observation. It seems that, in many ways, the decisions being made by the government on our behalf these days in the name of "security" are really based on fear, on the idea that we have to take drastic measures in the name of national security. And what surprises me is the reaction, or non-reaction, of most Americans who say, "Oh, well, I'm willing to put up with this, I'm willing to do this, I'm willing to sacrifice certain civil liberties." And then I go back to the Declaration of Independence, and I think it's the second or third sentence that talks about "inalienable rights." All people, not just Americans, have certain inalienable rights that, by definition, cannot be taken away. And yet some of these rights are being taken away without any kind of dialogue or response other than saying, "Oh well, that's okay."

TTW: I think that's been the terrifying and disappointing thing. It felt like, for a time, we were in a period of conversation. Now, all of a sudden, the conversations have stopped in the name, as you say, of "national security." I was fascinated that, every time a discussion did come forth in this country, we were put on high alert by "General Ashcroft." I think that this has been a very interesting coincidence.

Certainly on the environmental front, there is no discussion. It's not "if" we will drill in the Arctic, but "when." Maybe I have a skewed viewpoint living in Utah, but it is really terrifying. You have someone like Representative McInnis of Colorado asking every environmental organization to denounce eco-terrorism, and I love that a message came from

WildLaw, a grass-roots organization, that said, "Congressman McGinnis, we'd love to denounce all eco-terrorists," and then they proceeded to mention Exxon, Mobile Oil, Weyerhaeuser—all the corporations that have been terrorizing the environment. Do we dare to say that there are many forms of terrorism and that environmental degradation is one of them. But there doesn't seem to be much of an appetite for that kind of discussion right now. It's viewed as anti-patriotic.

It's really troublesome. And I guess that's why I hope for daring acts of art this year. I was reading a book by Arthur Miller on politics, and he said art has always been the revenge of the human spirit upon the shortsighted. So I think it will be interesting to see what we do with this repression, this oppression, and to discover how we can bring these issues to the fore in creative, surprising ways that bypass rhetoric and pierce the heart.

MT: Give us that quote again from Arthur Miller.

TTW: "Art has always been the revenge of the human spirit upon the shortsighted."

MT: That's a great quote.

TTW: Isn't it? And especially coming from Arthur Miller, who went through the McCarthy era and refused to give in to this same kind of skewed patriotism.

MT: Yes, he wrote *The Crucible*, which was all about that.

TTW: Right. So, again, it goes back to Faulkner. We need to really be bold and to be brave and to speak out and to realize that it is our right to question. America was founded on that premise. And we need to understand the value of dissent. And I think we have to wake up and get our energy back. I think all of us grieved and were undone by what happened in September, and I find I am renewed. I have a renewed spirit, and I feel like I've got my soul back from the fatigue and from the grief. And now, what are we going to do with that?

MT: That's a good place to wind up. I think that's a good question for all of us, Terry.

TTW: And Michael, bless you for giving us an alternative way of seeing and being in the world. That is its own form of courage and engagement.

An Interview with Terry Tempest Williams

Jana Bouck Remy, *Irreantum*, 2002

Terry Tempest Williams is perhaps best known for her book Refuge: An Unnatural History of Family and Place *(Pantheon, 1991), in which she chronicles the epic rise of the Great Salt Lake and the flooding of the Bear River Migratory Bird Refuge in 1983, alongside her mother's diagnosis with ovarian cancer, believed to be caused by radioactive fallout from the nuclear tests in the Nevada desert in the 1950s and '60s.* Refuge *is now regarded as a classic in American nature writing, a testament to loss and the earth's healing grace.* The San Francisco Chronicle *wrote, "There has never been a book like* Refuge . . . *[It is] utterly original."*

Williams's most recent book, Red: Patience and Passion in the Desert *(Pantheon, 2001), traces her lifelong love of and commitment to the desert, inspiring a soulful return to "wild mercy" and the spiritual and political commitment of preserving the fragile redrock wilderness of Southern Utah.*

Departing from the natural landscape, another recent work, Leap *(Pantheon, 2000), is an unexpected pilgrimage into the habitat of Hieronymus Bosch's medieval triptych masterpiece* The Garden of Earthly Delights. *With spiritual candor, psychological immediacy, and emotional intensity, Williams uncovers deep connections between contemporary life and the world of this startling, 500-year-old painting depicting Paradise, Hell, and the Garden.*

Jana Bouck Remy, "An Interview with Terry Tempest Williams," *Irreantum* 4, no. 2 (Summer 2002): 14–22. Reprinted by permission. *Irreantum* is an official publication of the Association for Mormon Letters.

An Interview with Terry Tempest Williams

Her other books include a collection of essays, An Unspoken Hunger *(Pantheon, 1994);* Desert Quartet: An Erotic Landscape *(Pantheon, 1995);* Coyote's Canyon *(Gibbs Smith, 1989); and* Pieces of White Shell: A Journey to Navajoland *(Charles Scribner's Sons, 1984). She is also the author of two children's books:* The Secret Language of Snow *(Sierra Club/Pantheon, 1984) and* Between Cattails *(Little Brown, 1985).*

Her work has been widely anthologized, having appeared in The New Yorker, The Nation, Outside, Audubon, Orion, The Iowa Review, *and* The New England Review, *among other national and international publications.*

In 1991, Newsweek *identified Williams as someone likely to make "a considerable impact on the political, economic, and environmental issues facing the western states this decade." She has served on the governing council of the Wilderness Society and was a member of the Western team for the President's Council for Sustainable Development. She is currently on the advisory board of The Murie Center and the Southern Utah Wilderness Alliance. She has testified before the U.S. Congress twice regarding women's health and the environmental links associated with cancer and has been a strong advocate for America's Redrock Wilderness Act.*

As an editor of Testimony: Writers Speak on Behalf of Utah Wilderness, *she organized 20 American writers to pen their thoughts on why the protection of these wildlands matters. When President Clinton dedicated the new Grand Staircase-Escalante National Monument on September 18, 1996, he held up this book on the North Rim of the Grand Canyon and said, "This made a difference."*

Formerly naturalist-in-residence at the Utah Museum of Natural History, Williams now lives in Castle Valley, Utah, with her husband, Brooke Williams.

REMY: How did you find the courage to write so candidly about your family's experiences in *Refuge*? Was the writing process a healing experience for you? As you travel and meet other women with similar experiences, how do you reach out and comfort them?

WILLIAMS: In writing *Refuge*, I wanted to honor the memory of my mother, Diane Dixon Tempest, and my grandmother, Kathryn Blackett Tempest. I knew the first requirement in creating this memoir would be to try and tell the truth as I saw it, felt it, remembered it, in respect to the integrity of their lives. They were women of tremendous courage. I had to try and find that same kind of courage on the page, even if that meant risking my own comfort level within the boundaries of my emotional and cultural landscapes. I kept thinking of a passage in one of Emily Dickinson's letters.

A Voice in the Wilderness

She writes, "Life is a spell so exquisite, everything conspires to break it." How can we not respond? I had to believe that in writing about the death of a loved one, that which is most personal is most general. And so in a very real sense, "nakedness was my shield," to quote a Buddhist koan. With the publication of Refuge, that turned out to be true. Many people responded to our family's story because they too had gone through the process of cancer with someone close to them. I could see both the grief and compassion in their eyes. We are told a story, and then we tell our own. We are bound by our vulnerability as human beings. To make this connection on the page or in the world is its own form of comfort. It makes us feel less lonely, knowing that a shared grief is grief endured.

REMY: I read that your recent book tour became a series of "vigils" to honor the thousands killed on September 11. What were some of the highlights of that experience? How do you feel America has changed since 9/11?

WILLIAMS: The publication date of *Red: Passion and Patience in the Desert* was, in fact, September 11, 2001. I was in Washington, D.C., for the opening of the Nature Conservancy's photographic exhibit entitled "In Response to Place." I had written the foreword to the book published simultaneously with the exhibit. The photographers and myself were at the Corcoran Museum of Art that morning—scheduled for a press conference at 10:00 a.m.—when we received the news that the World Trade Center had been hit by planes and that the Pentagon had just been struck. We were directly across from the White House. The security guard basically said, "We have reason to believe the White House is next. Run." Chills shot through us all as we vacated the museum. It was chaos outside. Gridlock. People running across the White House lawn with their cell phones to their ears. The next thing I recall is seven of us crammed into a cab. The driver turned around very matter-of-factly and said, "And just where would you all like to go?" It was at that moment I realized there's no place to go; we are here.

We ended up in the lobby of the Mayflower Hotel and watched the horror on television with all other Americans, not being able to distinguish what sirens were on the TV and what were outside on the streets of Washington. Within minutes, Washington, D.C., became a police state.

Stories. We all have our stories. But the terror of that day, that week in D.C., not being able to get home, still registers in my bones. This was the beginning of the book tour for *Red*. My publisher wanted to know if I wanted to cancel the six-week tour. I said I simply wanted to be of use, that perhaps this was the fate of *Red*, to take these words and find a context for where we found ourselves now as a nation.

Much of *Red* focuses on issues of democracy and why America's redrock wilderness matters to the soul of this country. Pantheon was very supportive. The reading scheduled that Friday in Washington, D.C., at [the bookstore] Politics and Prose became a vigil. The booksellers were wonderful. Together, we tried to create an atmosphere of safety where people felt comfortable to speak. Over two hundred people gathered together. Candles were lit as we sat in silence. I read a short passage and then turned the microphone in the other direction, as we all listened to people share their thoughts and feelings. Stories. It was incredibly moving. I remember a cab driver from Afghanistan came in with the person he was driving to the bookstore.

"I am afraid," he said. "There is a hole in my heart. We all share this same wound."

For the remainder of my book tour, I tried to be sensitive to where I was and what the situation required. It literally changed day to day, place to place. Many times, the planes were empty, the security severe. The time from September 11 to October 6 seemed like a grace period where we faced our vulnerability and love of country together. It felt like as Americans we were truly contemplating what mattered in our lives. It was a time of pondering the questions together with great compassion.

When the United States began bombing Afghanistan on October 7, something shifted. The conversations became something different. "You are either with us or against us." The rhetoric of war replaced the thoughtful deliberations. And then with the anthrax scares, fear entered the public discourse, once again. I tried to read passages from *Red* that offered some kind of solace in the name of the natural world and all that endures in wildness. I also tried to read passages that focused on the power of democracy, that to question even in times of war is another form of patriotism.

This was a very tender time, a very intense time. There were many days and nights when I was both exhausted and scared, but I found great strength in the people I met, in the power of community. Perhaps the most meaningful encounter was in Boulder, Colorado, where Hopi elders were in attendance at a particular gathering. They spoke of what we might do to help bring about the transition from the Fourth World to the Fifth World. It was a gift to hear native wisdom at a time when there was so much hysteria in the media flying about.

How has September 11 changed us? I think it is too early to tell. The attacks on the Twin Towers registered on the Richter scale as an earthquake, a seismic shift. Is it too much to suggest that we may be in the midst of a shift in consciousness, as well? Do we dare to see this wave of destruction as a wave of renewal?

REMY: In *Leap*, you make some pretty clear connections between environmental ethics and artistic ethics. Could you speak to how that ought to affect LDS writers and their attempts to write about their faith?

WILLIAMS: "Oughts and shoulds" always make me nervous. I think each writer finds his or her own path within the questions that propel him or her to write. In *Refuge*, the question I was holding was "How do we find refuge in change?" With *Leap* (which I view as a sequel to *Refuge* in many ways), the question keeping me up at night was "What do I believe?"

The medieval triptych painted by Hieronymus Bosch inspired me, allowed me to see various patterns and connections within my own religion and homeland. The painting became a meditation. Each panel began a different conversation. I recognized that wildness exists in both art and landscape and both the work of the artist and the activist draws on spiritual beliefs; call it inspiration, motivation. And it is deeply personal.

My father will give anyone who has finished *Leap* a prize. When I asked him what he thought of the book, he said, "I'm stuck in Hell, and I don't want to talk about it!"

I know it's a difficult and strange book, but it is the book I had to write. Hélène Cixous says, "The only book worth writing is the book that threatens to kill us." I believe her.

There was one very gratifying moment that I will share with you. You never know if a reader will understand what you are attempting to do, especially if you are experimenting with form, which I was in *Leap*. Shortly before Elder Hugh Pinnock died, my father and I went to visit him.[1] He was a childhood friend of my father and a very close friend to our family. When we arrived, he invited us into their living room. On his table was a copy of *Leap*, with dozens of marked pages and passages. For

---

1. Elder Hugh Pinnock (1934-2000) was a member of the First Quorum of the Seventy of the Church of Jesus Christ of Latter-day Saints from 1977 until his death. The First Quorum of the Seventy is the ecclesiastical body directly below the Quorum of the Twelve Apostles in the LDS Church hierarchy.

over two hours, he asked me questions and gave me his impressions of the book. It was an exhilarating discussion on religious ideology, concepts, and principles that ranged from personal visions to authority to the Creation and how an ethic of place might be realized within the Church. He truly understood the spirit of the book, particularly the notion of restoration, whether it is the restoration of a painting, a landscape, a body, or of the restoration of the gospel of The Church of Jesus Christ of Latter-day Saints. He gave me an extraordinary gift through his faith and belief in the creative process, which is a spiritual process.

Each of us must follow our own creative hunger in our own way, with our own gifts. I believe this is a matter of conscience and consequence. *Leap* brought me to a place of peace out of a place of struggle.

REMY: Some theorists have suggested that the body is perhaps a better source of language and understanding than the mind. What do you think about these ideas, and how do you think an LDS writer could use them to overcome something like the use of religious clichés or institutional thinking?

WILLIAMS: The body does not lie. Therefore, if we write out of the body, we are writing out of the truth of our lives. This creates a language that is organic and whole. Original. We listen to what is coursing through our veins, what is held within our hearts, what is registered in our bones. Call it cellular knowledge. Something akin to instinct. It is here, perhaps, where we write muscular prose that lifts our ideas to both a higher and deeper place where the full range of our intelligence can be found. If we are simply writing out of our heads, there is no weight to our words. They become abstractions that dissipate into the air. This is the realm of rhetoric. The body is the realm of the story. And it is in story that we bypass rhetoric and pierce the heart. We feel it first and understand it later. Memory resides in the body. Memorization resides in the mind.

I think we fall into religious clichés when we become afraid of the deep reflective work that organic writing requires. Clichés follow answers and almost always lead us to sentimentality. Nothing surprises or delights. Original prose that breathes and bleeds follows the questions, the mysteries, the place where we dare to say, "I don't know where I am going on the page." It is the place of discovery and revelation. This is where we can begin to trust the body. The body carries the physical reality of our spirits like a river. Institutional thinking is fearful of rivers because rivers inevitably follow their own path, and that channel may change from day to day, even though the muscle of the river, the property of water remains consistent, life sustaining, fierce, and compassionate, at once. To write out of the body is to write ourselves into a freedom. It is here we can let go of fear and trust the joy that is held in each movement of the hand, word by word by word.

REMY: Is there an antagonism in the Church toward the tag "environmentalist"? If so, why is that? And do you think it has had an effect on many LDS writers' choices to skirt environmental topics in their writing?

WILLIAMS: Maybe I am in denial, but I don't believe there is an antagonism in the Church toward environmentalists. If we read Genesis about the power and beauty of Creation, if we read about the obligation and responsibility of stewardship toward the land, if we think about what community really means in the broadest sense—I think you can find all these ideas and tenets, if you will, rooted deeply within the principles of the gospel.

True, there may be individuals within the Church who do not respond to ecological concerns or who may view environmentalists with suspicion of one kind or another. I certainly have encountered that kind of hostility. But that belongs to the realm of politics, not religion. And for the most part, I do believe there is a desire to move toward more respectful conversation and dialogue between differing parties. In the end, I believe there is more that brings us together than separates us. As writers, one of our challenges is how to create narratives that open hearts rather than close them. How to write in a language that can be heard.

There is a very strong movement in this country centering around the greening of Christianity. I think we are finding it within Mormonism as well. It is about not compartmentalizing spiritual concerns here or environmental concerns over there. We are talking about the dignity and sacredness of life.

REMY: Why are there not more LDS writers writing about the environment or practicing what is called "nature writing?"

WILLIAMS: Again, I think it is choosing to compartmentalize literature into various genres, categories, and self-imposed distinctions. We don't have to do that. Some of our strongest LDS writers are creating beautiful, complex characters in tangible landscapes that we can see and hear, taste and feel. Levi Peterson is a writer of place. His characters wear the character of the landscape they inhabit. Certainly Eugene England was a writer of place whose evocations of the natural world were rooted in the sacred whether he was fly-fishing or hiking in the Wasatch Mountains. I think of Marilyn Arnold's work, particularly her novels; they are filled with a love of the land, particularly the subtleties and erosional power of the desert. Susan Howe's poetry is infused with the lyricism and hope of nature. Emma Lou Thayne's poetry and prose is a celebration of Creation in every line or sentence. Her voice is a voice of praise, and it is grounded in her passionate familial embrace of Mount Aire, Sun Valley, or Bear Lake. We may not think of these writers as nature writers, but they are writers whose work carries its own sense of wildness. Orson Scott Card is another example. His novels create other worlds with their own natural histories.

REMY: Has the publication of *New Genesis: A Mormon Reader on Land and Community* effected change related to the Church and environmental issues?

WILLIAMS: I honestly don't know. What pleases me is that it is being used as a text in various classes and departments at Brigham Young University, which means it is creating a discussion around environmental issues and the Church. This is all we were hoping for with *New Genesis*: to create conversation. I also know it is being used in book groups and study groups. When we conceived of this idea, Bill Smart and Gibbs Smith and I wanted to dispel the stereotype that only Democrats and non-Mormons cared about the environment. We didn't believe that. We wanted to bring together a diverse group of LDS people who love the land. We wanted to show that this is a bipartisan issue that transcends party lines. And we wanted to ask the question, How has the natural world influenced your testimony of the gospel and, conversely, how has the gospel influenced your view of nature? Again, we felt the most powerful way we could engage in this kind of dialogue would be through personal stories. I love the stories that are held in that collection, from "The Natural History of a Quilt" by Martha Young Moench to the story told by world-renowned biologist Clayton White of going to see peregrine falcons on top of a hospital in New York City and walking through an AIDS ward before he could find his way to the birds.

We have received some very moving letters from readers saying that the essays in this anthology provided them with "cover," that they could bring forth their views on conservation issues more freely without ridicule. And other readers have said they have appreciated the scriptural references that support a stewardship toward the Earth within Church doctrine. It gives us a sense of history, a people in place, something we can build on in creating an ethic of place.

REMY: In *Leap*, you discuss your relocation to southern Utah. How has this move affected your spirit and/or your writing? What advice do you have for someone contemplating a similar change, whether geographical or occupational?

WILLIAMS: Moving to the redrock country of southern Utah has been a great gift for both Brooke and me. It is a much slower pace. We live in a landscape where rocks tell time differently. Time and space. In the desert, there is space. Space is the twin sister of time. If we have open space, then we have time to breathe, to dream, to dare, to create, to play, to pray, to move freely, so freely. This is a landscape of the imagination. You can hear yourself think in the desert. I have become completely addicted to stillness. I am not so easily seduced by speed. I find I just can't move so quickly in the world. It's the silence. This deep, resonate silence. Very humbling.

I love living in an erosional landscape where the lesson of the day is change. It encourages our own changes. I love the extremes of the desert, the intense heat and the intense cold. The wind. There is a reason this country looks the way it does. Wind is the architect of beauty, movement in the midst of peace. This is what I seek as a writer. Art is created through the collision of ideas, forces that shape, sculpt, and define thought. There is a physicality to beauty, to any creative process. The wind reminds me of Spirit—what we feel, what has the power to change stone, yet we cannot see.

Living in these redrocks and near the Colorado River has brought the necessity of wildness and why wilderness matters out of the abstract into the real. It terrifies me to think what would have happened to us if we hadn't moved. Movement. Yes, it takes courage to leave the known for the unknown, especially when you are comfortable and established. But both Brooke and I love taking risks, to make ourselves a bit uncomfortable, to see the world with beginner's eyes. This is how we grow. And if we are growing as human beings, then our writing is growing alongside us.

Brooke and I did not plan this—it just happened, or rather we allowed it to happen. When the opportunity or possibility presented itself, we took it. We didn't really think about the security we were leaving behind, certainly not the practicality of what this move would mean. We honestly didn't have a clue how radically our lives would change. We were rooted in Salt Lake City. We had a voice. Here, we will forever be newcomers. I am just beginning to learn the language of what it means to live in rural Utah. But it felt right. Maybe it goes back to what the body knows, that cellular knowledge that carries its own wisdom.

We are in the middle of our lives; why not shake things up a bit? Every morning I wake up here in this beautiful valley, I think to myself, I don't have enough time to see all I want to see here, to learn all I want to learn. And I love the diversity of our neighbors. It's a real community, rural and raw. We are in the process of defining together what it means to weave together a village adjacent to wilderness.

It's very different living in the desert versus visiting it. There is an intensity here that can be very difficult. You are exposed in an exposed landscape. Nothing hidden. It's good to get away at times. And then there is always the blissful return to silence, that ringing silence. This is the source and inspiration of my writing.

REMY: How do you feel that your Mormon-ness is reflected in your writing? Have you ever encountered problems with your editors about the Mormon elements of your books? On the other hand, are LDS readers uncomfortable with the "unorthodox" behaviors you describe in your books?

WILLIAMS: Mormonism is one of the lenses I see the world through. We cannot escape our conditioning. Why would we want to? I grew up in a Mormon household where that was the focus of our lives. It was the fabric that held everything else together.

I think it's still so much a part of me. I cannot separate out the various strands again; it's my connective tissue. Given that, there are other lenses that I see the world through as well, and that creates an artistic tension in my work.

I have worked with the same editor for over 15 years, beginning with *Refuge*. He is extraordinary in his support of the Mormon elements of my work. In both *Refuge* and *Leap*, he advocated for more material regarding the Church, to always go deeper and further than I may have felt comfortable. We don't see how interesting and peculiar our religion is, so much is taken for granted, a given.

I remember distinctly with *Refuge* in one of the later drafts, he said, "Write against your instincts . . . When you feel you have said too much about the Church or your feelings, say more, go deeper, take us further into the ideas." He was right. But I can tell you, it was not easy. It is never easy to push against the rigidity of the status quo, but in the end, I believe it's about your own integrity. Again, telling the truth as you feel it. One of the curious situations I have found myself in as a writer is that outside of Utah, I am seen as Mormon, whereas inside Utah I am seen as an "edge walker," an unorthodox Mormon. What that says to me is that we just have to write out of the center of our own lives.

155

A Voice in the Wilderness

I love what the writer Clarice Lispector says: "I now know what I want: to stand still in the middle of the sea." If you worry about what other people are going to think about you, you better just put down your pencil for good. Writing will always offend someone and provoke powerful emotions. It can also inspire. I believe writing has the capacity to save our lives, both as writers and as readers.

Regarding LDS readers being uncomfortable with the "unorthodox" behaviors in my books (this makes me smile; it sounds like some kind of aberrant sexual behavior), there's no question some people have been offended. I can think of the scene where Brooke and I break open a bottle of champagne on the edge of Great Salt Lake. I realized that would bother some people, but I also realized that at that particular moment, it was a gesture within our own marriage to celebrate that which was ours. It was what we did. It would be a lie to pretend Brooke and I are devout, practicing Mormons; we are not. But there are many aspects of our religion that we cherish and hold on to. Must it always be all or nothing? I think life is a continual accommodation and adjustment of our beliefs, if we are honest.

There have been so many offensive moments in my books for some LDS readers, now that you bring it up, that there are too many to list, from criticizing Mormon crafts like glass grapes to the fact that Brooke and I don't have children to theological complaints centered around my asking the question "If there is a Godhead, where is the Motherbody?" These critiques don't bother me. I think it is good to have these kinds of discussions. I certainly don't have any answers.

I think of the passage in *Leap* when Brooke and I choose to burn up our marriage certificate. Again, it was a gesture on behalf of renewal. Anyone who has been married for a long time understands the need to rewrite the script one wrote in one's youth. For us it was about growth, daring to ask some tough questions about what we want in our life together now in our forties, which is very different from our needs in our twenties. It is allowing each other to bow to not only their own potential, but the potential of the marriage. I think it is about stepping back and taking a deep breath and saying, "What is working here, and what is not?"

I have to say, on the other hand, I have also had very beautiful and poignant letters from LDS readers that are very supportive, where they have found strength and recognition within my books that gave them the courage to continue on their own individual path within the context of the Church. I believe it is healthy to have a diversity within our beliefs

156

and interpretations. To me, that is the sign of a gracious, compassionate, and expansive theology. I believe there is room within The Church of Jesus Christ of Latter-day Saints for all of us.

REMY: Some Mormon authors believe that inspiration plays a part in their artistic creation. Do you ever feel that what you are writing is inspired?

WILLIAMS: I do not feel my writing is inspired by God, if that is what you mean. I do feel, however, that any serious, deliberate act of writing is inspired by the burning white heat of our desires, our questions, our passions.

And there are many sources of inspiration.

REMY: What works of Mormon literature have you personally most enjoyed?

WILLIAMS: To tell you the truth, I am not exactly sure what constitutes Mormon literature. Again, I'm uncomfortable with these distinctions. I loved *The Giant Joshua* by Maurine Whipple. I loved the biography of Annie Clark Tanner, *A Mormon Mother*. Judith Freeman has written some powerful novels with insight into the culture, such as *The Chinchilla Farm* and her most recent book, *Red Water*. Freeman's voice has a literary elegance. Laurel Ulrich is an exquisite writer of great depth and perception. Dorothy Solomon is a voice of grace, integrity, and wisdom. I admire her writing tremendously.

I have appreciated Levi Peterson's voice in his short stories, the humanity of his characters. Certainly, Emma Lou Thayne's poetry is a compassionate embrace of tolerance and peace. I think Carol Lynn Pearson's poems are full of courage and insight. I also appreciate the writing of Walter Kirn, Orson Scott Card, Linda Sillitoe, Marilyn Arnold, and Lyman Hafen. Eugene England has given us all courage and inspiration to continue on the path of individual truth while still standing tall within the faith. In working with students around the country, I am seeing some brave and beautiful narratives written by younger Mormon women, Louisa Bennion from Spring City, Utah, among them. But to limit any one of these writers to "Mormon literature" is to diminish the fullness of their work as writers.

REMY: Tell us about your writing habits: how often do you write, how do you balance it with other things, any rituals or conditions you must have for a good writing session, and perhaps some comments about whether you use notes, outlines, research, multiple drafts, etc.

WILLIAMS: I do not write every day. I write to the questions and issues before me. I write to deadlines. I write out of my passions. And I write to make peace with my own contradictory nature. For me, writing is a spiritual practice.

A Voice in the Wilderness

A small bowl of water sits on my desk, a reminder that even if nothing is happening on the page, something is happening in the room—evaporation. And I always light a candle when I begin to write, a reminder that I have now entered another realm, call it the realm of the Spirit. I am mindful that when one writes, one leaves this world and enters another. My books are collages made from journals, research, and personal experience. I love the images rendered in journal entries, the immediacy that is captured on the page, the handwritten notes. I love the depth of ideas and perspective that research brings to a story, be it biological or anthropological studies or the insights brought to the page through the scholarly work of art historians. When I go into a library, I feel like I am a sleuth looking to solve a mystery. I am completely inspired by the pursuit of knowledge through various references. I read newspapers voraciously. I love what newspapers say about contemporary culture. And then, you go back to your own perceptions, your own words, and weigh them against all you have brought together. I am interested in the kaleidoscope of ideas, how you bring many strands of thought into a book and weave them together as one piece of coherent fabric, while at the same time trying to create beautiful language in the service of the story. This is the blood work of the writer.

Writing is also about a life engaged. And so, for me, community work, working in the schools or with grassroots conservation organizations is another critical component of my life as a writer. I cannot separate the writing life from a spiritual life, from a life as a teacher or activist or my life intertwined with family and the responsibilities we carry within our own homes. Writing is daring to feel what nurtures and breaks our hearts. Bearing witness is its own form of advocacy. It is a dance with pain and beauty.

REMY: What are your favorites among your works? Which one has been the hardest to write?

WILLIAMS: I suppose that is like asking a mother which one of her children is her favorite. I couldn't say. Each book was conceived through its own question. Each book sent me on my own pilgrimage. Each book brought about its own sense of inquiry and liberation. Each book wedged its own struggle inside my heart and then released me into another peace of mind. Each book has its own fingerprint and character and audience. Each book has a life of its own, apart from me.

REMY: How did you become a writer? In what ways do you think you've developed as a writer during the course of your career? Are there things you can do now that you don't think you could have pulled off successfully when you were first starting to write? What do you do to keep developing as a writer?

WILLIAMS: These are tough questions. How does anyone "become" a writer? You just write. I have always written, always kept a journal, always loved to read. Perhaps as writers, we are really storytellers, finding that golden thread that connects us to the past, present, and future at once. I love language and landscape. For me, writing is the correspondence between these two passions.

It is difficult to ever see yourself. I don't know how I've developed or grown as a writer. I hope I am continuing to take risks on the page. I hope I am continuing to ask the hard questions of myself. If we are attentive to the world and to those around us, I believe we will be attentive on the page. Writing is about presence. I want to be fully present wherever I am, alive to the pulse just beneath the skin. I want to dare to speak "the language women speak when there is no one around to correct us."

REMY: What's ahead for you? What's coming up in the near future, and what are you working on now?

WILLIAMS: I honestly have no idea what's ahead, what's coming up for me. I find that very exciting. What I can tell you is that the next year is wide open. I am not working on anything in particular. I have made a conscious decision to retreat and focus on home. We are restoring the place where we live with native plants so it blends more naturally into the juniper and sagebrush flats. I am reading a great deal of poetry. It is time for me to lay low and listen.

For now, I just want to walk in the desert.

Coffee Talk

A Chat with Terry Tempest Williams

Aria Seligmann, *Eugene Weekly*, 2003

Environmental writer and poet Terry Tempest Williams sat at a table at the Excelsior Inn about 8 o'clock on a Friday morning a couple of weks ago. In town to lecture and lead some writing workshops at the UO, she squeezed me into her busy schedule. Too early for me, I'd arrived at the restaurant several minutes prior just to get enough coffee down my gullet to be able to ask some questions. Williams, on the other hand, was already put together and naturally beautiful at that early hour, her unique combination of wisdom and grace readily apparent.

A lifetime resident of Utah, environmental writer and poet Terry Tempest Williams writes from her own experiences as a Mormon woman living in that state. She has authored six books, as well as An Unspoken Hunger, *a collection of essays, and two children's books.*

Her work has been anthologized widely and reproduced in The New Yorker, The Nation, Outside, Audubon *and* Orion *and she's best known for* Refuge, *a book that tells the parallel tales of the degradation of the environment and her mother's battle with cancer.*

She's been inducted into the Rachel Carson Honor Roll and has received the National Wildlife Federation's Conservation Award for Special Achievement. On May 2,

Aria Seligmann, "Coffee Talk: A Chat with Terry Tempest Williams," *Eugene Weekly*, May 8, 2003. Reprinted by permission.

she received an honorary doctorate from the University of Utah—a huge step for the university to make for that state's own "wayward" daughter.

The waitress arrives, and I'm ecstatic to hear Williams say, "Coffee—yes, please."

So she's human.

"I love Eugene: the water, the freedom of thought, and it's the first place I drank coffee," she reveals. But it's not the coffee, it's the Pacific yew that first introduced her to the Emerald Valley.

TTW: Shortly after my mother died, I received a call, then a letter about the Pacific yew and its properties for healing cancer. I ignored the letter because it was too close, my grandmother had just been diagnosed with cancer as well. Then I received another letter, only this time it had a branch in it of Pacific yew and I couldn't ignore that. I came here to walk in the woods, see the Pacific rainforest along the McKenzie and it really was life-changing.

EW: What is the most pressing environmental concern we face?

TTW: The Bush Administration. There are many forms of terrorism and environmental degradation is one of them. We're being hit on all counts. It's not enough that last month the Senate voted not to drill in the Arctic—it went back to the House floor and passed. Bush said he's going door to door himself. I believe our country is being run as a business, not as a democracy and they don't understand that this is a public process. Whether it's Bush/Cheney's energy policy behind closed doors or the desire to exploit everything they possibly can on every possible level—the environment, social issues or the economy—I think it's devastating. Now there's this atmosphere of war where we aren't allowed to criticize our president. To be called a traitor or a patriot—this is one of the darkest times we've faced in this country.

EW: What light do you see that will get us out of this scenario, besides the 2004 elections? What do you think the individual can do?

TTW: Speak. Shatter the silence. Question everything. Redefine. Reimagine patriotism. Reimagine hatred and take back the language. I think we can do this each in our own ways, each with our own gifts. I realize that since Sept. 11 I've been writing mostly for newspapers. Books are too slow and they don't get read. I've wanted to be part of the dialogue and this dialogue is taking place daily and on a national and local level, that's where we are having this public discourse. It's critical that we engage in this form of democracy; it literally is happening at our kitchen table. That's an exciting thing to see. We're struggling. I'm struggling. I don't know whom to believe I don't know what to believe. And everyday I hear myself saying over and over again, "I don't know."

We watch Saddam toppled and we're told this is in the same category as Stalin and Hitler and I think, "Am I losing it?" But on the other hand, I believe it is an occupation. It's about American Imperialism and I do think they have their eyes on Syria, this fundamentalist government. On one hand they tell us they're liberating Iraq, and on the other hand we're watching the erosion of democracy in our own country. There's this paradox going on. I wonder how the Patriot Act will go over in Iraq as the first document of democracy.

EW: And here?

TTW: I believe we are in this atmosphere of terror and that they are imposing and propagating and elevating fear to create compliance and complacency. It's all the more critical for us to be highly attentive and to really ground ourselves, to stay in the center in the thick of our lives and in the thread of our own communities. That's the only place I know where hope truly lives. And the only place we can have an impact is within our own community.

I was arrested in Washington during the Code Pink rally. That's certainly not something we anticipated, planned, or expected. There was a wall of Washington, D.C., police there saying "You cannot come into Lafayette Park" and "No, you cannot stand in front of the White House and protest this war." That was a week before it started. And we looked through their arms and saw pro-life protesters standing in front of the White House with ghastly images and that appeared not to be a problem. Again, the incredible irony and paradox. There is no room for diplomacy.

EW: What can citizens do who want to change this administration's priorities and agenda?

TTW: I don't know. We can vote. It seems really important that the 2004 election be held with as much integrity as possible. A great idea was given by Granny D at the Code Pink rally. She said, "Vote absentee in your state and then become a swing state suffragette and go to the states that are close and help get the vote out." I thought that was really smart.

She also said—again, we listen to our elders, she's what, in her nineties—she said the Green Party needs to be patient with this next election

162

and that yes, the Greens can organize locally and build up state legislatures and start from the ground up but this next election we have to try to get a Democratic candidate that can defeat George Bush. Otherwise, we have four more years. I thought that was a brave thing to say. And that may be controversial, but I agree.

EW: Who would you support for the Democratic candidate?

TTW: I'm waiting. It may even be a Republican candidate. I don't know. I'm looking for someone who has a vision and who dares to speak out against these corporate ideas of democracy. I still have great faith in democracy. I have great belief in the power of community. And I also have a strong belief in dinner parties. In people's homes, where you create an atmosphere where people feel comfortable speaking their minds and are literally nourished. Wouldn't it be wonderful if we had them in our own homes where we are safe and we can have these dinner parties of real discussion among our friends and also invite people with different ideas so we can listen? If we can teach ourselves how to listen to the other viewpoint, what a great idea. If we can get democracy around our own dinner tables.

I'm also thinking of the whole idea of shadow. Whether we like it or not, George Bush is our shadow: arrogance, impatience, entitlement, greed capitalism; we are all complicit in that. I'm interested in looking at what that shadow means. This is a time of reflection, contemplation, calming down and settling. As a writer, I'm trying to find places that test my own courage and comfort.

We are a nation at war. Can we have the courage to stay in that place of darkness and not be undone by it, not be undone by despair? I have enormous faith in the capacity to transform. This is a powerful time in the evolution of the human psyche—like the Renaissance and the Reformation. Look at the global response of humans to this war. That is powerful. It's never happened before.

EW: It's interesting to me that we started this conversation talking about the environment, but we couldn't help but talk about the war.

TTW: These are core issues at the heart of the land. We can't separate them but we have separated them and that's the problem. So when we talk about the Earth, the animals as one consideration—when you talk about issues of water and politics, every being has a right to clean water, we incorporate conversations about democracy.

We need to be able to treat each other well in order to treat the animals and plants well. It's a cycle, the embrace. We need to see our limitations as human beings. I don't think the Bush Administration sees any limitations. And how do you create democracy without humility?

EW: This country was founded on the idea that anyone, well, white people, could come here and be equal. And be welcomed. And tame the land.

TTW: We have to speak out now on behalf of our community and on behalf of the land and say they're the same thing and say "No, we are not rolling over" and "No, this is not a corporate enterprise. This is democracy in the fullest sense and we must have regard and reverence and those are the cornerstones of a just society."

EW: Terry, why aren't more people out on the streets striking, protesting, and refusing to pretend that life goes on as normal, at least for the duration of the war?

TTW: Again, it's those words, I don't know. We have to ask ourselves, "What do I have to give?" and then, "How do I give it?" Whether it's as a writer, an organic gardener, as a teacher, a social worker, a mother or father, we can exercise that courage and insistence, resistance, and say there's another way of being, another way of seeing, and I do think that counts. And numbers count. In many ways it comes down to that. We need to step forward. Question. Stand. Speak. Act.

A Conversation with Terry Tempest Williams

Delicious Living magazine, 2003

Naturalist, writer, and conservationist Terry Tempest Williams has written numerous books including the esteemed Refuge *(Pantheon, 2000) and her most recent books* Leap *(Pantheon, 2000) and* Red *(Pantheon, 2001). Williams is currently on the board of directors of the Murie Center and the Southern Utah Wilderness Alliance. This month she is also a featured speaker at the 2003 Bioneers Conference in San Rafael, California. She spoke with us from her home among the red rocks of Castle Valley, Utah.*

A Voice in the Wilderness

DELICIOUS LIVING: You recently returned from the Arctic. What was that experience like?

TERRY TEMPEST WILLIAMS: The Arctic was life-changing in ways I am still trying to understand. It had been a 30-year dream to visit the Arctic National Wildlife Refuge, a dream I had been holding ever since I met Mardy Murie at the Teton Science School when I was 18 years old. Mardy gave a slideshow of the trip she and her husband, Olaus, took to the Sheenjek River in 1956. It was this trip taken with friends like George Schaller that inspired the creation of the Arctic National Wildlife Refuge and its protection in 1960. After imagining this landscape for so long, to actually stand there and breathe in that kind of vast, pure, raw, wild beauty, well, it took the Arctic from a place of abstraction to a place of the real. When the plane dropped us off in the heart of the Brooks Range, the first thought that came into my mind was that I was perfectly safe. Never have I felt that kind of calm and deep peace.

DL: What did you think about the wildness there?

TTW: My husband, Brooke, and I have spent the majority of our lives seeking out wild places, and I think both of us, in those short two weeks, realized we had never really been in a truly pristine place until then. We saw no other human beings or virtual signs of humanity until we flew into Kavik, a small outpost on the North Slope, at the end of our trip. To stand on a knoll in the tundra at 2 o'clock in the morning with the depth of Arctic light creating double rainbows as thousands upon thousands of caribou move across the coastal plain is to stand in the presence of the divine with total awe and humility. No words. That kind of motion creates an emotion that binds us to all life. We remember what we are connected to as a species. We forget we belong to a world of such complete wholeness. We live in such a fragmented world, even a fragmented state of mind. We forget what is still possible, what still lives and breathes on this planet with no thought of modernity or global economies or war.

DL: How do you feel about the proposed oil drilling in the region?

TTW: The shortsightedness is stunning. Our lack of restraint is chilling and the diabolical environmental agenda of the Bush administration should outrage all Americans who care about the health and integrity of our public lands. We no longer have the luxury of not becoming involved in these issues. So much is at stake. Our voices matter. If we let our congressmen and congresswomen and senators know how we feel, they are obliged to represent our views. This is how the Arctic National Wildlife has been protected in the past and this is how these sacred lands will be preserved in the future. Call it The Open Space of Democracy.

DL: What do you think we should be focusing on in terms of the environment?

TTW: I feel like we are at a time of great creativity if we choose to embrace it as such, if we choose to engage the will of our imaginations and imagine another way of being in the world. Democracy requires our participation. The land trust movement in this country is a beautiful example of how we can find hope within our own communities because it bypasses government and creates a diverse and truly bipartisan conversation on behalf of the land. We dare to define community to include all life alongside human beings. Whether it is the Castle Rock Collaboration in the red rock desert of southern Utah or the Blue Hill Heritage Trust in coastal Maine, these small groups made up of neighbors and friends from all walks of life are having an extraordinary influence on our creation of an ethic of place. I believe radical change occurs through the care of our relationships.

An Interview with Terry Tempest Williams

David Kupfer, *The Progressive, 2005*

The sun was setting on a late October afternoon when I met with author Terry Tempest Williams in a hotel conference room built over a saltwater marsh near San Pablo Bay in San Rafael, California. She was in my hometown that day to deliver a Sunday morning keynote lecture about her latest book, The Open Space of Democracy, *to 4,000 people attending the 15th annual Bioneers Conference. Following her morning plenary lecture, she hosted a press conference with several dozen journalists, spoke as part a workshop on her book, and signed copies for a long line of fans.*

Despite her rather intense schedule that day, she was bright, evocative, introspective, and quite poignant. Like Edward Abbey, she is very much aware of her place in the world and her community in the American West. A fifth-generation Mormon and native of Utah, she takes inspiration from her church and from nature.

Among her books are Desert Quartet, Leap, Unspoken Hunger, *and* Red: Passion and Patience in the Desert. *Her sixth,* Refuge: An Unnatural History of Family and Place, *tells the story of how the Great Salt Lake once rose to historic levels and flooded the wetlands that serve the migratory birds in northern Utah. She also weaves in her own family's struggle with cancer as a result of living downwind from the Nevada Nuclear Test Site near Las Vegas. A recipient of both a Guggenheim and a Lannan literary fellowship, Williams lives with her husband, Brooke, far from the concrete jungle in*

David Kupfer, "An Interview with Terry Tempest Williams," *The Progressive* 69, no. 2 (February 2005): 35–40. Reprinted by permission of *The Progressive*, 409 E. Main Street, Madison, WI 53703, www.progressive.org.

An Interview with Terry Tempest Williams

Castle Valley, Utah. She has been passionately active in social and environmental issues for decades. She is currently the Annie Clark Tanner fellow at the Environmental Humanities Program at the University of Utah.

DAVID KUPFER: How do you plug into your muse?

TERRY TEMPEST WILLIAMS: I live in a very, very quiet place. I have a sequence to my creative life. In spring and fall, I am above ground and commit to community. In the summer, I'm outside. It is a time for family. And in the winter, I am underground. Home. This is when I do my work as a writer—in hibernation. I write with the bears.

KUPFER: How has your sense of place affected your outlook?

WILLIAMS: I come from an old Mormon family, six generations. Our ancestors came across the plains with Brigham Young in 1847, when he settled the Salt Lake Valley. I was raised in the interior American West. The space seemed infinite. It was a wonderful place to grow up. Our family spent most of our time together outside, so there was never a separation between the land, our family, and our spiritual life. For four generations, the Tempest family has made a living by putting in natural gas lines, water lines, sewage lines, optic fiber cables. Our family has made its livelihood from the land, digging trenches for hundreds of miles cross-country. You could say this is a real paradox, to destroy the land, yet love it at the same time. This is a typical story of Westerners, how we build community through change. For me, it always comes back to the land, respecting the land, the wildlife, the plants, the rivers, mountains, and deserts, the absolute essential bedrock of our lives. This is the source of where my power lies, the source of where all our power lies. We are animal. We are Earth. We are water. We are a community of human beings living on this planet together. And we forget that. We become disconnected, we lose our center point of gravity, that stillness that allows us to listen to life on a deeper level and to meet each other in a fully authentic and present way.

As children, we had access to all the open space imaginable. We would set up camps in rural Utah where the Tempest Company was at work laying pipe. We spent time around the West in Wyoming, Idaho, Nevada, and Colorado. Wild beautiful places. Now, many of these natural places have disappeared under the press of development.

Every day, my heart breaks living in Southern Utah on the edge of America's Redrock Wilderness, witnessing what the Bush Administration's policies regarding oil and gas exploitation are doing to our public lands that belong to all Americans. In Utah alone, ten million acres are open for business. Their policy is not about the public or the public's best interest. It is about the oil and gas corporations' best interests. The Secretary of the Interior, under Bush and Cheney's thumb, is urging the Bureau of Land Management to support the gas and oil industry's most extreme drilling scenario in some of the American West's most pristine and fragile areas without proper legal and public input. Community after community is rising up, ranchers, developers, environmentalists, and local commissioners, all saying this is not the best use of our public lands. It is a story that is largely unknown in the rest of the country. It is a disturbing and community-destroying example of domestic imperialism being waged against people in places deeply connected to the public lands that are our public commons. The Bush energy policy is a short-term strategy based on corporate greed instead of a sustainable vision of what best supports local economies and healthy ecosystems.

KUPFER: It seems to me that being an American right now has never been more shameful. How do you deal with that?

WILLIAMS: I don't think of myself as an American; I see myself as a human being. On the other hand, you're right, I am an American, I do live in Utah, and I am deeply ashamed about the decisions our President is making around the world, in our name: the war in Iraq, his continued denial about global warming, the wholesale degradation of the environment on every level. Since September 11, 2001, I have come to believe that there are many forms of terrorism, and environmental degradation is one of them.

We have to transcend our government and relate to each other as human beings first and Americans second and feel both our local and global responsibilities. No one lives in isolation anymore.

KUPFER: You've said our language has been taken hostage. What do you mean by that?

WILLIAMS: Not only has our language been taken hostage, but individual words like "patriot," "patriotism," "democracy," and "liberty" have been bound and gagged, forced to perform indecent acts through the abuse of slogans like "Liberty and freedom will prevail." As a writer, I cannot in good conscience use the word "prevail" anymore because I keep hearing the clichés circling around it. Take the word "resolve." I am so tired of hearing George W. Bush use it *ad nauseum* like a verbal weapon. He speaks in this mind-numbing, heart-tearing litany of clichés. Our symbols have also been taken hostage: the American flag, the Statue of Liberty, the list goes on and on. Joseph Campbell warns us to beware of those who take our deeply held symbols and turn them into signs of intolerance, signs of shallowness, coercion, and control.

KUPFER: You yourself encountered some of this coercion. Talk about your brush with censorship at Florida Gulf Coast University.

WILLIAMS: I was invited to give the Freshmen Convocation at Florida Gulf Coast University on October 24, 2004. My book *The Open Space of Democracy* had been selected as one of the "common readers" for the university's 1,050 entering freshmen. On October 6, William Merwin, the president of Florida Gulf Coast (along with his board of trustees appointed by Governor Jeb Bush), made the decision to "postpone" the convocation because, in the president's words, "I in good conscience cannot permit an unbalanced political commentary." He cited negative statements I had made in print about President Bush.

What was so upsetting about this situation is the fact that if our colleges and universities are no longer the champions and protectors of free speech, then no voice in this country is safe.

In a telephone conversation, which I had with him prior to his public announcement, he had said that I was "threatening to the students and the university."

Earlier in the month, President Merwin asked me to sign an agreement creating the conditions that would enable me to speak at Florida Gulf Coast University. The agreement demanded that 1) I would not represent a particular point of view and 2) I would not publicly criticize the President of the United States. I refused.

Luckily, the students rose to the occasion. They immediately recognized the violation of their own free speech and how this was compromising their own education. They exerted true courage and leadership creating a bipartisan coalition of over 12 student organizations ranging from the Young Republicans to the New Democrats to the Model U.N. They issued their own invitation to me to speak on campus at the same date, which I readily accepted. And then they publicly denounced the president's decision to postpone their convocation as a violation of the First Amendment and their understanding of the precepts of Florida Gulf Coast University.

KUPFER: And then what happened?

A Voice in the Wilderness

WILLIAMS: What happened was even more disturbing. The following week, Vice President Dick Cheney spoke on campus. Evidently, this was not a problem. Turns out, Merwin was a known contributor to the Republican Party and a Bush supporter. The students and faculty became outraged; the Faculty Senate called a meeting with Merwin where impassioned speeches were made and hard questions asked. In the end, the president agreed never to make a unilateral decision like this again without input from students and faculty. In the end, I did speak at Florida Gulf Coast University at the student-organized event, and it was an extraordinary gathering, a true healing inspired by the students' wise leadership. I thanked them for their true civil disobedience and spoke about how what power fears most is the naked beauty of a singular voice—what they had exercised. I thanked them for not only reading *The Open Space of Democracy* but for embodying it.

KUPFER: Who have been your role models?

WILLIAMS: Rachel Carson. I remember as a child, my grandmother read to me *Silent Spring*. It was incomprehensible to me that there could be a world without birdsong. Rachel Carson was not only an influence on me but felt like family because of the regard my grandmother had for her. It was the same with the writer Loren Eiseley. Certainly, I've been influenced by the Transcendentalists: Thoreau, Emerson, and Walt Whitman. Lately, I have returned to Whitman's poetry, his notion of what a spiritual democracy is and can be. These ideas are part of a great continuum, both literary and political. Consider the writings of Willa Cather, Mary Austin, Aldo Leopold, James Baldwin, Edward Abbey, Wallace Stegner, Maxine Hong Kingston, and the poetry of Mary Oliver.

KUPFER: What is the best advice you have ever received from a role model or mentor?

WILLIAMS: Wangari Maathai, one of my teachers to whom I dedicated *The Open Space of Democracy*, comes to mind most readily. She said to me in Castle Valley last spring, "Those who help create these openings of democracy must inhabit them." She was speaking about each of us getting involved in local and national politics. And then I asked her what she had learned in these last twenty years of activism on behalf of the Green Belt Movement in Kenya. Her reply was one word: patience.

KUPFER: Do you look to your writing as a tool for your activism in the effort to prevent the wholesale destruction of the environment?

WILLIAMS: I do. I never will forget when I crossed the line at the Nevada Test Site in the Mojave Desert just outside Las Vegas. Before arresting me, the officer searched my body and found a pen and a notepad tucked inside my boots. "And these?" she asked. "Weapons," I replied. She quietly slipped my pant leg over my boots and let me keep them. Writing can be a powerful tool toward justice. Story bypasses rhetoric and pierces the heart. We feel it. Stories have the power to create social change and inspire community. But good writing must stay open to the questions and not fall prey to the pull of a polemic, otherwise, words simply become predictable, sentimental, and stale.

KUPFER: What role should direct action play in the conservation and environmental movement?

WILLIAMS: It's a personal decision not to be taken lightly. I know when I chose to commit civil disobedience at the Nevada Test Site for the first time in 1988, it was not only a political decision but a spiritual one. I thought about this gesture, long and hard. I felt the gravity of its tradition, the seriousness of its action. I remember reading Gandhi's words and Martin Luther King's "Letter from Birmingham Jail," along with Thoreau's essay. I went through nonviolent training led by seasoned activists at the Test Site sponsored by the Nevada Desert Experience. And I was not alone; there was a great solidarity among the men and women who were far more experienced about social actions than I was, including the Shoshone elders whose land the Test Site is on. So I think direct political action, civil disobedience, in particular, is something to be taken very seriously. I belong to "a clan of one-breasted women," where nine women in my family have all had mastectomies; seven have died, as a result of nuclear testing and radioactive fallout. We are downwinders. As we speak, my brother is in the last stages of lymphoma. There are times we have to put our body on the line for what we believe, for the injustices we see even within our own families.

KUPFER: Could you speak to environmentalism in the Mormon Church and to other changes there?

WILLIAMS: At the heart of Mormonism is a high regard for community. That is its strength. I have great respect for that, and I think that for those of us living in Utah—for those of us who are Mormon, even if we are not orthodox—the way into an environmental conversation with the Mormon Church is through the door of community. And if we respect the Creator, then it logically follows that we respect Creation. In the early days of the Mormon Church, stewardship toward the land was a priority. It was a matter of survival in the desert.

173

If you waste water, you die. Brigham Young and others lectured about water and soil conservation and overgrazing. There are members of the church today who are still concerned about sustainability issues. They have gone back into church history and pulled out old references that have never been so relevant.

An example of this renaissance of environmental thought can be found in an anthology some of us put together called *New Genesis—A Mormon Reader on Land and Community*. It's a collection of forty essays written by members of the LDS faith on why wilderness and a healthy environment matter and why they are compatible with religious beliefs. It has provided some balance and provocation to the notion that all Mormons are Republicans and anti-wilderness.

I can only say that I believe the Mormon Church is changing because the people inside the church are changing, particularly the women. And if the women in the Mormon Church are changing, that means the men in the Mormon Church will change—slowly, reluctantly to be sure, but inevitably.

Our orthodoxies are no longer working for us, whether it is government, organized religion, or our schools. We are moving beyond the constraints that have held us for so long. There is an unraveling, a great unraveling that I believe is occurring. Not without its pain, not without its frustration. Perhaps the fundamentalism we see within America right now is in response to these changes. We fear change, and so we cling to what is known.

KUPFER: Where are we in history?

WILLIAMS: This is an incredibly creative time. It is a difficult time. It is a disparaging time. A time of cultural and global transitions based on the realization that the Earth cannot support nonsustainable practices anymore. I believe capitalism will eventually be replaced by a communitarian ethic where the rights and care of all beings will be taken into consideration, not just the greed of a corporate few. Thomas Berry calls this time the Ecozoic Era, a time when we recognize the imperative of caring for the planet as a means of compassionate survival. We do not know what the outcome is going to be, but we have an opportunity to make these kinds of creative and imaginative leaps of thought and actions both locally and globally. This is completely antithetical to the direction George W. Bush is leading this nation. I do trust that the open space of democracy is ultimately the open space of our hearts and that we can follow our own leadership that carries a long-term view way beyond "four more years."

174

KUPFER: No one has ever quite phrased it that way before in terms of the ideals of the nation.

WILLIAMS: There is such an atmosphere of fear right now, and it is being used aggressively against us. It seems to be in times of war, the only appropriate action is to bare our hearts relentlessly, fearlessly. Call it a reflective activism born out of humility, not arrogance, with deep time spent in the consideration of others, which can open the door to becoming a compassionate citizen in the world.

KUPFER: Why do you remain hopeful?

WILLIAMS: Hope is not attached to outcomes but is a state of mind, as Vaclav Havel says, "an orientation of the spirit." And I have faith; maybe more than hope, I have faith. I think of my great-grandmother, Vilate Lee Romney, who came from good pioneer Mormon stock. She always said to us that faith without works is dead, so I think if we have hope, we must work to further that hope. Maybe that is the most important thing of all, to have our faith rooted in action. Our community in Castle Valley, Utah, gives me hope. It is a group of people who have committed to caring for a place, both human and wild. If I walked forever, I would never be able to cover this native ground of wonder and awe. I really do believe if there is hope in the world, then it is to be found within our own communities with our own neighbors, and within our own homes and families. Hope radiates outward from the center of our concerns. Hope dares us to stare the miraculous in the eye and have the courage not to look away. I refuse to walk away.

The Wild Mind

Terry Tempest Williams and the Writing Process

Michael Austin, 2005

When I first contacted Terry Tempest Williams to discuss A Voice in the Wilderness, *she wrote me back and told me that the one interview that she had never given—but always wanted to—was an interview on the writing process itself. She said that she had always wanted to explore with an interviewer the nuts and bolts of how she nurtured an idea from an incipient thought to a published manuscript. The possibilities of such an interview immediately seized my imagination, and I set about to find a time that we both could meet.*

Over the next few months, I launched myself into the work of locating, reading, listening to, and transcribing 40 interviews that Terry gave between 1989 and 2005. Each interview I read led to more questions that I wanted to ask Terry, and more and more I looked forward to the chance to sit with her and talk about those issues. On March 25, 2005, Terry and I met for lunch in Salt Lake City. We talked for several hours and then drove to her office at the University of Utah, where the following interview about the writing process took place.

MA: I want to start with something that you said earlier in an interview, and it's something we've talked about as well. You said that during the seven years in which the events that took place in *Refuge* were occurring, you filled, I believe it was 22 journals. But you didn't realize you were writing a book. Is that correct?

TTW: That's correct.

MA: When did that "aha" moment come?

TTW: I wanted to write a book on the Bear River Migratory Bird Refuge. I always felt this to be a landscape of orientation for me. So it was always in my mind to write a book on the birds and on Bear River. But I had no idea that the story I was living would become the story I would write. Between 1983, to my mother's death in 1987, and Mimi's death in 1989, I did fill well over 20 journals. I think it's what kept me sane. It was probably a manic exercise to try and make sense of what made no sense at all. When did I know I was writing a book? I think it was my mother. We were in Jackson Hole, Wyoming in the fall of '86, shortly before she died. "Tell me how you are," she asked. I said, "I'm so frustrated because I haven't had any time to write this book that I wanted to write on Bear River." And she looked at me and said, "Is it not enough that you kept a family together? Maybe you are writing a different book."

MA: Did what you wrote in the moment resemble the book that ended up being produced?

TTW: That's a great question, Michael. There are passages that stand as they were written in my journal, infused with the immediacy of the moment. The book itself was very different. And again, I remember my mother, when I asked her permission shortly before she died if I could write this book, she said, "I think you must; it's a book of secrets." I didn't see it that way, but I think, coming from her generation regarding her own privacy, she did see it as a book of secrets among women. She gave me one piece of advice. She said, "Don't publish it right away. Whatever you do, sit on it, let it percolate, let it steep," and I think she was absolutely right. She passed away on January 16, 1987. *Refuge* came out in 1991. I can't tell you how many drafts and revision there were—hundreds? All I can tell you is that I was rewriting right up until the last copy edit in the spring of 1991. The book changed and grew as I did. May I tell you a story?

MA: Please.

TTW: In 1988, a year after Mother died, Brooke and I were flying to New York. My father had driven us to the airport. As we boarded the plane, I handed him the first draft of *Refuge*. When we got to the hotel in New York, I saw the red phone light flashing and I thought "Oh no, something has happened." I called home, and Dad said, "I finished your book, and I can't believe what a hothead you've made me out to be." There was a long pause—"Your brother wants to speak to you." And then my brother got on the phone and said, "I can't believe what a minor character I am." I realized I was in trouble. Not only did I have an editor that I had to please, but also a family. It was not just my story.

I view the manuscript as a collaboration with my editor, whom I love and respect. But it was not easy. It was a lonely and arduous process. He was not complimentary, to say the least, with the first draft of *Refuge*. He said, "You've basically written a cheap *Death Be Not Proud*." I began again and rewrote and rewrote and rewrote. And then in 1990, I felt I had a solid manuscript of 500 pages. I sent it to him and received a letter which I have almost memorized, which said something like, "Dearest Terry, although Christine Peavitt and I greatly admire what you've attempted to do, we feel it fails on every level." And then he wrote about how it read like reeds and cattails going "hither and thither" and finished the letter by saying, "If you still wish to go forward with this manuscript, you might begin on page 496." That meant, in my editor's eyes, there were four pages that were worthwhile. Needless to say, I went to bed, and into a deep depression. A friend of mine, Christopher Merrill, called and said, "You sound terrible," and I said, "I am." I told him what happened, said "I'm taking my manuscript and myself to Great Salt Lake and jumping in," and he said, "Don't bother, you'll both just float." Humor brings us back to center. We can be grateful for dear friends.

I wrote a long letter to my editor and said, "Although I agree with you this book is still in process, it is not linear; it is circular. This is what I know as a Mormon woman living on the edge of the Great Salt Lake in the American West." He wrote back to me and said, "Terry, you were right to rebuke me, but you must trust me. You are not present in this manuscript yet." And with that I called him. We had a very lively, spirited conversation on the phone. I heard truth in his voice. "Terry, you're not there. You've managed to tell this story in the third-person, almost in the manner of a journalist. I want you to go back into the manuscript and, when you think you've gone too far, go further, when you think you've talked about the church, go deeper. Write against your instincts." I believed him. I went back into the manuscript, page by page by page and rewrote the book. It took six months, and I saw that he was correct. After I sent in the manuscript, I called him and told him that. He said "50 percent." We had completed our collaboration. He is still my editor today.

MA: Do ideas move onto the page for you in the same way for each book, or is it a completely different process that you go through each time that you write?

TTW: No, each book is different. There is always a question gnawing at me—an obsession that is growing. I live my life and the story unfolds, images appear.

MA: So does the question—and I like the way you phrase it that each book begins with a question—do you find yourself surprised at how many things that question relates to as the idea gestates?

TTW: Yes, each book is an exploration, a discovery. I have no idea where I'm going, and with a book like *Refuge*, with *Leap*, and *Red*, these are books that have taken years to formulate. Halfway through, I have no idea what I'm doing. I have to trust that it will come. It wasn't until the very end of *Refuge* that I finally realized the structure was found within the lake levels. And it wasn't until the last six months of *Leap* that I realized this was not going to be written in the voice of "the traveler" but in the first-person narrative. This became clear when I was working at the Sundance Playwright Lab. I was writing a monologue. The actress Elizabeth Marvel read the script, through the voice of the traveler. She was five minutes into the reading when I realized it was all wrong, and I ended up rewriting the entire book, leaving only one fragment of the traveler as a reminder of where my voice came from.

MA: Let me ask you another question. I'm very curious about what is physically going on as you write. Where do you do most of your writing? Where are you comfortable writing? Do you have different physical environments for different kinds of writing?

TTW: The starting point for all my work is in my journals. Anything I have ever written, whether it's an op-ed piece, an essay, or a book, it's in my journals first: the images, the experience. My writing begins there. And then I'll sit down at my desk and work on a sustained piece of writing. My process is ritualistic: I light a candle. I have a bowl of water to remind me that even if nothing is happening on the page, I know something is happening in the bowl—call it the process of evaporation—and it supports my mind and heart. And then I just work. I go to work, and it's a balance—no, maybe weaving is a better word—between personal experience and the creation of imagery grounded with facts, as the narrative voice begins to tell a story. I enter the writer's trance to see and feel my words.

MA: Another question—again I want to ask this right, but it's just a matter related to knowing about you and about your writing in general—and that is, how do you integrate writing with living with other facets of life? And you understand what I'm saying there? How does it come together? There are so many Terry Tempest Williamses—the writer, the activist, the naturalist, the wife, the speaker, the educator—how does writing integrate with other facets of your life?

TTW: Well I only know one me [laughing]. I don't know those other people you are talking about. It's one life and it's a life engaged.

MA: That's so admirable.

TTW: Well I don't know if it's admirable; I just think it's how we live our lives, and different days call for a different focus. I schedule my writing time as seriously as I schedule time teaching at the University of Utah. So I know, for example, that this year I have six weeks of absolutely undisturbed time, from mid-July till August, that is inviolate. No one enters that time. And it may even be extended until October 1; that's what I'm hoping for. So my scheduled time, my free time to write, is as fiercely protected as any other time. (Of course, there are family situations that arise that will take priority, like my brother's illness this past year.)

MA: Okay. And here is the question that I've been dying to ask for years. When do you find time to read as much as your work so clearly shows that you do read?

TTW: I feel extremely un-read, but I love to read; it's like breathing to me. We live in a very quiet place, we don't have a television, we don't have neighbors nearby, and so there's a lot of time to read. Also, if I'm traveling somewhere, planes are very private quarters, and my fear of flying is transcended by my love of reading.

MA: When you read and then write about the books you have read, do you sense yourself as a part of a much larger literary dialogue or conversation?

TTW: I certainly view reading as a conversation you have with the writer. And I really did feel I was in correspondence with Hieronymus Bosch when I was researching *Leap*. I feel great affinity with the American romantics: Thoreau, Emerson, Dickinson, Melville, and especially, Whitman. I feel there is a tremendous community of writers that are alive today, writers of place, located in place, concerned with environmental and social issues.

They are concerned about these larger issues illuminating what it means to be human. Each of us is a tessera in a larger mosaic.

MA: When you read a writer that you admire tremendously, someone like Whitman or Thoreau, and you dialogue in the margins, and then you also realize that you're a writer, too, do you imagine people sitting with your books dialoguing with you in the margins?

TTW: No, only disagreeing [laughing]. You know, I guess I don't, because I've never seen anyone read a book of mine. I would like to think that happens. I can tell you all the margins in the books that I read look like road maps.

MA: I can show you my copy of *Refuge*. It's as marked-up as anything I own.

TTW: I remember there was a period when I was reading everything I could get my hands on by Virginia Woolf. I was so steeped in her life and work that everything I did was colored by her presence. One day, Brooke and I were having an argument and he was exasperated. I turned to him and said, "Well I'm sure Leonard Woolf had it worse than you!" Brooke looked at me as though I had gone mad. Then we both started laughing. I'd so internalized her life into my own that she was a constant companion to me. Writers can have a profound effect on us. I guess I never imagined people entering my books this way.

MA: When you write for publication, who is in your mind, the ideal reader of your book? Who are you writing to, when you think about who you're writing to, and who do you imagine is reading?

TTW: I'm still intrigued by how you said that when you write in a journal, you're writing to an audience of yourself. I've never thought about it that way. When I'm writing in my journal, it's again that exploration on the page. My journals have everything in them from note-taking on a lecture, to a shopping list, to a journal entry about something I experienced, to reading notes from books. I really view my journal as a sketchbook. And in many ways, my journal is less personal than my books are.

MA: That's very intriguing.

TTW: I think that I am more afraid that someone will find my journals. Maybe it was because living in a family of brothers, I was terrified that they were going to read my journal and find out who my boyfriend was, and that fear was extended to having my parents reading it. So I'm very cautious in my journals and very loyal not to talk about other people. So I think in many ways I'm much freer when I write in an essay or a book because I don't perceive that it's going to be read. A book I write feels more private than my notebooks. Isn't that strange?

MA: So, in your books, do you have an ideal reader in mind? Do you have somebody who is the person who gets all the jokes and catches all the references? I just want to know who you imagine is reading your books as you're writing them.

TTW: Again, I think each book is a different . . . With *Refuge* I was writing for myself, as I said, to make sense of what made no sense at all. When it was about to be published, I called my father in a panic and said, "Dad, the book's going to be out. I don't know what I'm going to do; this could be read as gossip by people in the ward." And he said, "Don't worry about it; no one's going to read it, anyway." And that actually was a great relief. There is nothing like family to ground you. On my birthday, the same day my copy of *Refuge* arrived, he gave me a pistol.

MA: Was it a dueling pistol?

TTW: It was this beautiful, pearl-handled Lady Wesson. I think in some way it was my father's unconscious attempt to say, "Protect yourself, you're very vulnerable here." When *The Open Space of Democracy* came out, in 2004, he gave me a cell phone, which was his way of saying, "You're still vulnerable, keep in touch." So, families, I think, keep us both rooted in the real and protected. But back to your question, in some ways, I always imagine that my audience is a Mormon one. *Leap* is a book that certainly has a Mormon reader in mind, and *Refuge* has different reference points for Mormon readers as well, but I would hope that there's a universality to these stories that transcends the Mormon community. I think I am more conscious about the audience in the political work that I do. If it's an op-ed piece—for example, when Vice-President Dick Cheney was operating behind closed doors and not giving the names of those sitting around the table defining our nation's energy policy, and we knew that four miles beyond Arches National Park, the Bush-Cheney energy plan was being enacted, I wrote "Chewing Up A Fragile Landscape" as an op-ed piece for the *New York Times*. I had a definite audience in mind: the American public. I wanted to expose and inform. We may not know what's going on behind closed doors in Washington, but in Utah, this energy policy is a ground-thumping experience. So I am very mindful of who the audience is, in those pieces. In this instance, I wrote to change public opinion.

MA: Okay, I want to read you a list to see if you can guess where this list came from. This is a list of descriptors: "Anthropology, Medicine, Religion and Spirituality, Women's Studies, Literature, Poetry, Native American Studies, Children's Literature, Personal Essays, Science, Politics and

182

Government, Sexuality, Photography, Environmental Studies, Mormon Literature, Literary History and Criticism, Folklore, Art History, Nature Writing, Autobiography, and the Occult." What does that list represent?

TTW: Tell me.

MA: That list represents every section in the bookstore in which I have encountered your work.

TTW: That's very funny.

MA: Or the categories on the backs of your books. And it's always struck me, ever since I read *Refuge*, that on the back of *Refuge* it says I think something like, "autobiography/personal essay/science/medicine/women's studies/ecology." I think that's the descriptor. It strikes me that the people who are the booksellers and publishers who are attaching those labels to your books are fundamentally missing a point. They're trying to put you into boxes, or put your work into boxes where they just don't like to go.

TTW: Again, that doesn't concern me. That's about something else called marketing. What concerns me is how do we address these ideas? How do we write the vision we hold. The creative process and how we articulate our own story is without category.

MA: You know, if you write a science-fiction novel you would be in every aisle of Borders.

TTW: [laughing] There are some people that would view the epilogue to *Refuge* as science-fiction. Unfortunately, "The Clan of One-Breasted Women" is not.

MA: We in academics are so obsessed with these questions of categorizing and genre, and people who write textbooks and people who sell books and a lot of people who buy books are always—the first question they ask is what box can I put this in? What category can I put this in? And I think you're right—I've never gotten the sense that you've ever been even the slightest bit concerned about that.

TTW: I'm not. I'm concerned about how we see the world whole. I think the compartments, the categories, we have ascribed to the world have caused us a lot of problems. It goes all the way back to Descartes, how we compartmentalize, how we theorize, how we abstract the world, and I think when we see the world whole, when we feel the organic nature of the self as part of this larger community, then we don't allow ourselves to be confined or restricted to particular organization or genre. It's about staying open.

MA: That's something I find very admirable, actually. It's very rare that a writer writes without a bookstore knowing what shelf to put it on. And that's a

183

lot of our market, how a lot of our market economy works. We start with the question of what kind of book is it, and we write the book.

TTW: And I never know what book I'm writing until it's done.

MA: Let's go back to something that you said earlier, when your publisher told you to "write against your instincts." What does that mean?

TTW: I think our instinct, as human beings, is to be safe. And when my editor said "write against your instincts," what I think he was saying was "dare to tell the truth as far as you can." And I think when we write against our instincts we avoid sentimentality. Because writing against our instincts is walking out and standing on the precipice. At any moment we might fall, fail. Writing against our instincts is daring to write the book that as Hèléne Cixous says, "threatens to kill us."

MA: Where do you think those instincts come from, the ones that tell us to be safe and not to tell the truth?

TTW: We are mammals. We want to survive. It's part of our evolution. But it is also in our evolutionary interest to take risks. Whether we are Mormon, Catholic, Buddhist, or whatever our spiritual tradition is, there are conditionings that create an "ought" and a "should." As writers, we have to bypass the oughts and shoulds to the "what is." I think this really goes to the heart of the matter of exposing our true selves. Inherently, we don't think people are interested in what we have to say, and we don't have any confidence that our voice matters. So writing against our instincts is also believing that maybe we do have something to say. We think that nobody cares. Well, we really do care about the details of one another's lives. It's why we love gossip—the inside secret story. So I think it's a very complicated set of instructions to write against our instincts.

MA: Do you think that has something to do with, and I'm probably trying to draw too many connections here, but with wildness or wilderness—is there a wilderness of ideas? Is there such a thing as an idea in the wild compared to an idea that's been constrained?

TTW: That is a very evocative idea, Michael. When I hear that it says to me don't be afraid of the paradoxical nature of the mind. Because I was thinking, if we're talking about writing against our instincts and if I'm specifically talking about my editor's directions for *Refuge*, that goes in direct contrast to when I said to him, "I am writing from my instinctual self, I'm writing from my instincts, this book is not linear; its circular." So you write *out of your instincts* and you write *against your instincts*.

MA: And you're comfortable with that paradox.

184

TTW: I am. I am very comfortable with paradox. Perhaps it is what I trust most. I write from what I trust in my heart. I write out of my body, as Hèléne Cixous asks us to do as women. But by the same token, we have strong, self-protective mechanisms so we have to go beyond fear. Again, it's embracing the paradoxical nature. We are both fearful and courageous. We must enter the realm of the unknown as writer, and surrender to the mysteries. I think that is the nature of wild mind—to be comfortable with chaos. And my writing process is extremely chaotic. I look at friends of mine whose offices and studies look so organized and orderly. Mine is a disaster. And yet I know where everything is. So again, it's just understanding the shape of one's mind, and my mind is a mind of chaos and intuition. But there's an order in that. I accept paradox as a constant in my life. Great Salt Lake is a great teacher of paradox.

MA: Let's talk a little bit about September 11. Is it fair to say that the events of September 11, and the subsequent events—the invasion of Afghanistan, the invasion of Iraq—changed the trajectory of your writing?

TTW: Yes. Let me correct that. Yes, for the time being.

MA: What was the change?

TTW: The change in my writing was a change in America. I felt that our language after September 11 had been hijacked. And talk about being constricted. We were being restricted at the level of our language: the definition of what a patriot was, what a terrorist was, what a dissident was, the language of war that seeped into our culture. I felt my pen became my own exacto knife to try to cut through the lies we were hearing and made to believe.

MA: Where has your sense of responsibility to use your writing to respond to these issues come from? What created the urgency for you? And I know the events are very urgent, but writers have gone on to write exactly the way they used to write.

TTW: You know, when any type of book comes out, you're given a "pub. date," and I've always viewed that as the book's birthday. I had a box of books that arrived from Pantheon that had *Red*, 9-11-01 stamped on it, so I'd been staring at that date for about a month. What that means is that the bookstores can't sell that particular book until that particular date. In my mind, *Red* and 9/11 were inextricably linked. In truth, they were. I was in Washington, D.C., on September 11, 2001, at the Corcoran Gallery directly across from the White House. We not only witnessed the terror but felt it. My first reading of *Red* was at the Politics and Prose Bookstore.

185

We had a candlelight vigil and sat both in silence and story together. So *Red* was inextricably tied to that moment, and I was in motion during the days that followed, watching the country react to the events. I think I traveled through 23 cities during the six weeks that followed. I remember specifically at one of the readings, in Park City, Utah, when President Bush was scheduled to give his speech about September 11, we brought in a television set to the reading, turned it on, and watched it. Afterwards we talked about our impressions. Each person there offered a question. It was very powerful. There were differences of opinions. But we listened to one another. So what were scheduled as readings became town meetings. We didn't need to hear my words; we needed to hear one another's words. I experienced these events all in a public setting, so my voice became public in the process.

MA: And you think you became a more public writer because of those events?

TTW: I have simply chosen to speak and to write, and I am not alone. There is a strong tradition among writers in this country and abroad to raise essential questions during times of war. And we are a nation at war.

Albert Camus writes, "To create today is to create dangerously."

MA: So what's next?

TTW: I want to listen. I want to pay attention to the world in which we belong. I want to be in the service of story and not be fearful of where it leads me.

Appendix

Interviews with Terry Tempest Williams

The following lists most interviews with Terry Tempest Williams that were published or recorded between 1989 and 2005. It includes all print interviews that the editor has been able to locate and all radio interviews available on cassette tapes or as transcripts. It does not include a number of interviews available or once available on the Internet in streaming audio because of the impermanent nature of these, a half dozen or so of which are now no longer available to the public. A website about Terry Tempest Williams and her work, www.coyoteclan.com, contains an ongoing list of interviews with the author and activist as well as much else of interest.

1989

Lueders, Edward, ed. "Dialogue Two: Landscape, People, and Place." In *Writing Natural History: Dialogues with Authors*, 37–65. Salt Lake City: University of Utah Press, 1989.

1991

Toms, Justine. "The Meaning of Refuge." New Dimensions radio interview, November 14, 1991. Program 2294. Cassette tape available at http://www.newdimensions.org.

*Petersen, David. "Memory Is the Only Way Home: A Conversational Interview with Terry Tempest Williams." *Bloomsbury Review* 11, no. 8 (December 1991): 8-9

1993

Pearlman, Mickey. "Terry Tempest Williams." In *Listen to their Voices: Twenty Interviews with Women Who Write*, 121–33. New York: Norton, 1993.

---

*   Interviews compiled in *A Voice in the Wilderness.*

Daniel, Lucille. "Standing Our Ground: Conversations with Terry Tempest Williams." *Sojourner* 18, no. 6 (February 1993): 1, 17-19.

1994

Mencimer, Stephanie. "A Fierce Responsibility." *Mother Jones*, March–April 1994, 17.

*Toms, Justine. "Wild Heart: The Politics of Place." New Dimensions radio interview, December 30, 1994. Program 2460. Cassette tape available at http://www.newdimensions.org.

1995

Ives, Susan. "A Conversation with Terry Tempest Williams." *Land and People Magazine*, 1995. Archived at http://www.tpl.org/tier3_cdl.cfm?content_item_id=1220&folder_id=831.

*Jensen, Derrick. "Terry Tempest Williams." In *Listening to the Land: Conversations About Nature, Culture, and Eros*, 310–26. San Francisco: Sierra Club Books, 1995.

Skog, Susan. *Embracing Our Essence: Spiritual Conversations with Prominent Women*, 89–100. Deerfield Beach, Fla.: Health Communications International, 1995.

*London, Scott. "The Politics of Place: An Interview with Terry Tempest Williams." *Insight & Outlook*, National Public Radio, May 1995. Archived at http://www.scottlondon.com/interviews/williams.html.

1996

Shaw, Jean Walkin, producer. *Westwords: Six Western Writers*. PBS Home Video, 1996.

"An Interview with Terry Tempest Williams." *Timeline*, January–February 1996, 10.

Regan, Margaret. "Piercing the Heart." *Tucson Weekly*, March 14, 1996. Archived at http://www.tucsonweekly.com/tw/03-14-96/review1.htm.

Reed, Susan. "Friend of the Earth." *People Weekly*, July 15, 1996, 145.

*Siporin, Ona. "Terry Tempest Williams and Ona Siporin: A Conversation." *Western American Literature* 31, no. 2 (August 1996): 99–113.

1997

*Bartkevicius, Jocelyn and Mary Hussmann. "A Conversation with Terry Tempest Williams." *The Iowa Review* 27, no.1 (Spring 1997): 1–23.

1999

*Lynch, Tom. "Talking to Terry Tempest Williams about Nature, the Environment, and Being a Mormon." *Desert Exposure*, March 1999, 18.

Paul, Steve. "On Hemingway and His Influence: Conversations with Writers." *Hemingway Review* 18, no.2 (Spring 1999): 115–32.

2000

Olsen, Karen. "Terry Tempest Williams." *UTNE Reader*, May–June 2000, 102. Archived at http://www.utne.com/pub/2000_99/view/1159-1.html.

*Toms, Michael. "The Transformative Power of Art." New Dimensions radio interview, June 29, 2000. Program 2821. Cassette tape available at http://www.newdimensions.org.

2001

*Caldwell, Susie. "Lighting the Match." *Whole Terrain 9 (2000–2001): 48–51.*

"A Conversation with Terry Tempest Williams, author of *Leap*." Author interview on Random House website, 2001. http://www.randomhouse.com/catalog/display.pperl?isbn=9780 679752578&view=qa.

Wortman, Julie. "Erosional Spirituality: An Interview with Terry Tempest Williams." *The Witness*, April 2001, 18. Archived at http://thewitness.org/archive/april2001/williamsinterview.html.

Nizalowski, John. "Terry Tempest Williams: The Emerson of the West." *Inside/Outside Southwest*, September 2001. Archived at http://www.insideoutsidemag.com/archives/articles/2001/09/terry_tempest_williams.asp?archive_year=2001&archive_month=09.

*Toms, Michael. "Wild Mercy," *A Time for Choices*. New Dimensions radio interview, September 25 2001. Program 2891. Cassette tape available at http://www.newdimensions.org.

2002

*Toms, Michael. "Restoring the Dialogue." *A Time for Choices*. New Dimensions radion interview, January 10, 2002. Program 2913. Cassette tape available at http://www.newdimensions.org.

*Remy, Jana Bouk. "An Interview with Terry Tempest Williams."*Irreantum* 4, no.2 (Summer 2002): 14–22.

2003

*Sumner, David Thomas. "*Testimony, Refuge,* and the Sense of Place—A Conversation with Terry Tempest Williams." *Weber Studies* 19, no.3 (Spring–Summer 2003). Based on a 1999 interview. Archived at http://weberstudies.weber.edu/archive/archive%20D%20Vol.%201 8.2-21.1/Vol.%2019.3/Sumner%20Williams.htm

*Seligmann, Aria. "Coffee Talk: A Chat with Terry Tempest Williams." *Eugene Weekly*, May 8, 2003. Archived at http://www2.eugeneweekly.com/2003/050803news.html#news.

Brick, Tricia. "Q&A Terry Tempest Williams: Every Story Has a Context." *Etude*, Summer 2003. Archived at http://etude.uoregon.edu/summer2003/williams.

*"A Conversation with Terry Tempest Williams." *Delicious Living*, October 2003, 82. Archived at http://www.deliciouslivingmag.com/magazine/index.cfm?fuseaction=article&arti cleid=617

Seaman, Donna. "A Spell So Exquisite: An Interview with Terry Tempest Williams." *Ruminator Review* 16 (Winter 2003–4): 18–201.

2005

*Kupfer, David. "An Interview with Terry Tempest Williams." *The Progressive* 69, no.2 (February 2005): 35–40. Archived at http://www.progressive.org/?q=node/334.

Index

191